Studying
Aging
and
Social
Change

This book is dedicated to the memory of my mother and father,

Claire W. and John R. Hardy.

Studying Aging and Social Change

Conceptual and Methodological Issues

Edited by

Melissa A. Hardy

SAGE Publications
International Educational and Professional Publisher
Thousand Oaks   London   New Delhi

For information:

SAGE Publications, Inc.
2455 Teller Road
Thousand Oaks, California 91320
E-mail: order@sagepub.com

SAGE Publications Ltd.
6 Bonhill Street
London EC2A 4PU
United Kingdom

SAGE Publications India Pvt. Ltd.
M-32 Market
Greater Kailash I
New Delhi 110 048 India

Printed in the United States of America

Library of Congress Cataloging-in-Publication Data

Main entry under title:

Studying aging and social change: Conceptual and methodological issues/
   editor, Melissa A. Hardy
      p. cm.
   Includes bibliographical references (p.   ) and index.
   ISBN 0-7619-0590-1 (cloth: acid-free paper).—ISBN
   0-7619-0591-X (pbk.: acid-free paper)
    1. Historical sociology. 2. Social change. 3. Generations.
   4. Cohort analysis. I. Hardy, Melissa A., 1952-
   HM104.S76 1997   97-4740
   303.4'01—dc21

This book is printed on acid-free paper.

97 98 99 00 01 02 03 10 9 8 7 6 5 4 3 2 1

Acquiring Editor:	Margaret Zusky
Editorial Assistant:	Corinne Pierce
Production Editor:	Sherrise M. Purdum
Production Assistant:	Denise Santoyo
Typesetter/Designer:	Marion Warren
Cover Designer:	Candice Harman
Print Buyer:	Anna Chin

Contents

Acknowledgments

I would like to express my thanks to Steve Cutler, Lawrence Hazelrigg, and Jill Quadagno for their advice and support; to Sandra Gillespie for her assistance in preparing the manuscript; and to Margaret Zusky for her guidance.

A man cannot become a child again, or he becomes childish. But does he not find joy in the child's naïveté, and must he himself not strive to reproduce its truth at a higher stage? Does not the true character of each epoch come alive in the nature of its children? Why should not the historic childhood of humanity, its most beautiful unfolding, as a stage never to return, exercise an eternal charm? There are unruly children and precocious children. Many of the old people belong in this category. The Greeks were normal children. The charm of their art for us is not in contradiction to the undeveloped stage of society on which it grew. [It] is its result, rather, and is inextricably bound up, rather, with the fact that the unripe social conditions under which it arose, and could alone arise, can never return.

Karl Marx (1973, p.111)

The facts of contemporary history are also facts about the success and the failure of individual men and women. . . . Neither the life of an individual nor the history of a society can be understood without understanding both.

C. Wright Mills (1959, p. 3)

The normalizing task in history is to mobilize the remedial powers of imagination by the velvet hand of reason. . . . Histories are revisioned retrospectively, and while the revisioning may be justified by "discoveries" of previously unseen or unappreciated chains of events, anticipations, precursive stages, evolving objects, and the like, nothing

*of the installations escapes the contingencies of the
classificatory practices that have fashioned the difference
of a revision. In other words, revisioning is always built
not merely as a response to current circumstances but
in/of current circumstances.*

Lawrence Hazelrigg (1995, p. 316)

*What sort of a life, what sort of a world, what sort of a self,
can be preserved in a man who has lost the greater part of his
memory and, with this, his past, and his moorings in time? It
immediately [makes] me think of a patient of mine in whom
these questions were precisely exemplified. . . . Jimmie was a
fine-looking man, with a curly bush of grey hair, a healthy and
handsome forty-nine-year-old. "Hiya, Doc!" he said. "Nice
morning!". . . . He talked with enthusiasm of his days in the
navy—he was seventeen, had just graduated from high school
when he was drafted in 1943. . . . With recalling, reliving,
Jimmie was full of animation; he did not seem to be speaking
of the past but of the present. . . . "Jimmie, how old would you
be?" "Why, I guess I'm nineteen, Doc." I . . . thrust a mirror
toward him. "Look in the mirror and tell me what you see. Is
that a nineteen-year-old looking out from the mirror?" He
suddenly turned ashen and gripped the sides of the chair.
"Jesus Christ, . . . what's going on? What's happened to me?
Is this a nightmare? Am I crazy?". . . . He regained his colour
and started to smile, and I stole away, taking the hateful
mirror with me. Two minutes later I re-entered the room.
"Hiya, Doc" he said. "Nice morning!"*

Oliver Sacks (1985, pp. 22-23),
discussing a patient named Jimmie
who suffered from a severe case of
Korsakov's syndrome, a profound
loss of memory such that whatever
occurred in the present was forgotten
in a few moments' time.

CHAPTER ONE

Doing Time: Reconciling Biography With History in the Study of Social Change

MELISSA A. HARDY
LINDA WAITE

◇ INTRODUCTION

The juxtapositions of "aging" and "social change" or "biography" and "history" are merely alternate formulations of the basic duality of "self and world" or "personality and social structure" or, more recently, what has been framed as the issue of "micro/macro linkage" that presents sociology with its defining problematic. We need no further evidence of the importance and complexity of these issues than our own reactions to two famous thought experiments. In 1927, Karl Mannheim (1927/1952b) asked that we imagine "what . . . the social life course of man [would] be like if one generation lived on forever and none followed to replace it?" (p. 277). In response, we imagine a world in which the very concept of "generation" is absent; where no "new" cohorts challenge the ideas of older generations; where, once members have aged to adulthood, children no longer exist except in the memories of grown children. We imagine a world where the history of the social and the biography of the individual occupy the same time line.

Mannheim (1927/1952b) posed this question as a particular framing of an earlier thought experiment suggested by David Hume. Hume (1777/ 1985) asked us to "suppose that the type of succession of human generations was completely altered so that the older generation disappears at one stroke and

1

the new one is then born all at once" (p. 476). In Hume's counterfactual world, we have a continuous sequence of "fresh starts," a series of open choices whereby each successive generation creates its own social institutions anew, makes its own decisions about the social organization of production and distribution; where each new generation defines "good" and "right" and "fair" as it deems appropriate. Both thought experiments suggest a single generation society. By proposing a society composed of members of a single age, both experiments focus us on the role of cohort succession in the production of social organization and social history. Mannheim's generation lives forever as the cumulative social history and lived experience of biography continue to build, one event or experience upon another. Though past experiences may well be reinterpreted in light of new information, one can only reinterpret memory but cannot view transpired events through the lens of those born in another time. In contrast, Hume's imagined social world consists of a set of nonoverlapping generations that operate behind a true veil of ignorance. By the time the new generation is born, the social history of the old has been lost. If documents exist, there are no sages to explain their content. And whatever material artifacts remain as a testament to past generations, the meaning and purpose of those objects must be forged anew, without benefit of a "past" set of experiences—direct or indirect—on which to draw.

The very fact that we find these questions significant tells us something about how we understand the intersection of biography and history, how we construct the distinction between lived experience and historical experience. We see from these examples that history does not simply provide a context in which lived experience occurs. Rather, history is an integral part of that lived experience, but it is that very point that causes us discomfort. We want to believe that we can learn the lessons of history, act as history makers, and react as history consumers, yet at the same time stand outside the reach of history. It is this desire for separation that has led many researchers to try to map one pole of the duality—biography or self or agency—in terms of the other pole—social change, social world, or social structure.

The use of the conjunction "and" in these dualities serves to link and to contrast the concepts. The concepts differ in number and scale: whereas "aging" and "biography" and "self" all refer to individual experiences, "social change," "history," and "world" make sense only for collectives. But moving from one pole to the other is not a simple matter of aggregation. If we cannot simply sum behaviors or experiences across all individuals, how do we conceptualize the linkage between the two? To answer that question, we must understand how people are organized in and through social experiences, how these organizing features of society shape behaviors and attitudes, and how the connections across levels are articulated.

Three concepts—generation, cohort, and the life course—have been offered by theorists to explain how aging and social change are articulated across time. All three concepts reflect intersections of age and history; they are viewed as dimensions of social structure that mediate and reflect change. The remainder of this chapter provides a discussion of these three concepts and describes some of the methodological issues embedded in their use.

◇ LINKING INDIVIDUAL DEVELOPMENT
TO HISTORICAL EXPERIENCE

Mannheim and the Generation
as a Historical Unit

In the late 1800s, social theorists attempted to link micro- and macrolevels of analysis by drawing analogies between the functioning of an individual organism and collectives of individuals. The rapid changes taking place in society were viewed, in some quarters, as a process of development—often seen unilinearly—that could be tied to the life span of individuals. For although social collectives had "life spans" of a sort—cultures were born, went through a process of growth and development, and then died out—this social process did not occur within the time frame of an individual's life span. In fact, the importance of this difference was framed by Mannheim (1927/1952b) through the thought experiment of the single generation society. New members were born into society, aged as part of the collective, and then died. The vitality of the society came from the continuous production of new members and replacement of current members, and the rhythm of that process was linked to the duration and limitation of the individual life span. It was this linkage between "generational replacement" and social change that Mannheim wanted to explore in his essay.

Mannheim's (this volume) dissatisfaction with what he termed the "positivist" and "romantic historical" approaches to the problem of generations led him to formulate a different understanding of generation as a historical unit. The positivist view regarded generations as quantifiable natural facts and emphasized an "externalized concept of time." The utility of this concept of generations lay in accurately measuring the process of replacement.

Although the 30-year length of a generation seemed to be consistent with the periods of activity generally experienced during the standard life span—30 years for development, education, and training; 30 years to work in positions that allowed decision making and direction; and a subsequent withdrawal from positions of power—this (roughly) 30-year rhythm was more characteristic of family structure (with different generations of children, parents, and grandparents) than society, since new waves of births occurred continuously in society through overlapping and adjacent kinship structures. What was the link between this biological process and the trigger for social change?

To develop this linkage, Mannheim (this volume) turned to Dilthey's (1927/1958) work, particularly Dilthey's use of generations as an internal measure of time and as a crucial factor in defining the true meaning of contemporaneity. True contemporaries, he argued, do not simply live at the same time. Clearly, many different generations coexist at any one point in time, yet all these generations do not experience the same events in the same way. In other words, different generations do not live in the same world nor in the same time; subjective experience separates them. The biographical significance of historical experience lies in the creation of different stratifications of human consciousness, in which experiences are not simply layered, one on top of the other, but dialectically articulated—a process that allows new experiences to be interpreted in light of history and history to be revised in light of new experiences.

The biological process that defines generations creates the potential for the development of a shared consciousness that unites and motivates people. It provides them a similar location, much like social class, but does not guarantee that they will form a "generation as actuality." For a generation to trigger social change, they must share something more than simply copresence in time and space; they must forge an additional bond that allows a shared consciousness that motivates them to "participate in a common destiny." The basis for that additional bond lies in the (largely unconscious) cultural orientations developed in early life. Further, all members of a generation need not respond to historical circumstances in the same way. As a result, members form a "generational unit" that acts as an "actual" generation but may also react against the position of another generational unit, thereby allowing multiple and perhaps antagonistic generational units to coexist.

For Mannheim (this volume), then, generation as shared birth year simply creates the potential for a more powerful unit of behavioral consciousness—

the generation as actuality—whose consciousness has been shaped by experiences shared through similar locations in the historically-stratified structure of life in that society. Once adopted, this consciousness is resistant to revision, and though mobility into a different social location may prompt a different view of events and beliefs, our minds' "limited elasticity" make it impossible for us to truly look at something with "new" eyes. The continuous introduction of new members into a society provides the only real possibility of a "fresh look," although even the perspectives of new members are shaped by unconscious forces. The prominence Mannheim gave to the concept of a shared, similarly stratified consciousness in providing the link between generation and social change compromised the concept of generation as a clean analytic device adaptable to the scientific method. Perhaps recognizing the complexity of these issues, Mannheim chose not to return to this topic in his later writings.

Ryder and the Birth Cohort

Approximately 40 years—or somewhat longer than one generation—later, Norman Ryder (1965, this volume) revisited these issues, substituting the concept of "birth cohort" for Mannheim's "generation," and largely jettisoned the notion of shared consciousness and the distinction between "generation" and "generation-as-actuality" that was central to Mannheim's (this volume) view of the structural linkage between agency and social change. Ryder argued that structural transformations of society could be linked to population processes through the mechanisms of cohort succession and cohort replacement. Rather than emphasize the development of shared consciousness, Ryder spoke of equality in person-years of exposure; rather than attempt to untangle the mechanisms whereby the "fresh contact" of new members is translated into actions that ultimately transform social structure, Ryder argued that a comparison of different cohorts is a powerful strategy for studying social change. Cohorts are sharper analytic devices than Mannheim's "generation-as-actuality," that, Ryder argued, rarely developed and, when they did, likely encompassed a minority of generational members. Cohorts, in contrast, described age-homogeneous groupings that were inclusive and clearly bounded. They could be implicated in the process of social change without presuming the self-conscious development of a shared sense of purpose. Instead, compositional features of cohorts—intra- and intercohort dimensions of variability—and the "fit" between cohort composition and social institutions fueled and guided institutional development and social change.

The concept of the birth cohort has several advantages as an element in a classification system. Cohorts can be easily measured by collecting temporal data; they are fundamentally aggregate phenomena, characterized in ways that are not meaningful at the individual level of analysis; they are stamped with a pattern of variability that has consequences for the developmental trajectories of individual members and for their fit with the existing social structure. Cohort differentiation can be established on the basis of size, demographic composition, the strength of age-specific norms, historical events at key junctures, and the opportunities and constraints cohort members face as they confront social structures. Though cohorts may continue to diverge as members age, cohort variability in many features is present at birth and thereby represents a set of ascribed cohort characteristics, reflecting the characteristics and behaviors of parents.

Though he agrees with Mannheim (1927/1952b) that the concept of cohort (generation) is in many ways similar to the concept of social class—both serve to locate individuals relative to social institutions—Ryder argues that ethnic group membership is perhaps the better analogy. Ryder develops an argument similar to Mannheim's to explain the salience of the notion that age groups are uniquely embedded in historically specific sets of social relations and that, consequently, it is essential to specify when in historical time an age range was occupied. Defining cohorts thereby represents an important elaboration of an age classification system. In addition, although different cohorts may experience the same historical events, they often vary greatly in their reaction to them. A cohort that reached age 18 at the start of World War II had a different experience of that war than the cohort that was age one or age 60 in that same year. Recognizing the complexity of trying to detail these different impacts, Ryder notes that the simplicity of the cohort concept lies in the fact that its explanatory power derives from its surrogate status: cohort (like race/ethnicity or gender) provides a useful classification that serves as a proxy measure for what are, in fact, traits, dispositions, and behaviors—and more important, the social relationships in which those traits, dispositions, or behaviors are embedded—that actually carry the "effect" and provide theoretically meaningful interpretation.

Organizations such as schools and firms play an important role in mediating the fit between successive cohorts and existing social institutions. Cohort size has implications for the competitive environment in which cohort members vie for resources and opportunities. Cohort composition—in ascribed and achieved characteristics—shapes labor markets. Although cohort characteristics help to structure experiences of cohort members, their effects are not confined within cohorts. The characteristics of any single cohort may cast shadows onto prior and subsequent cohorts. These patterns of interdependence across cohorts are reflected in variations of social organization and variability in the incidence and patterning of individual experiences.

Riley and Age Stratification Theory

Attempting to refocus an increasingly social psychological "gerontology," Riley (1987) also invoked the ideas of Mannheim and those of Sorokin (1941) to shift attention away from aging-as-adjustment at the microlevel toward age as a central organizing principle of societies. The age stratification theory that Riley and her colleagues (Riley, Johnson, & Foner, 1972) developed promoted the idea that societies organize the distributions of rewards and opportunities and develop sets of behavioral expectations based on several stratifying characteristics of its members, with chronological age as a central element in these systems of stratification. In this framework, societies are structured on the basis of age; members of society are stratified on the basis of age. These age structures change over time, and individuals age in time. Riley argues that these processes of change are "separate and distinct" dynamisms. However, the aging of members of successive cohorts and the change in social structures as these cohorts pass through social institutions that are organized at least in part by age are also interdependent processes, though analytically distinct. The three research issues that follow from these propositions are: How do changes in social structure produce cohort differences in aging? How do cohorts—and the process of cohort succession—produce modifications in age structures at the societal level? How do we understand (model) the interdependence between changes in social structure and this process of cohort succession?

The first research issue posed by age stratification theory really has two parts: (a) Do cohorts age differently? and (b) how can differences in the processes of cohort aging be linked to changes in social structure?

Elder and the Life Course

The life course perspective offers one strategy for answering the first part of the question posed by age stratification theory. Providing a summary concept for the social process of aging, life course theory focuses on the interweave of age-graded trajectories, such as family and work careers, that are affected by changing social and economic conditions and on short-term transitions such as marriage or school completion (Elder, 1995). Typically defined as a sequence of connected transitions and changes in social roles that accompany movement across the age structure (Elder, 1985), the "life course"—much like the concept of "role"—was enacted by individuals but ordered relative to the organizational context of opportunities and constraints and the cultural context of expectations and social traditions. The life course represents the dynamic counterpart to the set of roles/positions that people occupy at any point in time. Research within the life course perspective investigates the timing and nature of transitions across positions or statuses and assesses how the types and rates of these movements are organized relative to stratifying characteristics of individuals or contextual characteristics of the groups (or organizations) in which people (or the positions they occupy) are embedded. It focuses on the dynamics of multiple, interconnected pathways.

This conceptualization has motivated studies of differences in aging across cohorts. By looking not only at measures of central tendency— average age of first marriage, average age of retirement—but also at measures of dispersion, we learn not only about changes in the center of gravity of the timing distribution (measured by age, or exposure, or duration) but also about changes in the congruity of cohort behavior, that is, the consistency with which cohort members make these transitions relative to the clock being used to organize these transitions in time.[1] The life course perspective thereby emphasizes the temporal organization of behaviors and positions and invites analyses of events-as-sequence, organized across time and space by social rules of allocation and individual preferences. In that way, the life course individualizes across time what the concepts of cohort and generation attempted to collectivize through the juxtaposition of time and space. Ironically, though much of the empirical work has attempted to map out individual-level variability in transitions and transition rates, the theoretical models motivating these analyses have ranged from highly individualized rational choice models to structural approaches in which human agency is severely limited (Dowd, 1987; Meyer, 1988). Although the "life course" was proposed as a concept that linked the micro- and macrolevels of analysis, research flowing from this perspective has concentrated on the aging of individuals without focusing more than tangentially on the dynamics of social change (Kohli, 1986; Marshall, 1996). But to focus on both would require analytic techniques that can assess the nature and temporal patterns of individual behavior while simultaneously attending to the manner in which this behavior is embedded in different organizational structures that are themselves changing. Have we developed the methodological tools to address problems of this sort?

◻ RESHAPING RESEARCH DESIGNS

The Limitations of Cross-Sectional Designs

At the time Ryder (1965, this volume) penned his essay, quantitative research was dominated by the analysis of large cross-sectional surveys with statistical techniques designed to partition variance. Ryder promoted longitudinal and time series designs, arguing that cross-sectional designs were ill-suited to the study of process and change. In addition, estimated age group differences based on cross-sectional designs were not unambiguously interpretable. This limitation is easily illustrated by considering three possible interpretations of a cross-sectional "age effect," any or all of which could be implicated in a relationship that we observe. Consider, for example, the relationship between age and wage for prime-aged workers (i.e., workers aged 16 to 64). On average, wages increase with age, plateau and then decline slightly. This relationship could result from developmental stage, serving as a proxy for such qualities as skill acquisition, personality plasticity, or changes in cognitive capacity; the relationship could reflect institutionalized opportunities or constraints linked to age through formal rules and regulations or through social convention; or the effect could reflect different cohort experiences with economic downturns, wars, or education, since age and birth cohort are inseparable in a cross-sectional design.

Riley (1973; Riley, Foner, & Waring, 1988) elaborated on the limitations of cross-sectional designs for studying ag*ing*. Cross-sectional designs are necessarily limited to a single distribution of characteristics and outcomes, and the variability that is "explained" is variability across sample elements, not across time, although time is differentially implied in the production of both distributions of characteristics and distributions of outcomes. But researchers often interpret these cross-sectional variations by age as though they applied to the same individual at different ages. Riley dubbed such misinterpretations examples of "life course fallacies" and emphasized that cross-sectional age-group differences were not necessarily *caused* by ag*ing*.

As a response to these limitations, Ryder (1965, this volume) argued for two lines of research, both of which required longitudinal information and temporal data. The two lines of research—the study of intracohort temporal development through the life cycle and the study of comparative cohort careers—continue to define major themes of quantitative research in aging and social change.

Challenges for Data and Measurement

Data Challenges

Studying the link between individual lives and social change requires information beyond that necessary to study either of these alone. As a result, we see a number of large surveys that follow individuals, couples, and families over extended periods, with frequent interviews and collection of extensive retrospective information. This approach provides researchers with information on the nature and the timing of transitions and with repeated measures of characteristics and attributes that may be connected to these transitions as either cause or effect.

At the same time that longitudinal and retrospective data create analytic opportunities, they present substantial challenges. Accurately locating events in time is a difficult task for most people, and definitions of one's past are revised in light of one's current situation. So some people "forget" failed marriages, children who died, businesses that closed, and refuse (implicitly) to report abortions, time in prison, or unemployment. Remembering the order of events is somewhat easier, and individuals can often sketch in details of fuzzier memories by timing them relative to events that were more noteworthy through a "life calendar" approach (Freedman, Thornton, Camburn, Alwin, & Young-DeMarco, 1988), although all are not motivated to do so. Nevertheless, we are limited by the ability of individuals to recall the timing of transitions and events, and their willingness to report them accurately, and by the association between other characteristics of people such as their sex, education, and age, and the accuracy of the information that they provide to researchers.

At the macrolevel, it is often difficult to distinguish between competing explanations of events because of the interrelatedness of political, social, and economic trends. For example, researchers continue to debate the impact of Social Security benefits on aggregate changes in labor force participation. Although bivariate analyses suggest a correlation between the age structure of declining labor force participation and the benefit structure of Social Security in the lumping of retirement transitions around ages of benefit entitlement, researchers disagree as to the importance of Social Security, per se, in causing these declines versus Social Security in conjunction with other trends that are arguably relevant to the retirement process. Because changes in Social Security benefits coincided with increasingly favorable attitudes toward retirement, improvements in employer pension policies, and increases in household wealth (to name a few), disentangling the unique effects of these various determinants is a difficult task.

Finally, to be able to examine individual behaviors within the various levels of social organization in which they occur, coordinated information on individuals, organizations, and social contexts must be collected. For example, retirement transitions have been studied at the level of the individual (i.e., what characteristics increase the likelihood of retirement at given ages) and at the aggregate level (i.e., what explains declines in labor force participation rates). The importance of the work environment, the job, or the labor market for retirement transitions has been assessed by mapping features of the work environment, average characteristics of jobs, or the size and unemployment rate of the local labor market to the individual data record. However, this approach does not coherently capture the organizational features of the firms from which workers retire. But to expand the research design to include characteristics of firms would require appropriate sampling frames at the individual and the organizational level and the cooperation of both individuals and organizations in furnishing the necessary information.[2]

Measurement Challenges

Specifying time paths of change is better suited to changes in status, that is, changes in discrete characteristics, than it is to changes in attitudes or beliefs. Even so, measuring changes in status has complications as well. For example, we can observe changes in marital status—from single to married, from married to divorced—and we can date these transitions to the day, perhaps even the hour, by noting the wedding date or the date on the divorce decree. We can even measure the duration of the marriage by differencing the two dates. To the extent that "marriage" implies legally recognized relationships between two people (with the various economic ramifications), then our measures of transition and duration are accurate. However, if the relevance of marital status for our study lies in the underlying relationship, the task is more complicated. How many people who experience divorce would argue that the marriage ended the day the divorce decree was issued? That date may be the legal end, but typically the change in the relationship occurred as a gradual process that began well before the actual date of the divorce. And what of people who are, for all practical purposes (and perhaps by common law), married? How will they date their relationship? By institutionalizing or ritualizing status changes, we provide measurement markers that allow us to accurately locate events in time and space, relying on institutional memory rather than respondent memory. The kinds of life course transitions that we can most easily investigate are very important and therefore memorable transitions that are already institutionalized. We have much less luck with fuzzy, gradual, or disputed transitions.

An important methodological tool in life course research has been the development of dynamic modeling techniques that allow researchers to trace the time paths of behaviors and events and identify factors implicated in the production of these time paths (Allison, 1984; Yamaguchi, 1991). Dynamic models are divided into "discrete" time and "continuous" time models—a distinction that is conceptually linked to the way changes can occur in the process under study. In practice, the choice is often governed by the structure of the data and the statistical techniques available to the researcher. But some events take place—or fail to do so—at a particular time for most people, whereas others may take place for cohort members at any point over an extended period. High school graduation is an example of the first type of transition; and marriage, a first birth, and death are examples of the second.

When we are interested in an underlying process that changes gradually and continuously, measuring change through membership in discrete categories presents additional difficulties. As an example, consider a favorite question on political attitudes: "How much of the time do you think you can trust the government to do what is right—just about always, most of the time, or only some of the time?" We could ask the same group of individuals that question every 5 years for a span of 30 years and track any changes in their attitudes. Framed in this way, we may observe a deterioration in the level of trust people place in the government. But the more subtle changes in attitude may be missed, since we can imagine respondents who voiced trust in government becoming increasingly disenchanted with a government they view as more isolated, less "in touch" with "the people." But that shift may be more or less resilient to the inertia of remembered responses, more or less susceptible to a set of recent events that either reinforced or undermined trust. The shift may occur at different thresholds for different people, but at some point that discomfort becomes sufficiently strong for respondents to shift into a different response category. Further, what would appear as stability during the series of same-category responses may measure a consistently positive reaction to a changing point of reference, since the people involved in government and the policies enacted by government also change across measurement periods, and people may differ in their tendency to respond in terms of an abstraction—the government—versus a specific president or congress.

These concerns would seem to argue for more refined measurement of attitudes—more categories of response to capture the degree of trust or distrust, more specificity in defining the object of evaluation. However, cognitive theorists argue that respondents are limited in the number of categories they can reliably distinguish, suggesting that we gain greater detail at the cost of losing reliability. This tradeoff highlights another complexity of studying change. We generally recognize that an important aspect of modeling is the management of error. One of the important advances in modeling software during the last decades has been the development of analysis programs that allow us to explicitly model error structures. When studying *changes* in attitudes or other characteristics, it is important to directly address the impact of measurement error and work to refine measures that provide adequately detailed yet reliable information. Yet it is possible to conceive of these problems as generated by two (possibly interrelated) processes: the process that is generating the distribution of the attitude or characteristic of interest and the process that is generating the (perhaps shifting) error structure. If we start from an assumption of stability, then we can define variability around a "true" score as the noise introduced by measurement error. If we can then make assumptions about the error structure, we can disentangle these two components. For example, researchers have argued that analyses of attitude change must attend to change in attitude structure and (potentially) change in the errors in these measures; as an additional complexity, the possibility of errors correlated over time should be investigated (Wiley & Wiley, 1970). In other words, in modeling attitudes across time, we are making assumptions about the time dependency of attitudes as well as assumptions about the time dependency of errors. If we can assume random measurement error and constant error variance, then change across time can be attributed to true change in attitudes. However, if errors are correlated over time, then any observed change in attitude is a combination of a true-score process and an error process, and both must be modeled dynamically.

⊠ CONCEPTUAL AND METHODOLOGICAL
    CHALLENGES IN STUDYING COHORTS

As sociologists continued to unfold the complexity of the conceptual linkage between biography and history, between aging and social change, they also accepted the challenge of developing analytic techniques for identifying separate and distinguishable components of this conceptual framework, for although Ryder's (1965, this volume) essay provided a provocative argument for the conceptual utility of the cohort perspective, he did not provide answers to the technical questions encountered in conducting this type of research. Ryder promoted cohort analysis as a compromise between time series analysis of aggregated data and life history studies of small samples. The cohort record was a kind of "macrobiography" or aggregate life history and offered a research strategy that included the collection of temporal information, comparative longitudinal analysis, and reasonable sample sizes. But aggregated information masks certain types of change. For example, different cohorts may be characterized by the same employment rates, but a comparison of group-specific rates may reveal important compositional differences in who is working and who is not. In other words, to the extent that subgroups within cohorts register change to different degrees or in different directions, cohort comparisons of aggregated outcome measures do not unambiguously support a conclusion of stability versus change, nor, if differences are noted, allow a clear conclusion as to the magnitude of the changes taking place. In addition, simple cohort comparisons did not allow researchers to determine whether observed trends were due to cohort differ-ences, to changes in age-specific behaviors, or to historical (i.e., period) shifts. Since all three explanations could be operating simultaneously, re-searchers are challenged to distinguish the three types of effects. Though conceptually distinct, estimating quantitative models that identified all three effects was more difficult. The identification problem that came to charac-terize the study of aging and social change was the linear dependency of age, period, and cohort effects (Fienberg & Mason, 1985).

Researchers had discovered that by pooling together a series of survey panels, they could construct data sets that not only displayed age variability but also variability in when, historically, these age groups existed. Cross-sectional surveys allowed the comparison of 40-year-olds to 50-year-olds, but by pooling cross-sections it was possible to compare 40-year-olds in 1950 with 40-year-olds in 1960. Within these designs, the year in which data were collected typically defined the point in historical time (i.e., period); each member of the sample reported chronological "age"; and the difference between the two defined "cohort" or birth year. Given that we often have relatively few individuals born in any given year (and, by definition, any one-year birth cohort), respondents were frequently classified into age or cohort categories of broader width. Ideally, classifying respondents into age and birth year categories met the methodological requirements of any clas-sification scheme—that groups remained homogeneous with regard to observable and unobservable characteristics implicated in the process under study, and the number of observations was sufficiently large to preserve statistical power. In addition, if one constructed 5-year birth cohorts, for example, and collected information at 5-year intervals, one could create an age by period matrix that allowed visual comparison of same-aged people at different points in time (across rows), different-aged people at a single point in time (down columns), and "aging" cohorts across time (on the diagonal). The problem, however, was that each of these comparisons necessarily confounded two of the three effects, since each comparison holds only one of the three constant: comparing same-aged people across time confounded period and cohort effects; comparing different-aged people within periods confounded age and cohort effects; and performing intracohort comparisons across time confounded age and period effects. When researchers pursued more formal modeling techniques, the problem of identifying three separate and estimable effects within this framework remained. Mason, Mason, Winsborough, and Poole (1973) demonstrated the impossibility of estimating separate effects for age, period, and cohort in a generalized linear model without imposing some kind of linear restriction on the function. These restrictions frequently took the form of equality constraints on two or more adjacent age groups, periods, or cohorts, thereby limiting variability in one of the three dimensions.

Our experiences with age-period-cohort (APC) models provide a useful illustration of the power of modeling techniques developed on the basis of careful a priori conceptual and theoretical reasoning and the limitations of applying readily available modeling software to what are essentially technical exercises. The age, period, and cohort classifications provide "accounting categories" that allow researchers to locate category differences on these dimensions but provide little insight into the underlying social mechanisms that link different outcomes to different biographic/historic locations. Identifying these differences represents only a first step in a more extensive investigative process; explaining how the differences were produced is the ultimate goal. The identification problem that characterizes APC models is resolved—ideally—by replacing the classification schemes with substantive variables that measure the underlying phenomena (Mason & Fienberg, 1985). The APC models, therefore, should be based on carefully constructed conceptual models designed to answer *why* the outcome distribution should be organized on the basis of age, period, and/or cohort membership. But in meeting this last requirement, researchers must necessarily move across levels for, by definition, the kinds of substantive measures that should be nominated to replace age, period, or cohort categories are not individual-level measures. Cohort analysis requires a multilevel approach—one that allows us to treat organizational contexts as more than exogenous characteristics of individuals. Conceptually, one must see that cohort or period effects occur because macrolevel phenomena influence microlevel behaviors. Articulating the linkage across levels of aggregation requires that we conceptualize the mechanisms through which social structure affects individual behavior. Then we must develop adequate methodological tools to test our hypotheses and allow us to discriminate among competing explanations.

By way of example, consider four competing explanations that can account for why members of a given cohort may behave similarly. Cohort members may manifest the same behavior of interest because of (a) correlated individual effects, (b) ecological effects, (c) contextual effects, and (d) endogenous effects.[3] Correlated individual effects provide the most individualistic explanation, suggesting that people who share similar characteristics behave in similar ways. An ecological explanation emphasizes social structural arrangements in which groups exist: individuals-as-group-members face similar constraints and opportunities; therefore, their behaviors are shaped in similar ways.

The remaining two categories of effects are arguably more sociological, since they invoke the importance of the reference group in shaping individual behavior. The key to the difference between the first two effects and the remaining two is the extent to which the individual is influenced by group characteristics and group dynamics. Contextual effects link individual behaviors to the distribution of background characteristics in the reference group. As an example, Abrahamse, Morrison, and Waite (1988) find that the likelihood that teenage girls have a child in the 2 years after their sophomore year in high school depends on the attitudes toward unmarried childbearing of the other girls in their school. In contrast, endogenous effects refer to situations in which the likelihood that an individual behaves in a certain way is linked to the prevalence of that behavior in the reference group. As Manski (1993) describes, attempts to discriminate among these various explanations is thwarted by the problem of underidentification—too little information to support the detailed specification. Ecological effects cannot be differentiated from correlated individual effects; endogenous effects cannot be distinguished from contextual effects. If contextual effects describe the mechanism by which cohort membership shapes individual behavior, then the distinction between "exogenous" determinants and "endogenous" outcomes is legitimate: for any given cohort, the response of any member is a function of group characteristics, not group behavior. However, as the name implies, endogenous effects indicate that a cohort member's behavior is a function of the group's behavior, but any one member's response is simultaneously implicated in the response distribution of the cohort. Whereas contextual effects suggest that cohort members operate independently and the choice of any one member does not have ramifications for remaining cohort members, endogenous effects imply possible multiplier or feedback effects. Though many of the models we estimate operate as if the former were true, many theoretical perspectives (e.g., neoclassical economics) argue that choices made by any one individual are constrained by the simultaneous choices of all other individuals.

The notion that the behavior of individuals is, at least in part, shaped by characteristics of the groups to which they belong was behind the development of contextual models. Recent extensions of these techniques are designed to better address the part/whole relationships implied in social processes and to deal with implications of these relationships for the error structures. For example, the idea that individuals and social groupings at various levels of aggregation should be viewed as a hierarchically organized system of relationships fueled the development of hierarchical linear modeling techniques, also called multilevel models. Multilevel models provide a way of making explicit the contention that group dynamics reflect more than a simple aggregation of individual behaviors, that at increasingly complex levels of social organization, individuals and their relationship to one another may be more than an additive phenomenon. Instead, these approaches regard relationships among individuals as socially structured and argue that relevant group characteristics cannot necessarily be reduced to individual-level variation. Rather than defining concepts (and measuring variables) at different levels of aggregation and then analyzing relationships within a single level, multilevel models attend explicitly to group memberships and the social organization of individuals by treating parameters from micro- or individual-level models as variables that may be explained by more macrolevel system features involved in structuring the microprocess.

Although the utility of multilevel models for studying aging and social change has been questioned because of the "static" nature of these models (see, e.g., Mason, 1991), some researchers have been developing extensions of multilevel modeling techniques to analyze trends. DiPrete and Grusky (1990a) use a multilevel approach to analyze repeated surveys, allowing the year to define the "context" and using time series information on macrolevel variables to explain variation in patterns across years. Development within this general category of models has included applications to longitudinal data with repeated measures of the same subjects (Bryk & Raudenbush, 1992), factorial designs (Hox, Kreft, & Hermkens, 1991), and structural equation models (McDonald, 1994; Muthén, 1994). The fact that macrolevel variables (e.g., system characteristics) are treated as exogenous in these models—microlevel relationships *depend on* macrocharacteristics—is a different sort of limitation and returns us to one of Mannheim's concerns: how do we understand the process whereby individuals are shaped by social structure while, at the same time, they are involved in its production, reproduction, and revision? This issue, which historically defined the problematic of sociology, has also proved stubbornly intractable to our analytic tool kit. We have developed strategies to move beyond static, cross-sectional representations in favor of adopting a dynamic approach that allows us to look directly at process, but we are confined to one level of analysis; we look at individuals, or at organizations, or at nation states, but our only means of introducing other levels into the analysis is through the assumption of contextual effects. We have developed techniques that allow us to directly model individual behavior as it is embedded in organizations, or regions, or cohorts, but we cannot escape the limitation of assuming exogeneity. Though some techniques for dealing with endogeneity issues are also being developed, we cannot at present extend those techniques across time or across levels.

Asking the Right Questions

Clearly, many important issues remain unresolved in the study of aging and social change. The chapters that follow provide different perspectives on how these issues can be framed most productively and what methodological tools currently available hold the most promise for moving us forward. The reprinted papers by Karl Mannheim and Norman Ryder are regarded as classics in this literature; these writings have motivated the thinking of many of the contributors to this volume as they have tried to wrestle with the questions posed, the answers proposed, and the practical considerations involved in testing the propositions that flow from their ideas.

In his chapter on the importance of age, Hazelrigg questions the power of "age" as an explanatory factor, rather than a descriptive one, in furthering our understanding of social processes. What is it about a social process of aging that does more than simply reframe parallel processes of development or self formation, more than temporalize other socially constructed allocation processes? In asking how we conceptualize aging as a unique process, he forces us to examine more carefully conventional conceptions of the temporal properties of the processes we study. Although aging provides a convenient clock for measuring events or transitions, age may be no more than an arbitrary timing device for organizing information about processes that are, in some sense, time dependent. Though age may be useful in establishing temporal boundaries—before and after—and temporal orders—younger and older—the use of increasingly refined categories of age has been evacuating their substantive meaning and promoting further individualization of the life course.

Pavalko picks up on the theme of life course analysis and, in particular, the importance of framing transitions as elements of longer-term processes, rather than viewing them as isolated events of change, mobility or alteration. To be able to study these longer-term processes, we must know more than simply the origin and destination states and their timing relative to some temporal frame. She suggests we attend to the pattern, the sequence, the pace, and the reversibility of transitions in assessing how transitions may be organized in time and space to expand or limit the options of individuals to change course. In other words, how does the weight of past experiences shape the range of alternatives from which individuals may choose? How does it influence the probability of success in alternate ventures?

Firebaugh and Haynie shift our attention from the unfolding of individual life histories to the study of cohort behavior and cohort replacement as a reflection of social change. Arguing the utility of repeated survey designs, they note the catch-22 reflected in the two major data collection strategies used in social science. By studying the same individuals over time, it is possible to build a record of correlated characteristics and events, study the determinants of behaviors and transitions within a prospective framework, and address questions of intraindividual change over time. In other words, we can document the process of individual aging as it is manifested in the distributions of characteristics we measure. But, with time, these samples become less and less representative of the total population, since they generally do not allow cohort replacement; repeated measurements can introduce "study effects" in the information collected; and we are necessarily limited to studying the experiences of a single cohort. By using repeated surveys in combination with various analytic strategies, we can make cohort comparisons, study trends in attitudes or behaviors, assess the relative contributions of cohort succession and within-cohort change to the production of observed trends, and study changing individual-level effects. But by addressing issues of group change within the repeated survey design, we cannot speak directly about the nature of intraindividual change.

In his examination of the relationship between aging and political conservatism, Alwin directly confronts this conundrum. Alwin initially uses a repeated surveys design in analyzing a series of National Election Studies and National Opinion Research Center (NORC) General Social Surveys to identify trends in political party identification. He uses Firebaugh's (1989) decomposition technique to separate the net change in party identification that results from cohort replacement from that linked to intracohort change. However, the interpretation of results is ambiguous with regard to the issue of life span stability in political party identification, since the cohort replacement effect also reflects the compositional effects of aging and the intracohort change effect confounds aging and period effects. In other words, the effect of aging is not limited to one element in the decomposition but is implied in both, a limitation noted by Firebaugh (1989). In order to gain additional leverage on the question of whether and how aging processes contribute to political orientations, Alwin moves from a repeated surveys design to a synthetic cohort design in order to examine the life span stability in three measures of party choice and attachment. Key to his approach is the separation of measurement unreliability from "true" instability. Alwin argues that the linkage between cohort differentiation and social change rests on assumptions of human stability—the persistence of characteristics or attitudes on which cohort differentiation occurs.

The distinction between concepts of stability and concepts of intraindividual change is taken up by Nesselroade and Featherman in the final chapter. Whereas Alwin argues that stability provides a useful backdrop against which changes are assessed, Nesselroade and Featherman view variability as "the norm" and the absence of change as requiring explanation. Arguing that concepts of stability have enjoyed a privileged position in the theoretical and methodological literatures, they suggest that concepts of intraindividual variability should be more fully incorporated into developmental research and theorizing. Their assertion that intraindividual variation should be viewed as adaptation to changing contexts is consistent with Hazelrigg's discussion of the development of self as a process of change over which individuals attempt to exert control. This gestalt shift in perspective has profound implications for the way we theorize aging/development and for how we design analytic techniques to test our propositions.

Though we face frustrating limitations in our ability to model dynamic systems in all their complexity, the questions we ask are pushing on the conceptual boundaries as we develop additional methodological tools to test our ideas. Sometimes we find it difficult to adequately verbalize the issues. We lapse into a syntax that treats the different levels as analytically distinct pieces of the puzzle, joined by the conjunction "and" (as in the individual and society, aging, and social change) and simultaneously recognize that this part/whole relationship belies that separation. And we find ourselves rediscovering insights that have been offered and forgotten, then resurrected and reframed, reminding ourselves that "the materialistic doctrine that men are products of circumstances and upbringing, and, therefore, that changed men are the products of other circumstances and changed upbringing, forgets that it is men [and women] that change circumstances" (Marx, 1976, p. 3-5).

◈ **NOTES**

1. Utilizing information on the functional form of the transition curves rather than simply relying on measures of central tendency is essential in making comparisons of experiences across cohorts. For example, average age of retirement may remain constant—or nearly so—over a decade, but over the same period the variation in when people take retirement may increase or decrease and the general shape of the distribution may be altered substantially. As is the case with any distribution, as dispersion increases the utility of measures of central tendency is reduced.

2. This argument could be extended to units other than firms. As labor force participation rates for married women have climbed, researchers have been developing models of joint retirement that attempt to assess individual retirement transitions within a household framework.

3. For a more detailed discussion of these and related issues see Manski (1993).

CHAPTER TWO

The Problem of Generations

KARL MANNHEIM

◇ HOW THE PROBLEM STANDS AT THE MOMENT

The Positivist Formulation of the Problem

The first task of the sociologist is to review the general state of investigation
into his problem. All too often it falls to his lot to deal with stray problems
to which all the sciences in turn have made their individual contribution
without anyone having ever paid any attention to the continuity of the
investigation as a whole. We shall need to do more, however, than give a
mere survey of past contributions to the problem of generations. We must try
to give a critical evaluation of the present stage of discussion (in Part One);
this will help us in our own analysis of the problem (in Part Two).

Two approaches to the problem have been worked out in the past: a
"positivist" and a "romantic-historical" one. These two schools represent two
antagonistic types of attitudes towards reality, and the different ways in
which they approach the problem reflect this contrast of basic attitudes. The
methodical ideal of the Positivists consisted in reducing their problems to
quantitative terms; they sought a quantitative formulation of factors ultimately determining human existence. The second school adopted a qualitative approach, firmly eschewing the clear daylight of mathematics, and
introverting the whole problem.

EDITOR'S NOTE: Reprinted by permission of Routledge & Kegan Paul. The bibliographic
information in this chapter has been modified to conform to the style used in this book.

To begin with the former. The Positivist is attracted by the problem of generations because it gives him the feeling that here he has achieved contact with some of the ultimate factors of human existence as such. There is life and death; a definite, measurable span of life; generation follows generation at regular intervals. Here, thinks the Positivist, is the framework of human destiny in comprehensible, even measurable form. All other data are conditioned within the process of life itself: they are only the expression of particular relationships. They can disappear, and their disappearance means only the loss of one of many possible forms of historical being. But if the ultimate human relationships are changed, the existence of man as we have come to understand it must cease altogether—culture, creativeness, tradition must all disappear, or must at least appear in a totally different light.

Hume actually experimented with the idea of a modification of such ultimate data. Suppose, he said, the type of succession of human generations to be completely altered to resemble that of a butterfly or caterpillar, so that the older generation disappears at one stroke and the new one is born all at once. Further, suppose man to be of such a high degree of mental development as to be capable of choosing rationally the form of government most suitable for himself. (This, of course, was the main problem of Hume's time.) These conditions given, he said, it would be both possible and proper for each generation, without reference to the ways of its ancestors, to choose afresh its own particular form of state. Only because mankind is as it is—generation following generation in a continuous stream, so that whenever one person dies off, another is born to replace him—do we find it necessary to preserve the continuity of our forms of government. Hume thus translates the principle of political continuity into terms of the biological continuity of generations.

Comte[1] too toyed with a similar idea: he tried to elucidate the nature and tempo of progress (the central problem of his time) by assuming a change in the basic data of the succession of generations and of the average length of life. If the average span of life of every individual were either shortened or lengthened, he said, the tempo of progress would also change. To lengthen the life-span of the individual would mean slowing up the tempo of progress, whereas to reduce the present duration of life by half or a quarter would correspondingly accelerate the tempo, because the restrictive, conservative, "go-slow" influence of the older generation would operate for a longer time, should they live longer, and for a shorter time, should they disappear more quickly.

An excessively retarded pace was harmful, but there was also danger that too great an acceleration might result in shallowness, the potentialities of life never being really exhausted. Without wishing to imply that our world is the best of all possible worlds, Comte nevertheless thought that our span of life and the average generation period of 30 years were necessary correlatives of our organism, and that further, the slow progress of mankind was directly related to this organic limitation. The tempo of progress and the presence of conservative as well as reforming forces in society are thus directly attributed to biological factors. This is, indeed, how the problem looks in broad daylight. Everything is almost mathematically clear: everything is capable of analysis into its constituent elements, the constructive imagination of the thinker celebrates its triumph; by freely combining the available data, he has succeeded in grasping the ultimate, constant elements of human existence, and the secret of History lies almost fully revealed before us.

The rationalism of positivism is a direct continuation of classical rationalism, and it shows the French mind at work in its own domain. In fact, the important contributors to the problem are for the most part French. Comte, Cournot, J. Dromel, Mentré, and others outside Germany are positivists or, at any rate, have come under their influence. Ferrari, the Italian, and O. Lorenz, the Austrian historian, all worked at a time when the positivist wave encompassed all Europe.[2]

Their formulations of the problem had something in common. They all were anxious to find a general law to express the rhythm of historical development, based on the biological law of the limited life-span of man and the overlap of new and old generations. The aim was to understand the changing patterns of intellectual and social currents directly in biological terms, to construct the curve of the progress of the human species in terms of its vital substructure. In the process, everything, so far as possible, was simplified: a schematic psychology provided that the parents should always be a conservative force.

Presented in this light, the history of ideas appears reduced to a chronological table. The core of the problem, after this implication, appears to be to find the average period of time taken for the older generation to be superseded by the new in public life, and principally, to find the natural starting-point in history from which to reckon a new period. The duration of a generation is very variously estimated—many assessing it at 15 years (e.g., Dromel), but most taking it to mean 30 years, on the ground that during the first 30 years of life people are still learning, that individual creativeness on an average begins only at that age, and that at 60 a man quits public life.[3] Even more difficult is it to find the natural beginning of the generation series, because birth and death in society as a whole follow continuously one upon the other, and full intervals exist only in the individual family where there is a definite period before children attain marriageable age.

This constitutes the core of this approach to the problem: the rest represents mere applications of the principle to concrete instances found in history. But the analytical mind remains at work all the time, and brings to light many important ramifications of the problem while working on the historical material.

Mentré[4] in particular, who first reviewed the problem historically, placed the whole formulation on a more solid basis.[5] He takes up the analysis of the problem of generations in the human family after a discussion of the same phenomenon among animals, based on the work of Espinas (*Les Sociétés animales,* Paris, 1877). It is only after having investigated these elementary aspects of the problem that he takes up more complex aspects, such as the question of social and intellectual generations.

We also must take into account a refinement of the problem due to Mentré which flows from the distinction he makes (in common with Lévy-Bruhl) between "institutions" and "*séries libres.*" A rhythm in the sequence of generations is far more apparent in the realm of the *séries*—free human groupings such as salons and literary circles—than in the realm of the institutions which for the most part lay down a lasting pattern of behaviour, either by prescriptions or by the organization of collective undertakings, thus preventing the new generation from showing its originality. An essential part of his work is concerned with the question as to whether there is what he calls a *pre-eminent sphere* in history (for example, politics, science, law, art, economic, etc.) which determines all others. He comes to the conclusion that there is no such dominant sphere imposing its own rhythm of development upon the others, since all alike are embedded in the general stream of history,[6] although the aesthetic sphere is perhaps the most appropriate to reflect overall changes of mental climate. An analysis of the history of this sphere in France since the 16th century led him to the view that essential changes had come about at intervals of 30 years.

Mentré's book is useful as the first comprehensive survey of the problem, although in reality it yields little, considering its volume, and fails to probe deeply enough or to formulate the problem in systematic terms. That the French recently became so interested in the problem of change from one generation to another was largely due to the fact that they witnessed the sudden eclipse of liberal cosmopolitanism as a result of the arrival of a nationalistically-minded young generation. The change of generations appeared as an immediately given datum and also as a problem extending far outside the academic field, a problem whose impact upon real life could be observed in concrete fashion, for example, by issuing questionnaires.[7]

Although Mentré occasionally makes remarks which point beyond a purely quantitative approach, we may consider him as a positivist whose treatment of the problem of generations thus far represents the last word of the school on this subject.

We must now turn our attention to the alterative romantic-historical approach.

The Romantic-Historical
Formulation of the Problem

We find ourselves in a quite different atmosphere if we turn to Germany and trace the development of the problem there. It would be difficult to find better proof of the thesis that ways of formulating problems and modes of thought differ from country to country and from epoch to epoch, depending on dominant political trends, than the contrasting solutions offered to our problem in the various countries at different times. It is true that Rümelin, who attacked the problem from the statistical viewpoint, and O. Lorenz, who used genealogical research data as his starting-point, both remained faithful to the positivist spirit of their epoch. But the whole problem of generations took on a specifically "German" character when Dilthey tackled it. All the traditions and impulses which once inspired the romantic-historical school were revived in Dilthey's work; in Dilthey we witness the sudden re-emergence, in revised form, of problems and categories which in their original, romantic-historicist setting helped found the social and historical sciences in Germany.

In Germany and France, the predominating trends of thought in the last epoch emerged closely related with their respective historical and political structures.

In France a positivist type of thought, deriving directly from the tradition of the enlightenment, prevailed. It tended to dominate not merely the natural but also the cultural sciences. It not only inspired progressive and opposi-tional groups, but even those professing conservatism and traditionalism. In Germany, on the other hand, the position was just the reverse—the romantic and historical schools supported by a strong conservative impulse always held sway. Only the natural sciences were able to develop in the positivist tradition: the cultural sciences were based entirely on the romantic-historical attitude, and positivism gained ground only sporadically, insofar as from time to time it was sponsored by oppositional groups.

Although the antithesis must not be exaggerated, it is nevertheless true that it provided rallying points in the struggle which was conducted round practically every logical category; and the problem of generations itself constituted merely one stage in the development of this much wider campaign. Unless we put this antithesis between French positivism and German romanticism into its wider context, we cannot hope to understand it in relation to the narrower problem of generations.

For the liberal positivist type, especially at home, as stated, in France, the problem of generations serves above all as evidence in favour of its unilinear conception of progress.

This type of thought, arising out of modern liberal impulses, from the outset adopted a mechanistic, externalised concept of time, and attempted to use it as an objective measure of unilinear progress by virtue of its expressibility in quantitative terms. Even the succession of generations was considered as something which articulated rather than broke the unilinear continuity of time. The most important thing about generations from this point was that they constituted one of the essential driving forces of progress.

It is this concept of progress, on the other hand, that is challenged by the romantic and historicist German mind which, relying on data furnished by a conservative technique of observation, points to the problem of generations precisely as evidence against the concept of unilinear development in history.[8] The problem of generations is seen here as the problem of the existence of an interior time that cannot be measured but only experienced in purely qualitative terms.

The relative novelty of Dilthey's work consists in just this distinction which he made between the qualitative and quantitative concept of time. Dilthey is interested in the problem of generations primarily because, as he puts it, the adoption of the "generation" as a temporal unit of the history of intellectual evolution makes it possible to replace such purely external units as hours, months, years, decades, etc., by a concept of measure operating from within (*eine von innen abmessende Vorstellung*). The use of generations as units makes it possible to appraise intellectual movements by an intuitive process of re-enactment.[9]

The second conclusion to which Dilthey comes in connection with the phenomenon of generations is that not merely is the succession of one after another important, but also that their *co-existence* is of more than mere chronological significance. The same dominant influences deriving from the prevailing intellectual, social, and political circumstances are experienced by contemporary individuals, both in their early, formative, and in their later years. They are contemporaries, they constitute one generation, just because they are subject to common influences. This idea that, from the point of view of the history of ideas, contemporaneity means a state of being subjected to similar influences rather than a mere chronological datum, shifts the discussion from a plane on which it risked degenerating into a kind of arithmetical mysticism to the sphere of interior time which can be grasped by intuitive understanding.

Thus, a problem open to quantitative, mathematical treatment only is replaced by a qualitative one, centred about the notion of something which is not quantifiable, but capable only of being experienced. The time-interval separating generations becomes subjectively experienceable time; and contemporaneity becomes a subjective condition of having been submitted to the same determining influences.

From here it is only one step to the phenomenological position of Heidegger, who gives a very profound interpretation of this qualitative relationship—for him, the very stuff and substance of Fate. "Fate is not the sum of individual destinies, any more than togetherness can be understood as a mere appearing together of several subjects. Togetherness in the same world, and the consequent preparedness for a distinct set of possibilities, determines the direction of individual destinies in advance. The power of Fate is then unleashed in the peaceful intercourse and the conflict of social life. The inescapable fate of living in and with one's generation completes the full drama of individual human existence."[10]

The qualitative concept of time upon which, as we have seen, Dilthey's approach was based, also underlies the formulation given the problem by the art historian Pinder.[11] Dilthey with a happy restraint is never led to develop any but genuine possibilities opened up by the romantic-qualitative approach. As a matter of fact, he was able to learn also from positivism. Pinder, on the other hand, becomes thoroughly enmeshed in all the confusions of romanticism. He gives many deep insights, but does not know how to avoid the natural excesses of romanticism. *The non-contemporaneity of the contemporaneous* is what interests Pinder most in relation to generations. Different generations live at the same time. But since experienced time is the only real time, they must all in fact be living in qualitatively quite different subjective eras. "Everyone lives with people of the same and of different ages, with a variety of possibilities of experience facing them all alike. But for each the "same time" is a different time—that is, it represents a different *period of his self,* which he can only share with people of his own age."[12]

Every moment of time is therefore in reality more than a point-like event—it is a temporal volume having more than one dimension, because it is always experienced by several generations at various stages of development.[13] To quote a musical simile employed by Pinder: the thinking of each epoch is polyphonous. At any given point in time we must always sort out the individual voices of the various generations, each attaining that point in time in its own way.

A further idea suggested by Pinder is that each generation builds up an "entelechy" of its own by which means alone it can really become a qualitative unity. Although Dilthey believed the inner unity of a generation to exist in the community of determining influences of an intellectual and social kind, the link of contemporaneity as such did not assume a purely qualitative form in his analysis. Heidegger tried to remedy this with his concept of "fate" as the primary factor producing unity; Pinder, then, in the tradition of modern art history, suggested the concept of "entelechy."

According to him, the entelechy of a generation is the expression of the unity of its "inner aim"—of its inborn way of experiencing life and the world. Viewed within the tradition of German art history, this concept of "entelechy" represents the transfer of Riegl's concept of the "art motive" (*Kunstwollen*)[14] from the phenomenon of unity of artistic styles to that of the unity of generations, in the same way as the concept of the "art motive" itself resulted from the rejuvenation and fructification, under the influence of positivism, of the morphological tendency already inherent in the historicist concept of the *spirit of a people* (*Volksgeist*).

The concept of a *spirit of the age* (*Zeitgeist*) with which one had hitherto principally worked, now turns out to be—to take another of Pinder's favourite[15] musical analogies—an accidental chord, an apparent harmony, produced by the vertical coincidence of notes which in fact owe a primary horizontal allegiance to the different parts (i.e., the generation-entelechies) of a fugue. The generation-entelechies thus serve to destroy the purely temporal concepts of an epoch over-emphasized in the past (e.g., spirit of the age or epoch). The epoch as a unit has no homogeneous driving impulse, no homogeneous principle of form—no entelechy. Its unity consists at most in the related nature of the means which the period makes available for the fulfillment of the different historical tasks of the generations living in it. Periods have their characteristic colour—"such colours do in fact exist, but somewhat as the colour-tone of a varnish through which one can look at the many colours of the different generations and age-groups."[16]

Although this denial of the existence of an entelechy peculiar to each epoch means that epochs can no longer serve as units in historical analysis and that the concept of *Zeitgeist* becomes inapplicable and relativized, other terms customarily used as units in the history of ideas are left valid. According to Pinder, in addition to entelechies of generations, there exist entelechies of art, language, and style; entelechies of nations and tribes—even an entelechy of Europe; and finally, entelechies of the individuals themselves.

What then, according to Pinder, constitutes the historical process? The interplay of constant and transient factors. The constant factors are civilization, nation, tribe, family, individuality, and type; the transient factors are the entelechies already mentioned. "It is maintained that growth is more important than experience ("influences," "relationships"). It is maintained that the life of art, as seen by the historian, consists in the interactions of *determining entelechies, born* of mysterious processes of nature, with the equally essential frictions, influences, and relations *experienced* in the actual development of these entelechies."[17] What is immediately striking here is that the social factor is not even alluded to in this enumeration of determining factors.

This romantic tendency in Germany completely obscured the fact that between the natural or physical and the mental spheres there is a level of existence at which social forces operate. Either a completely spiritualistic attitude is maintained and everything is deduced from entelechies (the existence of which, however, is not to be denied), or there is a feeling of obligation to introduce some element of realism, and then some crude biological data like race and generation which, again, must be admitted to exist) are counted upon to produce cultural facts by a "mysterious natural process." Undoubtedly, there are mysteries in the world in any case, but we should use them as explanatory principles in their proper place, rather than at points where it is still perfectly possible to understand the agglomeration of forces in terms of social processes. Intellectual and cultural history is surely shaped, among other things, by social relations in which men get originally confronted with each other, by groups within which they find mutual stimulus, where concrete struggle produces entelechies and thereby also influences and to a large extent shapes art, religion, and so on. Perhaps it would also be fruitful to ask ourselves whether society in fact can produce nothing more than "influences" and "relationships," or whether, on the contrary, social factors also possess a certain creative energy, a formative power, a social entelechy of their own. Is it not perhaps possible that this energy, arising from the interplay of social forces, constitutes the link between the other entelechies of art, style, generations, etc., which would otherwise only accidentally cross paths or come together? If one refuses to look at this matter from this point of view, and assumes a direct relationship between the spiritual and the vital without any sociological and historical factors mediating between them, he will be too easily tempted to conclude that especially productive generations are the "chance products of nature,"[18] and "the problem of the times of birth will point towards the far more difficult and mysterious one of the times of death."[19] How much more sober, how much more in tune with the genuine impulses of research, is the following sentence in which Dilthey, so to speak, disposed of such speculations in advance: "For the time being, the most natural assumption would appear to be that on the whole, both the degree and the distribution of ability are the same for each generation, the level of efficiency within the national society being constant, so that two other groups of conditions[20] would explain both the distribution and the intensity of achievement."

Valuable, even a stroke of genius, is Pinder's idea of the *non-contemporaneity of the contemporaneous,* as well as his concept of entelechies—both the result of the romantic-historical approach and both undoubtedly unattainable by positivism. But his procedure becomes dangerously inimical to the scientific spirit where he chooses to make use of the method of analogy. This mode of thought, which actually derives from speculations about the philosophy of nature current during the Renaissance, was revived and blown up to grotesque proportions by the Romantics; it is used currently by Pinder whenever he tries to work out a biological world-rhythm. His ultimate aim also is to establish measurable intervals in history (although somewhat more flexibly than usual), and to use this magical formula of generations in order to discover birth cycles exercising a decisive influence on history. Joel,[21] otherwise an eminent scholar, indulges in even more unwarranted constructions in this field. His latest publication on the secular rhythm in history reminds the reader immediately of the romantic speculations.

It is a complete misconception to suppose, as do most investigators, that a real problem of generations exists only insofar as a rhythm of generations, recurring at unchanging intervals, can be established. Even if it proved impossible to establish such intervals, the problem of generations would nevertheless remain a fruitful and important field of research.

We do not yet know—perhaps there is a secular rhythm at work in history, and perhaps it will one day be discovered. But we must definitely repudiate any attempt to find it through imaginative speculations, particularly when this speculation—whether biological or spiritual in its character—is simply used as a pretext for avoiding research into the nearer and more transparent fabric of social processes and their influence on the phenomenon of generations. Any biological rhythm must work itself out through the medium of social events: and if this important group of formative factors is left unexamined, and everything is derived directly from vital factors, all the fruitful potentialities in the original formulation of the problem[22] are liable to be jettisoned in the manner of its solution.

◇ THE SOCIOLOGICAL PROBLEM OF GENERATIONS

The problem of generations is important enough to merit serious consideration. It is one of the indispensable guides to an understanding of the structure of social and intellectual movements. Its practical importance becomes clear as soon as one tries to obtain a more exact understanding of the accelerated pace of social change characteristic of our time. It would be regrettable if extra-scientific methods were permanently to conceal elements of the problem capable of immediate investigation.

It is clear from the foregoing survey of the problem as it stands today that a commonly accepted approach to it does not exist. The social sciences in various countries only sporadically take account of the achievements of their neighbours. In particular German research into the problem of generations has ignored results obtained abroad. Moreover, the problem has been tackled by specialists in many different sciences in succession; thus, we possess a number of interesting sidelights on the problem as well as contributions to an overall solution, but no consciously directed research on the basis of a clear formulation of the problem as a whole.

The multiplicity of points of view, resulting both from the peculiarities of the intellectual traditions of various nations and from those of the individual sciences, is both attractive and fruitful; and there can be no doubt that such a wide problem can only be solved as a result of co-operation between the most diverse disciplines and nationalities. However, the co-operation must somehow be planned and directed from an organic centre. The present status of the problem of generations thus affords a striking illustration of the anarchy in the social and cultural sciences, where everyone starts out afresh from his own point of view (to a certain extent, of course, this is both necessary and fruitful), never pausing to consider the various aspects as part of a single general problem, so that the contributions of the various disciplines to the collective solution could be planned.

Any attempt at over-organization of the social and cultural sciences is naturally undesirable: but it is at least worth considering whether there is not perhaps one discipline—according to the nature of the problem in question—which could act as the organizing centre for work on it by all the others. As far as generations are concerned, the task of sketching the layout of the problem undoubtedly falls to sociology. It seems to be the task of Formal *Sociology* to work out the simplest, but at the same time the most fundamental facts relating to the phenomenon of generations. Within the sphere of formal sociology, however, the problem lies on the borderline between the static and the dynamic types of investigation. Whereas formal sociology up to now has tended for the most part to study the social existence of man exclusively *statically,* this particular problem seems to be one of those which have to do with the ascertainment of the origin of social dynamism and of the laws governing the action of the dynamic components of the social process. Accordingly, this is the point where we have to make the transition from the formal static to the formal dynamic and from thence to applied historical sociology—all three together comprising the complete field of sociological research.

In the succeeding pages we shall attempt to work out in formal sociological terms all the most elementary facts regarding the phenomenon of generations, without the elucidation of which historical research into the problem cannot even begin. We shall try to incorporate any results of past investigations, which have proved themselves relevant, ignoring those which do not seem to be sufficiently well founded.

Concrete Group—Social Location *(Lagerung)*

To obtain a clear idea of the basic structure of the phenomenon of generations, we must clarify the specific inter-relations of the individuals comprising a single generation-unit.

The unity of a generation does not consist primarily in a social bond of the kind that leads to the formation of a concrete group, although it may sometimes happen that a feeling for the unity of a generation is consciously developed into a basis for the formation of concrete groups, as in the case of the modern German Youth Movement.[23] But in this case, the groups are most often mere cliques, with the one distinguishing characteristic that group-formation is based upon the consciousness of belonging to one generation, rather than upon definite objectives.

Apart from such a particular case, however, it is possible in general to draw a distinction between generations as mere collective facts on the one hand, and *concrete social groups* on the other.

Organizations for specified purposes, the family, tribe, sect, are all examples of such *concrete groups*. Their common characteristic is that the individuals of which they are composed do actually *in concrete* form a group, whether the entity is based on vital, existential ties of "proximity" or on the conscious application of the rational will. All "community" groups (*Gemeinschaftsgebilde*), such as the family and the tribe, come under the former heading, while the latter comprises "association" groups (*Gesellschaftsgebilde*).

The generation is not a concrete group in the sense of a community, i.e., a group which cannot exist without its members having concrete knowledge of each other, and which ceases to exist as a mental and spiritual unit as soon as physical proximity is destroyed. On the other hand, it is in no way comparable to associations such as organizations formed for a specific purpose, for the latter are characterized by a deliberate act of foundation, written statutes, and a machinery for dissolving the organization—features serving to hold the group together, even though it lacks the ties of spatial proximity and of community of life.

By a concrete group, then, we mean the union of a number of individuals through naturally developed or consciously willed ties. Although the members of a generation are undoubtedly bound together in certain ways, the ties between them have not resulted in a concrete group. How, then, can we define and understand the nature of the generation as a social phenomenon?

An answer may perhaps be found if we reflect upon the character of a different sort of social category, materially quite unlike the generation but bearing a certain structural resemblance to it—namely, the class position (*Klassenlage*) of an individual in society.

In its wider sense class-position can be defined as the common "location" (*Lagerung*) certain individuals hold in the economic and power structure of a given society as their "lot." One is proletarian, *entrepreneur,* or *rentier,* and he is what he is because he is constantly aware of the nature of his specific "location" in the social structure, i.e., of the pressures or possibilities of gain resulting from that position. This place in society does not resemble membership of an organization terminable by a conscious act of will. Nor is it at all binding in the same way as membership of a community (*Gemeinschaft*), which means that a concrete group affects every aspect of an individual's existence.

It is possible to abandon one's class position through an individual or collective rise or fall in the social scale, irrespective for the moment whether this is due to personal merit, personal effort, social upheaval, or mere chance.

Membership of an organization lapses as soon as we give notice of our intention to leave it; the cohesion of the community group *ceases to exist* if the mental and spiritual dispositions on which its existence has been based cease to operate in us or in our partners; and our previous class position loses its relevance for us as soon as we acquire a new position as a result of a change in our economic and power status.

Class position is an objective fact, whether the individual in question knows his class position or not, and whether he acknowledges it or not.

Class-consciousness does not necessarily accompany a class position, although in certain social conditions the latter can give rise to the former, lending it certain features, and resulting in the formation of a "conscious class."[24] At the moment, however, we are only interested in the general phenomenon of social *location* as such. Besides the concrete social group, there is also the phenomenon of similar location of a number of individuals in a social structure—under which heading other classes and generations fall.

We have now taken the first step towards an analysis of the "location" phenomenon as distinct from the phenomenon *"concrete group,"* and this much at any rate is clear—*viz.* the unity of generations is constituted essentially by a similarity of location of a number of individuals within a social whole.

The Biological and Sociological Formulation
of the Problem of Generations

Similarity of location can be defined only by specifying the structure within which and through which location groups emerge in historical-social reality. Class-position was based upon the existence of a changing economic and power structure in society. Generation location is based on the existence of biological rhythm in human existence—the factors of life and death, a limited span of life, and ageing. Individuals who belong to the same generation, who share the same year of birth, are endowed, to that extent, with a common location in the historical dimension of the social process.

Now, one might assume that the sociological phenomenon of location can be explained by, and deduced from, these basic biological factors. But this would be to make the mistake of all naturalistic theories which try to deduce sociological phenomena directly from natural facts, or lose sight of the social phenomenon altogether in a mass of primarily anthropological data. Anthropology and biology only help us explain the phenomena of life and death, the limited span of life, and the mental, spiritual, and physical changes accompanying ageing as such; they offer no explanation of the relevance these primary factors have for the shaping of social interrelationships in their historic flux.

The sociological phenomenon of generations is ultimately based on the biological rhythm of birth and death. But to be *based* on a factor does not necessarily mean to be *deducible* from it, or to be implied in it. If a phenomenon is *based* on another, it could not exist without the latter; however, it possesses certain characteristics peculiar to itself, characteristics in no way borrowed from the basic phenomenon. Were it not for the existence of social interaction between human beings—were there no definable social structure, no history based on a particular sort of continuity, the generation would not exist as a social location phenomenon; there would merely be birth, ageing, and death. The *sociological* problem of generations therefore begins at that point where the sociological relevance of these biological factors is discovered. Starting with the elementary phenomenon itself, then, we must first of all try to understand the generation as a particular type of social location.

The Tendency "Inherent In" a Social Location

The fact of belonging to the same class, and that of belonging to the same generation or age group, have this in common, that both endow the individuals sharing in them with a common location in the social and historical process, and thereby limit them to a specific range of potential experience, predisposing them for a certain characteristic mode of thought and experience, and a characteristic type of historically relevant action. Any given location, then, excludes a large number of possible modes of thought, experience, feeling, and action, and restricts the range of self-expression open to the individual to certain circumscribed possibilities. This *negative* delimitation, however, does not exhaust the matter. Inherent in a *positive* sense in every location is a tendency pointing towards certain definite modes of behaviour, feeling, and thought.

We shall therefore speak in this sense of a tendency "inherent in" every social location; a tendency which can be determined from the particular nature of the location as such.

For any group of individuals sharing the same class position, society always appears under the same aspect, familiarized by constantly repeated experience. It may be said in general that the experiential, intellectual, and emotional data which are available to the members of a certain society are not uniformly "given" to all of them; the fact is rather that each class has access to only one set of those data, restricted to one particular "aspect." Thus, the proletarian most probably appropriates only a fraction of the cultural heritage of his society, and that in the manner of his group. Even a mental climate as rigorously uniform as that of the Catholic Middle Ages presented itself differently according to whether one were a theologizing cleric, a knight, or a monk. But even where the intellectual material is more or less uniform or at least uniformly accessible to all, the *approach* to the material, the way in which it is assimilated and applied, is determined in its direction by social factors. We usually say in such cases that the approach is determined by the special traditions of the social stratum concerned. But these traditions themselves are explicable and understandable not only in terms of the history of the stratum but above all in terms of the location relationships of its members within the society. Traditions bearing in a particular direction only persist so long as the location relationships of the group acknowledging them remain more or less unchanged. The concrete form of an existing behaviour pattern or of a cultural product does not derive from the history of a particular tradition but ultimately from the history of the location relationships in which it originally arose and hardened itself into a tradition.

Fundamental Facts in Relation to Generations

According to what we have said so far, the social phenomenon "genera-tion" represents nothing more than a particular kind of identity of location, embracing related "age groups" embedded in a historical-social process. While the nature of class location can be explained in terms of economic and social conditions, generation location is determined by the way in which certain patterns of experience and thought tend to be brought into existence by the *natural data* of the transition from one generation to another.

The best way to appreciate which features of social life result from the existence of generations is to make the experiment of imagining what the social life of man would be like if one generation lived on forever and none followed to replace it. In contrast to such a utopian, imaginary society, our own has the following characteristics:[25]

- (a) new participants in the cultural process are emerging, whilst
- (b) former participants in that process are continually disappearing;
- (c) members of any one generation can participate only in a temporally limited section of the historical process, and
- (d) it is therefore necessary continually to transmit the accumulated cultural heritage;
- (e) the transition from generation to generation is a continuous process.

These are the basic phenomena implied by the mere fact of the existence of generations, apart from one specific phenomenon we choose to ignore for the moment, that of physical and mental ageing.[26] With this as a beginning, let us then investigate the bearing of these elementary facts upon formal sociology.

*(a) The continuous emergence of new
    participants in the cultural process*

In contrast to the imaginary society with no generations, our own—in which generation follows generation—is principally characterized by the fact that cultural creation and cultural accumulation are not accomplished by the same individuals—instead, we have the continuous emergence of new age groups.

This means, in the first place, that our culture is developed by individuals who come into contact anew with the accumulated heritage. In the nature of our psychical make-up, a fresh contact (meeting something anew) always means a changed relationship of distance from the object and a novel approach in assimilating, using, and developing the proffered material. The phenomenon of "fresh contact" is, incidentally, of great significance in many social contexts; the problem of generations is only one among those upon which it has a bearing. Fresh contacts play an important part in the life of the individual when he is forced by events to leave his own social group and enter a new one—when, for example, an adolescent leaves home, or a peasant the country-side for the town, or when an immigrant changes his home, or a social climber his social status or class. It is well known that in all these cases a quite visible and striking transformation of the consciousness of the individual in question takes place: a change, not merely in the content of experience, but in the individual's mental and spiritual adjustment to it. In all these cases, however, the fresh contact is an event in one individual biography, whereas in the case of generations, we may speak of "fresh contacts" in the sense of the addition of new psycho-physical units who are in the literal sense beginning a "new life." Whereas the adolescent, peasant, emigrant, and social climber can only in a more or less restricted sense be said to begin a "new life," in the case of generations, the "fresh contact" with the social and cultural heritage is determined not by mere social change, but by fundamental biological factors. We can accordingly differentiate between two types of "fresh contact": one based on a shift in social relations, and the other on vital factors (the change from one generation to another). The latter type is *potentially* much more radical, since with the advent of the new participant in the process of culture, the change of attitude takes place in a different individual whose attitude towards the heritage handed down by his predecessors is a novel one.

Were there no change of generation, there would be no "fresh contact" of this biological type. If the cultural process were always carried on and developed by the same individuals, then, to be sure, "fresh contacts" might still result from shifts in social relationships, but the more radical form of "fresh contact" would be missing. Once established, any fundamental social pattern (attitude or intellectual trend) would probably be perpetrated—in itself an advantage, but not if we consider the dangers resulting from onesidedness. There might be a certain compensation for the loss of fresh generations in such a utopian society only if the people living in it were possessed, as befits the denizens of a Utopia, of perfectly universal minds— minds capable of experiencing all that there was to experience and of knowing all there was to know, and enjoying an elasticity such as to make it possible at any time to start afresh. "Fresh contacts" resulting from shifts in the historical and social situation could suffice to bring about the changes in thought and practice necessitated by changed conditions only if the individuals experiencing these fresh contacts had such a perfect "elasticity of mind." Thus the continuous emergence of new human beings in our own society acts as compensation for the restricted and partial nature of the individual consciousness. The continuous emergence of new human beings certainly results in some loss of accumulated cultural possessions; but, on the other hand, it alone makes a fresh selection possible when it becomes necessary; it facilitates re-evaluation of our inventory and teaches us both to forget that which is no longer useful and to covet that which has yet to be won.

*(b) The continuous withdrawal of previous
        participants in the process of culture*

The function of this second factor is implied in what has already been said. It serves the necessary social purpose of enabling us to forget. If society is to continue, social remembering is just as important as forgetting and action starting from scratch.

At this point we must make clear in what social form remembering manifests itself and how the cultural heritage is actually accumulated. All psychic and cultural data only really exist insofar as they are produced and reproduced in the present: hence past experience is only relevant when it exists concretely incorporated in the present. In our present context, we have to consider two ways in which past experience can be incorporated in the present:

(i) as consciously recognized models[27] on which men pattern their behaviour (for example, the majority of subsequent revolutions tended to model themselves more or less consciously on the French Revolution); or

(ii) as unconsciously "condensed," merely "implicit" or "virtual" patterns; consider, for instance, how past experiences are "virtually" contained in such specific manifestations as that of sentimentality. Every present performance operates a certain selection among handed-down data, for the most part unconsciously. That is, the traditional material is transformed to fit a prevailing new situation, or hitherto unnoticed or neglected potentialities inherent in that material are discovered in the course of developing new patterns of action.[28]

At the more primitive levels of social life, we mostly encounter unconscious selection. There the past tends to be present in a "condensed," "implicit," and "virtual" form only. Even at the present level of social reality, we see this unconscious selection at work in the deeper region of our intellectual and spiritual lives, where the tempo of transformation is of less significance. A conscious and reflective selection becomes necessary only when a semi-conscious transformation, such as can be effected by the traditionalist mind, is no longer sufficient. In general, rational elucidation and reflectiveness invade only those realms of experience which become problematic as a result of a change in the historical and social situation; where that is the case, the necessary transformation can no longer be effected without conscious reflection and its technique of de-stabilization.

We are directly aware primarily of those aspects of our culture which have become subject to reflection; and these contain only those elements which in the course of development have somehow, at some point, become problematical. This is not to say, however, that once having become conscious and reflective, they cannot again sink back into the a-problematical, untouched region of vegetative life. In any case, that form of memory which contains the past in the form of reflection is much less significant—e.g., it extends over a much more restricted range of experience—than that in which the past is only "implicitly," "virtually" present; and reflective elements are more often dependent on unreflective elements than *vice versa.*

Here we must make a fundamental distinction between *appropriated* memories and *personally acquired* memories (a distinction applicable both to reflective and unreflective elements). It makes a great difference whether I acquire memories for myself in the process of personal development, or whether I simply take them over from someone else. I only really possess those "memories" which I have created directly for myself, only that "knowledge" I have personally gained in real situations. This is the only sort of knowledge which really "sticks" and it alone has real binding power. Hence, although it would appear desirable that man's spiritual and intellectual possessions should consist of nothing but individual acquired memories, this would also involve the danger that the earlier ways of possession and acquisition will inhibit the new acquisition of knowledge. That experience goes with age is in many ways an advantage. That, on the other hand, youth lacks experience means a lightening of the ballast for the young; it facilitates their living on in a changing world. One is old primarily insofar as[29] he comes to live within a specific, individually acquired, framework of useable past experience, so that every new experience has its form and its place largely marked out for it in advance. In youth, on the other hand, where life is new, formative forces are just coming into being, and basic attitudes in the process of development can take advantage of the moulding power of new situations. Thus a human race living on for ever would have to learn to forget to compensate for the lack of new generations.

(c) Members of any one generation can only participate in a temporally limited section of the historical process

The implications of this basic fact can also be worked out in the light of what has been said so far. The first two factors, (a) and (b), were only concerned with the aspects of constant "rejuvenation" of society. To be able to start afresh with a new life, to build a new destiny, a new framework of anticipations, upon a new set of experiences, are things which can come into the world only through the fact of new birth. All this is implied by the factor of social rejuvenation. The factor we are dealing with now, however, can be adequately analysed only in terms of the category of "similarity of location" which we have mentioned but not discussed in detail above.[30]

Members of a generation are "similarly located," first of all, insofar as they all are exposed to the same phase of the collective process. This, however, is a merely mechanical and external criterion of the phenomenon of "similar location." For a deeper understanding, we must turn to the phenomenon of the "stratification" of experience (*Erlebnisschichtung*), just as before we turned to "memory." The fact that people are born at the same time, or that their youth, adulthood, and old age coincide, does not in itself involve similarity of location; what does create a similar location is that they are in a position to experience the same events and data, etc., and especially that these experiences impinge upon a similarly "stratified" consciousness. It is not difficult to see why mere chronological contemporaneity cannot of itself produce a common generation location. No one, for example, would assert that there was community of location between the young people of

China and Germany about 1800. Only where contemporaries definitely are in a position to participate as an integrated group in certain common experiences can we rightly speak of community of location of a generation. Mere contemporaneity becomes sociologically significant only when it also involves participation in the same historical and social circumstances. Further, we have to take into consideration at this point the phenomenon of "stratification," mentioned above. Some older generation groups experience certain historical processes together with the young generation and yet we cannot say that they have the same generation location. The fact that their location is a different one, however, can be explained primarily by the different "stratification" of their lives. The human consciousness, structurally speaking, is characterized by a particular inner "dialectic." It is of considerable importance for the formation of the consciousness which experiences happen to make those all-important "first impressions," "childhood experiences"— and which follow to form the second, third, and other "strata." Conversely, in estimating the biographical significance of a particular experience, it is important to know whether it is undergone by an individual as a decisive childhood experience, or later in life, superimposed upon other basic and early impressions. Early impressions tend to coalesce into a *natural view* of the world. All later experiences then tend to receive their meaning from this original set, whether they appear as that set's verification and fulfillment or as its negation and antithesis. Experiences are not accumulated in the course of a lifetime through a process of summation or agglomeration, but are "dialectically" articulated in the way described. We cannot here analyse the specific forms of this dialectical articulation, which is potentially present whenever we act, think or feel, in more detail (the relationship of "antithesis" is only one way in which new experiences may graft themselves upon old ones). This much, however, is certain, that even if the rest of one's life consisted in one long process of negation and destruction of the natural world view acquired in youth, the determining influence of these early impressions would still be predominant. For even in negation our orientation is fundamentally centered upon that which is being negated, and we are thus still unwittingly determined by it. If we bear in mind that every concrete experience acquires its particular face and form from its relation to this primary stratum of experiences from which all others receive their meaning, we can appreciate its importance for the further development of the human consciousness. Another fact, closely related to the phenomenon just described, is that any two generations following one another always find different opponents, both within and without. While the older people may still be combating something in themselves or in the external world in such fashion that all their feelings and efforts and even their concepts and categories of thought are determined by that adversary, for the younger people this adversary may be simply non-existent: their primary orientation is an entirely different one. That historical development does not proceed in a straight line—a feature frequently observed particularly in the cultural sphere—is largely attributed to this shifting of the "polar" components of life, that is, to the fact that internal or external adversaries constantly disappear and are replaced by others. Now this particular dialectic, of changing generations, would be absent from our imaginary society. The only dialectical features of such a society would be those which would arise from social polarities—provided such polarities were present. The primary experiential stratum of the members of this imaginary society would simply consist of the earliest experiences of mankind; all later experience would receive its meaning from that stratum.

(d) The necessity for constant transmission of the cultural heritage

Some structural facts which follow from this must at least be indicated here. To mention one problem only: a utopian, immortal society would not have to face this necessity of cultural transmission, the most important aspect of which is the automatic passing on to the new generations of the traditional ways of life, feelings, and attitudes. The data transmitted by conscious teaching are of more limited importance, both quantitatively and qualitatively. All those attitudes and ideas which go on functioning satisfactorily in the new situation and serve as the basic inventory of group life are unconsciously and unwittingly handed on and transmitted: they seep in without either the teacher or pupil knowing anything about it. What is consciously learned or inculcated belongs to those things which in the course of time have somehow, somewhere, become problematic and therefore invited conscious reflection. This is why that inventory of experience which is absorbed by infiltration from the environment in early youth often becomes the historically oldest stratum of consciousness, which tends to stabilize itself as the natural view of the world.[31]

But in early childhood even many reflective elements are assimilated in the same "a-problematical" fashion as those elements of the basic inventory had been. The new germ of an original intellectual and spiritual life which is latent in the new human being has by no means as yet come into its own. The possibility of really questioning and reflecting on things only emerges at the point where personal experimentation with life begins—round about the age of 17, sometimes a little earlier and sometimes a little later.[32] It is only then that life's problems begin to be located in a "present" and are experienced as such. That level of data and attitudes which social change has rendered problematical, and which therefore requires reflection, has now been reached; for the first time, one lives "in the present." Combative juvenile groups struggle to clarify these issues, but never realise that, however radical they are, they are merely out to transform the uppermost stratum of consciousness which is open to conscious reflection. For it seems that the deeper strata are not easily destabilized[33] and that when this becomes necessary, the process must start out from the level of reflection and work down to the stratum of habits.[34] The "up-to-dateness" of youth therefore consists in their being closer to the "present" problems (as a result of their "potentially fresh contact" discussed above), and in the fact that they are dramatically aware of a process of de-stabilization and take sides in it. All this while, the older generation cling to the re-orientation that had been the drama of *their* youth.

From this angle, we can see that an adequate education or instruction of the young (in the sense of the complete transmission of all experiential stimuli which underlie pragmatic knowledge) would encounter a formidable difficulty in the fact that the experiential problems of the young are defined by a different set of adversaries from those of their teachers. Thus (apart from the exact sciences), the teacher-pupil relationship is not as between one representative of "consciousness in general" and another, but as between one possible subjective centre of vital orientation and another subsequent one. This tension[35] appears incapable of solution except for one compensating factor: not only does the teacher educate his pupil, but the pupil educates his teacher too. Generations are in a state of constant interaction.

This leads us to our next point:

(e) The uninterrupted generation series

The fact that the transition from one generation to another takes place continuously tends to render this interaction smoother; in the process of this interaction, it is not the oldest who meet the youngest at once; the first contacts are made by other "intermediary" generations, less removed from each other.

Fortunately, it is not as most students of the generation problem suggest— the 30-year interval is not solely decisive. Actually, all intermediary groups play their part; although they cannot wipe out the biological difference between generations, they can at least mitigate its consequences. The extent to which the problems of younger generations are reflected back upon the older one becomes greater in the measure that the dynamism of society increases. Static conditions make for attitudes of piety—the younger generation tends to adapt itself to the older, even to the point of making itself appear older. With the strengthening of the social dynamic, however, the older generation becomes increasingly receptive to influences from the younger.[36] This process can be so intensified that, with an elasticity of mind won in the course of experience, the older generation may even achieve greater adaptability in certain spheres than the intermediary generations, who may not yet be in a position to relinquish their original approach.[37]

Thus, the continuous shift in objective conditions has its counterpart in a continuous shift in the oncoming new generations which are first to incorporate the changes in their behaviour system. As the tempo of change becomes faster, smaller and smaller modifications are experienced by young people as significant ones, and more and more intermediary shades of novel impulses become interpolated between the oldest and newest re-orientation systems. The underlying inventory of vital responses, which remains unaffected by the change, acts in itself as a unifying factor; constant interaction, on the other hand, mitigates the differences in the top layer where the change takes place, while the continuous nature of the transition in normal times lessens the frictions involved. To sum up: if the social process involved no change of generations, the new impulses that can originate only in new organisms could not be reflected back upon the representatives of the tradition; and if the transition between generations were not continuous, this reciprocal action could not take place without friction.

◈ GENERATION STATUS, GENERATION AS ACTUALITY, GENERATION UNIT

This, then, broadly constitutes those aspects of generation phenomena which can be deduced by formal analysis. They would completely determine the effects resulting from the existence of generation if they could unfold themselves in a purely biological context, or if the generation phenomenon could be understood as a mere location phenomenon. However, a generation in the sense of a location phenomenon falls short of encompassing the generation phenomenon in its full actuality.[38] The latter is something more than the former, in the same way as the mere fact of class position does not yet involve the existence of a consciously constituted class. The location as such only contains potentialities which may materialize, or be suppressed, or become embedded in other social forces and manifest themselves in modified form. When we pointed out that mere co-existence in time did not even suffice to bring about community of generation location, we came very near to making the distinction which is now claiming our attention. In order to share the same generation location, i.e., in order to be able passively to undergo or actively to use the handicaps and privileges inherent in a generation location, one must be born within the same historical and cultural region. Generation as an actuality, however, involves even more than mere co-presence in such a historical and social region. A further concrete nexus is needed to constitute generation as an actuality. This additional nexus may be described as *participation in the common destiny* of this historical and social unit.[39] This is the phenomenon we have to examine next.

We said above that, for example, young people in Prussia about 1800 did not share a common generation location with young people in China at the same period. Membership in the same historical community, then, is the widest criterion of community of generation location. But what is its narrowest criterion? Do we put the peasants, scattered as they are in remote districts and almost untouched by current upheavals, in a common actual generation group with the urban youth of the same period? Certainly not!—and precisely because they remain unaffected by the events which move the youth of the towns. We shall therefore speak of a *generation as an actuality* only where a concrete bond is created between members of a generation by their being exposed to the social and intellectual symptoms of a process of dynamic de-stabilization. Thus, the young peasants we mentioned above only share the same generation location, without, however, being members of the same generation as an actuality, with the youth of the town. They are similarly located, insofar as they are *potentially* capable of being sucked into the vortex of social change, and, in fact, this is what happened in the wars against Napoleon, which stirred up all German classes. Or these peasants' sons, a mere generation location was transformed into membership of a generation as an actuality. Individuals of the same age, they were and are, however, only united as an actual generation insofar as they participate in the characteristic social and intellectual currents of their society and period, and insofar as they have an active or passive experience of the interactions of forces which made up the new situation. At the time of the wars against Napoleon, nearly all social strata were engaged in such a process of give and take, first in a wave of war enthusiasm, and later in a movement of religious revivalism. Here, however, a new question arises. Suppose we disregard all groups which do *not* actively participate in the process of social transformation—does this mean that all those groups, which *do* so participate, constitute one generation? From 1800 on, for instance, we see two contrasting groups—one which became more and more conservative as time went on, as against a youth group tending to become rationalistic and liberal. It cannot be said that these two groups were unified by the *same* modern mentality. Can we then speak, in this case, of the same actual generation? We can, it seems, if we make a further terminological distinction. Both the romantic-conservative and the liberal-rationalist youth belonged to the same actual generation, romantic-conservatism and liberal-rationalism were merely two *polar forms* of the intellectual and social response to an historical stimulus experienced by all in common. Romantic-conservative youth, and liberal-rationalist group, belong to the same actual generation but form separate "generation units" within it. The *generation unit* represents a much more concrete bond than the actual generation as such. *Youth experiencing the same concrete historical problems may be said to be part of the same actual generation; while those groups within the same actual generation which work up the material of their common experiences in different specific ways, constitute separate generation units.*

⬦ THE ORIGIN OF GENERATION UNITS

The question now arises, what produces a generation unit? In what does the greater intensity of the bond consist in this case? The first thing that strikes one on considering any particular generation unit is the great similarity in the data making up the consciousness of its members. Mental data are of sociological importance not only because of their actual content, but also because they cause the individuals sharing them to form one group—they have a socializing effect. The concept of Freedom, for example, was important for the Liberal generation-unit, not merely because of the material demands implied by it, but also because in and through it, it was possible to unite individuals scattered spatially and otherwise.[40] The data as such, however, are not the primary factor producing a group—this function belongs to a far greater extent to those formative forces which shape the data and give them character and direction. From the casual slogan to a reasoned system of thought, from the apparently isolated gesture to the finished work of art, the same formative tendency is often at work—the social importance of which lies in its power to bind individuals socially together. The profound emotional significance of a slogan, of an expressive gesture, or of a work of art lies in the fact that we not merely absorb them as objective data, but also as vehicles of formative tendencies and fundamental integrative attitudes, thus identifying ourselves with a set of collective strivings.

Fundamental integrative attitudes and formative principles are all-important also in the handing down of every tradition, firstly because they alone can bind groups together, secondly, and, what is perhaps even more important, they alone are really capable of becoming the basis of continuing practice. A mere statement of fact has a minimum capacity of initiating a continuing practice. Potentialities of a continued thought process, on the other hand, are contained in every thesis that has real group-forming potency; intuitions, feelings and works of art which create a spiritual community among men also contain in themselves the potentially new manner in which the intuition, feeling, or work of art in question can be re-created, rejuvenated and reinterpreted in novel situations. That is why unambiguousness, too great clarity is not an unqualified social value; productive misunderstanding is often a condition of continuing life. Fundamental integrative attitudes and formative principles are the primary socializing forces in the history of society, and it is necessary to live them fully in order really to participate in collective life.

Modern psychology provides more and more conclusive evidence in favour of the *Gestalt* theory of human perception: even in our most elementary perceptions of objects, we do not behave as the old atomistic psychology would have us believe; that is, we do not proceed towards a global impression by the gradual summation of a number of elementary sense data, but on the contrary, we start off with a global impression of the object as a whole. Now if even sense perception is governed by the *Gestalt* principle, the same applies, to an even greater extent, to the process of intellectual interpretation. There may be a number of reasons why the functioning of human consciousness should be based on the *Gestalt* principle, but a likely factor is the relatively limited capacity of the human consciousness when confronted with the infinity of elementary data which can be dealt with only by means of the simplifying and summarizing *Gestalt* approach. Seeing things in terms of *Gestalt,* however, also has its social roots with which we must deal here. Perceptions and their linguistic expressions never exist exclusively for the isolated individual who happens to entertain them, but also for the social group which stands behind the individual. Thus, the way in which seeing in terms of *Gestalt* modifies the datum as such—partly simplifying and abbreviating it, partly elaborating and filling it out—always corresponds to the meaning which the object in question has for the social groups as a whole.

We always see things already formed in a special way; we think concepts defined in terms of a specific context. Form and context depend, in any case, on the group to which we belong. To become really assimilated into a group involves more than the mere acceptance of its characteristic values—it involves the ability to see things from its particular "aspect," to endow concepts with its particular shade of meaning, and to experience psychological and intellectual impulses in the configuration characteristic of the group. It means, further, to absorb those interpretive formative principles which enable the individual to deal with new impressions and events in a fashion broadly pre-determined by the group.

The social importance of these formative and interpretive principles is that they form a link between spatially separated individuals who may never come into personal contact at all. Whereas mere common "location" in a generation is of only potential significance, a generation as an actuality is constituted when similarly "located" contemporaries participate in a common destiny and in the ideas and concepts which are in some way bound up with its unfolding. Within this community of people with a common destiny there can then arise particular *generation-units.* These are characterized by the fact that they do not merely involve a loose participation by a number of individuals in a pattern of events shared by all alike though interpreted by the different individuals differently, but an identity of responses, a certain affinity in the way in which all move with and are formed by their common experiences.

Thus within any generation there can exist a number of differentiated, antagonistic generation-units. Together they constitute an "actual" generation precisely because they are oriented toward each other, even though only in the sense of fighting one another. Those who were young about 1810 in Germany constituted one actual generation whether they adhered to the then current version of liberal or conservative ideas. But insofar as they were conservative or liberal, they belonged to different units of that actual generation.

The generation-unit tends to impose a much more concrete and binding tie on its members because of the parallelism of responses it involves. As a matter of fact, such new, overtly created, partisan integrative attitudes characterizing generation-units do not come into being spontaneously, without a personal contact among individuals, but within *concrete groups* where mutual stimulation in a close-knit vital unit inflames the participants and enables them to develop integrative attitudes which do justice to the requirements inherent in their common "location." Once developed in this way, however, these attitudes and formative tendencies are capable of being detached from the concrete groups of their origin and of exercising an appeal and binding force over a much wider area.

The generation-unit as we have described it is not, as such, a concrete group, although it does have as its nucleus a concrete group which has developed the most essential new conceptions which are subsequently developed by the unit. Thus, for example, the set of basic ideas which became prevalent in the development of modern German Conservatism had its origin in the concrete association *Christlich-deutsche Tischgesellschaft*. This association was first to take up and reformulate all the irrational tendencies corresponding to the overall situation prevailing at that time, and to the particular "location," in terms of generation, shared by the young Conservatives. Ideas which later were to have recruiting power in far wider circles originated in this particular concrete group.

The reason for the influence exercised beyond the limits of the original concrete group by such integrative attitudes originally evolved within the group is primarily that they provide a more or less adequate expression of the particular "location" of a generation as a whole. Hence, individuals outside the narrow group but nevertheless similarly located find in them the satisfying expression of their location in the prevailing *historical configuration*. Class ideology, for example, originates in more closely knit concrete groups and can gain ground only to the extent that other individuals see in it a more or less adequate expression and interpretation of the experiences peculiar to their particular *social* location. Similarly, the basic integrative attitudes and formative principles represented by a generation-unit, which are originally evolved within such a concrete group, are only really effective and capable of expansion into wider spheres when they formulate the typical experiences of the individuals sharing a generation location. Concrete groups can become influential in this sense if they succeed in evolving a "fresh contact" in terms of a "stratification of experience," such as we have described above. There is, in this respect, a further analogy between the phenomenon of class and that of generation. Just as a class ideology may, in epochs favourable to it, exercise an appeal beyond the "location" which is its proper habitat,[41] certain impulses particular to a generation may, if the trend of the times is favourable to them, also attract individual members of earlier or later age-groups.

But this is not all; it occurs very frequently that the nucleus of attitudes particular to a new generation is first evolved and practiced by older people who are isolated in their own generation (forerunners),[42] just as it is often the case that the forerunners in the development of a particular class ideology belong to a quite alien class.

All this, however, does not invalidate our thesis that there are new basic impulses attributable to a particular generation location which, then, may call forth generation units. The main thing in this respect is that the proper vehicle of these new impulses is always a collectivity. The real seat of the class ideology remains the class itself, with its own typical opportunities and handicaps—even when the author of the ideology, as it may happen, belongs to a different class, or when the ideology expands and becomes influential beyond the limits of the class location. Similarly, the real seat of new impulses remains the generation location (which will selectively encourage one form of experience and eliminate others), even when they may have been fostered by other age-groups.

The most important point we have to notice is the following: not every generation location—not even every age-group—creates new collective impulses and formative principles original to itself and adequate to its particular situation. Where this does happen, we shall speak of a *realization of potentialities inherent* in the location, and it appears probable that the frequency of such realizations is closely connected with the tempo of social change.[43] When as a result of an acceleration in the tempo of social and cultural transformation basic attitudes must change so quickly that the latent, continuous adaptation and modification of traditional patterns of experience, thought, and expression is no longer possible, then the various new phases of experience are consolidated somewhere, forming a clearly distinguishable new impulse, and a new centre of configuration. We speak in such cases of the formation of a new generation style, or of a new *generation entelechy*.

Here too, we may distinguish two possibilities. On the one hand, the generation unit may produce its work and deeds unconsciously out of the new impulse evolved by itself, having an intuitive awareness of its existence as a group but failing to realize the group's character as a generation unit. On the other hand, groups may consciously experience and emphasize their character as generation units—as is the case with the contemporary German youth movement, or even to a certain extent with its forerunner, the Student's Association (*Burschenschaft*) Movement in the first half of the nineteenth century, which already manifested many of the characteristics of the modern youth movement.

The importance of the acceleration of social change for the realization of the potentialities inherent in a generation location is clearly demonstrated by the fact that largely static or very slowly changing communities like the peasantry display no such phenomenon as new generation units sharply set off from their predecessors by virtue of an individual entelechy proper to them; in such communities, the tempo of change is so gradual that new generations evolve away from their predecessors without any visible break, and all we can see is the purely biological differentiation and affinity based upon difference or identity of age. Such biological factors are effective, of course, in modern society too, youth being attracted to youth and age to age. The generation unit as we have described it, however, could not arise solely on the basis of this simple factor of attraction between members of the same age-group.

The quicker the tempo of social and cultural change, then, the greater are the chances that particular generation location groups will react to changed situations by producing their own entelechy. On the other hand, it is conceivable that too greatly accelerated a tempo might lead to mutual destruction of the embryo entelechies. As contemporaries, we can observe, if we look closely, various finely graded patterns of response of age groups closely following upon each other and living side by side; these age groups, however, are so closely packed together that they do not succeed in achieving a fruitful new formulation of distinct generation entelechies and formative principles. Such generations, frustrated in the production of an individual entelechy, tend to attach themselves, where possible, to an earlier generation which may have achieved a satisfactory form, or to a younger generation which is capable of evolving a newer form. Crucial group experiences can act in this way as "crystallizing agents," and it is characteristic of cultural life that unattached elements are always attracted to perfected configurations, even when the unformed, groping impulse differs in many respects from the configuration to which it is attracted. In this way the impulses and trends peculiar to a generation may remain concealed because of the existence of the clear-cut form of another generation to which they have become attached.

From all this emerges the fact that each generation need not evolve its own, distinctive pattern of interpreting and influencing the world; the rhythm of successive generation locations, which is largely based upon biological factors, need not necessarily involve a parallel rhythm of successive motivation patterns and formative principles. Most generation theories, however, have this in common, that they try to establish a direct correlation between waves of decisive year classes of birth—set at intervals of 30 years, and conceived in a purely naturalistic, quantifying spirit—on the one hand, and waves of cultural changes on the other. Thus they ignore the important fact that the realization of hidden potentialities inherent in the generation location is governed by extra-biological factors, principally, as we have seen, by the prevailing tempo and impact of social change.

Whether a new *generation style* emerges every year, every 30, every 100 years, or whether it emerges rhythmically at all, depends entirely on the trigger action of the social and cultural process. One may ask, in this connection, whether the social dynamic operates predominantly through the agency of the economic or of one or the other "ideological" spheres: but this is a problem which has to be examined separately. It is immaterial in our context how this question is answered; all we have to bear in mind is that it depends on this group of social and cultural factors whether the impulses of a generation shall achieve a distinctive unity of style, or whether they shall remain latent. The biological fact of the existence of generations merely provides the *possibility* that generation entelechies may emerge at all—if there were no different generations succeeding each other, we should never encounter the phenomenon of generation styles. But the question of which generation locations will realize the potentialities inherent in them, finds its answer at the level of the social and cultural structure—a level regularly skipped by the usual kind of theory which starts from naturalism and then abruptly lands in the most extreme kind of spiritualism.

A formal sociological clarification of the distinction between the categories "generation location," "generation as actuality," and "generation unit," is important and indeed indispensable for any deeper analysis, since we can never grasp the dominant factors in this field without making that distinction. If we speak simply of "generations" without any further differentiation, we risk jumbling together purely biological phenomena and others which are the product of social and cultural forces: thus we arrive at a sort of sociology of chronological tables (*Geschichtstabellensoziologie*), which uses its bird's-eye perspective to "discover" fictitious generation movements to correspond to the crucial turning-points in historical chronology.

It must be admitted that biological data constitute the most basic stratum of factors determining generation phenomena; but for this very reason, we cannot observe the effect of biological factors directly; we must, instead, see how they are reflected through the medium of social and cultural forces.

As a matter of fact, the most striking feature of the historical process seems to be that the most basic biological factors operate in the most latent form, and can only be grasped in the medium of the social and historical phenomena which constitute a secondary sphere above them. In practice this means that the student of the generation problem cannot try to specify the effects attributable to the factor of generations before he has separated all the effects due to the specific dynamism of the historical and social sphere. If this intermediary sphere is skipped, one will be tempted to resort immediately to naturalistic principles, such as generation, race, geographical situation, in explaining phenomena due to environmental or temporal influences.

The fault of this naturalistic approach lies not so much in the fact that it emphasizes the role of natural factors in human life, as in its attempt to explain *dynamic* phenomena directly by something *constant,* thus ignoring and distorting precisely that intermediate sphere in which dynamism really originates. Dynamic factors operate on the basis of constant factors—on the basis of anthropological, geographical, etc., data—but on each occasion the dynamic factors seize upon different potentialities inherent in the constant factors. If we want to understand the primary, constant factors, we must observe them in the framework of the historical and social system of forces from which they receive their shape. Natural factors, including the succession of generations, provide the basic range of potentialities for the historical and social process. *But precisely because they are constant and therefore always present in any situation, the particular features of a given process of modification cannot be explained by reference to them.*

Their varying relevance (the particular way in which they can manifest themselves in this or that situation) can be clearly seen only if we pay proper attention to the formative layer of social and cultural forces.

The Generation in Relation to Other Formative Factors in History

It has been the merit of past theorizing about generations that it has kept alive scientific interest in this undoubtedly important factor in the history of mankind. Its one-sidedness, however—this may now be said in the light of the foregoing analysis—lay in the attempt to explain the whole dynamic of history from this one factor—an excusable one-sidedness easily explained by the fact that discoverers often tend to be over-enthusiastic about phenomena they are the first to see. The innumerable theories of history which have sprung up so luxuriantly recently all manifest this one-sidedness: they all single out just one factor as the sole determinant in historical development. Theories of race, generation, "national spirit," economic determinism, etc., suffer from this one-sidedness, but it may be said to their credit that they bring at least one partial factor into sharp focus and also direct attention to the general problem of the structural factors shaping history. In this they are definitely superior to that brand of historiography which limits itself to the ascertainment of causal connections between individual events and to the description of individual characters, and repudiates all interest in structural factors in history, an attitude which eventually had to result in the conclusion that nothing after all can be learned from history, since all of its manifestations are unique and incomparable. That this cannot be so must be realized by anyone who takes the liberty to think about history rather than merely to collect data, and also observe in everyday life how every new departure or outstanding personality has to operate in a given field which, although in constant process of change, is capable of description in structural terms.

If in our attempts to visualize the structure of the historical dynamic we refuse to deduce everything from a single factor, the next question is whether it is not perhaps possible to fix some sort of definite order of importance in the structural factors involved, either for a particular period or in general— for of course it cannot be assumed *a priori* that the relative importance of the various social or other factors (economy, power, race, etc.), must always be the same. We cannot here attempt to solve the whole problem: all that can be done is to examine more closely our own problem of generation in relation to the other formative factors in history.

Petersen had the merit of breaking away from that historical monism which characterized most earlier theories of generations. In dealing with the concrete case of romanticism, he tried to treat the problem of generations in conjunction with other historical determinants such as the ethnic unit, the region, the national character, the spirit of the epoch, the social structure, etc.

But however welcome this break with monistic theory is, we cannot agree with a mere juxtaposition of these factors (apparently this is only a provisional feature of the theory); the sociologist, moreover, cannot yet feel satisfied with the treatment of the social factor, at least in its present form.

If we are speaking of the "spirit of an epoch," for example, we must realize, as in the case of other factors, too, that this *Zeitgeist,* the mentality of a period, does not pervade the whole society at a given time. The mentality which is commonly attributed to an epoch has its proper seat in one (homogeneous or heterogeneous) social group which acquires special significance at a particular time, and is thus able to put its own intellectual stamp on all the other groups without either destroying or absorbing them.

We must try to break up the category of *Zeitgeist* in another fashion than Pinder did. With Pinder, the *Zeitgeist* as a fictitious unit was dissolved, so as to make the real units, i.e., for Pinder, the generation entelechies, visible. According to him, the *Zeitgeist* is not one organic individuality, since there is no real, organic entelechy corresponding to it. It would seem to us, too, that there is no such *Zeitgeist* entelechy which would confer organic unity on the spirit of an epoch; but in our view the real units which have to be substituted for the fictitious unit of *Zeitgeist* are entelechies of social currents giving polar tension to each temporal segment of history.

Thus the nineteenth century has no unitary *Zeitgeist,* but a composite mentality made up (if we consider its political manifestations)[44] of the mutually antagonistic conservative-traditional and liberal impulses, to which was later added the proletarian-socialistic one.

We would, however, not go quite as far as Pinder does in his denial of any temporal unity, and in his determination to attribute any homogeneity found in the manifestations of an epoch to a quite accidental crossing of various otherwise separate entelechies (accidental chords). The *Zeitgeist* is a unitary entity (otherwise, it would be meaningless to speak of it), insofar as we are able to view it in a dynamic-antinomical light.

The dynamic-antinomical unity of an epoch consists in the fact that polar opposites in an epoch always interpret their world in terms of one another, and that the various and opposing political orientations only become really comprehensible if viewed as so many different attempts to master the same destiny and solve the same social and intellectual problems that go with it.[45] Thus from this point of view the spirit of an age is no accidental coincidence of contemporary entelechies (as with Pinder); nor does it constitute itself an entelechy (a unified centre of volition—or formative principle, as with Petersen) on a par with other entelechies. We conceive it, rather, as a dynamic relationship of tension which we may well scrutinize in terms of its specific character but which should never be taken as a substantial "thing."

Genuine entelechies are primarily displayed by the social and intellectual trends or currents of which we spoke above. Each of these trends or currents (which may well be explained in terms of the social structure) evolves certain basic attitudes which exist over and above the change of generations as enduring (though nevertheless constantly changing) formative principles underlying social and historical development. Successively emerging new generations, then, superimpose their own generation entelechies upon the more comprehensive, stable entelechies of the various polar trends; this is how entelechies of the liberal, conservative, or socialist trends come to be transformed from generation to generation. We may conclude from this: generation units are no mere constructs, since they have their own en-telechies, but these ontologies cannot be grasped in and for themselves; they must be viewed within the wider framework of the trend entelechies. It follows, furthermore, that it is quite impossible either to delimit or to count intellectual generations (generation units) except as articulations of certain overall trends. The trend entelechy is prior to the generation entelechy, and the latter can only become effective and distinguishable within the former—

but this does not mean to say that every one of the conflicting trends at a given point of time will necessarily cause new generation-entelechies to arise.

It is quite wrong to assume, for example, that in the first decades of the nineteenth century there existed in Germany only one romantic-conservative generation,[46] which was succeeded later by a liberal-rationalistic one. We should say, more precisely, that in the first decades of the nineteenth century the situation was such that only that section of the younger generation which had its roots in the romantic-conservative tradition was able to develop new generation-entelechies. This section alone was able to leave its own mark on the prevailing tone of the age. What happened in the thirties, then, was not that a "new generation" emerged which somehow happened to be liberal and rationalistic—but the situation changed, and it now became possible for the first time for the other section of the younger generation to reconstitute the tradition from which it derived in such a way as to produce its own generation-entelechy. The fundamental differentiation and polarization were undoubtedly always there, and each current had its own younger generation: but the opportunity for creative development of its basic impulse was granted first to the romantic conservatives, and only later to the liberal-rationalists.

We may say in this sense, that Petersen's[47] distinction between a *leading,* a *diverted,* and a *suppressed* type of generation is both correct and important, but it is not yet expressed in a sufficiently precise form, because Petersen failed to analyse the corresponding sociological differentiation.

Petersen assumes a direct interaction between supra-temporal character types on the one hand, and the *Zeitgeist* (which he considers as an unambi-guously ascertainable datum) on the other, as if the historic process consisted in these two factors struggling with each other, and the fate of the single individuals were actually determined by their reciprocal interpenetration. Let us take, as an illustration of Petersen's method, an individual of an emotional type; he would be what Petersen would call a "romantically inclined" character. If we further suppose that this man lives in an age the spirit of which is essentially romantic, this coincidence may well result in a height-ening of his romantic inclinations, so that he will belong to the "leading type" of his generation. Another individual, however, in whom emotional and rational inclinations tended more or less to balance one another, could in similar circumstances be drawn over into the romantic camp. Thus he would represent Petersen's *diverted* type. If we take finally, a third individual who by nature was rationalistically inclined but living in a romantic epoch, he would represent the *suppressed* type. Only two alternatives would be open to him: either he could swim with the tide and, against his own inclinations, follow the romantic tendencies of his time—a course which would lead to stultification—or, alternatively, if he insisted on maintaining his ground, he could remain isolated in his time, an epigone of a past, or the forerunner of a future generation.

Apart from the somewhat cursory way in which "emotional" and "romantically inclined" are taken as synonymous, there is something essentially correct in this classification of generation types into *leading, diverted,* and *suppressed.* But what occurs is no clash between supra-temporal individual dispositions existing in a supra-social realm on the one hand, and an undifferentiated unitary *Zeitgeist* (because no such thing really exists) on the other. The individual is primarily moulded by those contemporary intellectual influences and currents which are indigenous to the particular social group to which he belongs. That is to say, he is in the first instance in no way affected or attracted by the *Zeitgeist* as a whole, but only by those currents and trends of the time which are a living tradition in his particular social environment. But that just these particular trends and not others should have taken root and maintained themselves in his world is ultimately due to the fact that they afford the typical "chances" of his life situation their most adequate expression. There is therefore no question of an undifferentiated "spirit of the age" promoting or inhibiting the potentialities inherent in individual characters: *in concreto* the individual always exposed to differentiated, polarized trends or currents within the "global spirit of the age," and in particular to that trend which had found its home in his immediate environment. The individual's personality structure will be confronted, in the first place, with this particular trend.

The reason why literary historians tend to overlook the fact that most people are confined to an existence within the limits of one of the trends of their time, and that the "spirit of the age" is always split up into a number of tendencies rather than being now exclusively romantic, now exclusively rationalistic, is that their material consists primarily of biographies of *hommes de lettres,* a social group of a very particular character.

In our society only the *hommes de lettres* exist as a relatively unattached (*freischwebend*) group (this being, of course, a sociological determinant of their situation); hence, they alone can vacillate, joining now one trend, now another. In the first half of the nineteenth century, they tended to embrace trends supported by a young generation which, favoured by circumstances of the time, had just achieved an intellectually dominant position—i.e., trends which permitted the formation of entelechies. The period of the Restoration and the social and political weakness of the German bourgeoisie at the beginning of the nineteenth century favoured the development of entelechies at the romantic-conservative pole of the younger generation, which also attracted a large part of the socially unattached *literati*. From the thirties on, the July revolution and the growing industrialization of the country favoured the development of new liberal rationalist entelechies among the younger generation; and many of the *literati* promptly joined this camp.

The behaviour of these *hommes de lettres,* then, gives the impression that at one moment the "spirit of the age" is entirely romantic, and at the next entirely liberal-rationalist, and further that whether the spirit of the age is to be romantic or rationalist is exclusively determined by these *literati*—poets and thinkers. In actual fact, however, the decisive impulses which determine the direction of social evolution do not originate with them at all, but with the much more compact, mutually antagonistic social groups which stand behind them, polarized into antagonistic trends. This wave-like rhythm in the change of the *Zeitgeist* is merely due to the fact that—according to the prevailing conditions—now one, and then the other pole succeeds in rallying an active youth which, then, carries the "intermediary" generations and in particular the socially unattached individuals along. We do not wish to underrate the enormous importance of these literary strata (a social group to which many of the greatest thinkers and poets belong), for indeed they alone endow the entelechies radiating from the social sphere with real depth and form. But if we pay exclusive attention to them, we shall not be able really to account for this vector structure of intellectual currents. Taking the whole historical and social process into consideration, we can say that there has never been an epoch *entirely* romantic, or *entirely* rationalist in character; at least since the nineteenth century, we clearly have to deal with a culture polarized in this respect. It may very well be asserted, however, that it is now the one, now the other of these two trends that takes the upper hand and becomes *dominant.* In sociological terms, to sum up once more, this means simply that the circumstances of the time favour the formation of a new generation-entelechy at one or the other pole, and that this new entelechy always attracts the vacillating middle strata, primarily the literary people of the time. Thus the socially attached individual (to whatever psychological "type" he may belong) allies himself with that current which happens to prevail in his particular social circle; the socially unattached *homme de lettres* of whatever psychological type, on the other hand, generally must clarify his position with regard to the *dominant* trend of his time. The outcome for the individual of this battle between his own natural disposition, the mental attitude most appropriate to his social situation, and the dominant trend of his time, undoubtedly differs from case to case; but only a very strong personality will be in a position to maintain his individual disposition in face of the antagonistic mental attitude of the social circle of his origin, especially if his group happens to be in process of rising in the social scale. An irrationally inclined "bourgeois" would find it as difficult to come into his own in the forties of the nineteenth century as a young aristocrat with rational inclinations to preserve his rationalism in face of the rise of romanticism and religious revivalism in his social circle. We find for the most part that the opponents of a new generation-entelechy consist mainly of people who, because of their "location" in an older generation, are unable or unwilling to assimilate themselves into the new entelechy growing up in their midst.

The generation location always exists as a potentiality seeking realization—the medium of such realization, however, is not a unitary *Zeitgeist* but rather one or the other of the concrete trends prevailing at a given time.[48] Whether new generation-entelechies will be formed at one pole in the social vector space or another depends, as we have seen, on historical group destinies.

There remains one further factor which we have not yet considered and which must be added to the others, complicated enough as they are.

We have not yet considered the fact that a newly rising generation-entelechy has not equal possibilities of asserting itself in every field of intellectual pursuit. Some of these fields tend to promote the emergence of new entelechies; others, to hinder it. And we can grade the different fields according to the degree to which they evidence the existence of generation entelechies.

Thus, for example, the natural sciences in which factors of total orientation (*Weltanschauung*) play a less important part than in other fields, definitely tend to conceal generation-entelechies.

The sphere of "civilization"[49] in general, by virtue of the unilinear nature of developments falling within it, tends to conceal experiential and volitional transformations to a far greater extent than does the sphere of "culture." And within the sphere of "culture" itself, Pinder is certainly right in ascribing to linguistic manifestations (religion, philosophy, poetry, and letters) a role different from that played by the plastic arts and music.[50]

In this field, however, we need a finer differentiation. It will have to be shown how far the various social and generation impulses and formative principles have peculiar affinities to this or that art form, and also whether they do not in certain cases bring new art forms into existence.

We must also consider the degree to which *forms of social intercourse* show stratification according to generations. Here, too, we find that certain forms of intercourse are more adequate to one particular set of social and generation trends than others. Mentré has already shown that an association deliberately organized on the basis of written statutes is much less capable of being moulded by new generation impulses than are less formal groupings (such as literary *salons* for example). Thus, it appears that in the same way as factors in the social and historical realm exercise either a restrictive or encouraging influence on the emergence of generation-entelechies, the degree to which various cultural "fields" lend themselves to serving as sounding-boards for a new generation cannot be exactly determined in advance. All this indicates from yet another point of view that the generation factor— which at the biological level operates with the uniformity of a natural law—becomes the most elusive one at the social and cultural level, where its effects can be ascertained only with great difficulty and by indirect methods.

The phenomenon of generations is one of the basic factors contributing to the genesis of the dynamic of historical development. The analysis of the interaction of forces in this connection is a large task in itself, without which the nature of historical development cannot be properly understood. The problem can only be solved on the basis of a strict and careful analysis of all its component elements.

The *formal sociological* analysis of the generation phenomenon can be of help insofar as we may possibly learn from it what can and what cannot be attributed to the generation factor as one of the factors impinging upon the social process.

◇ NOTES

1. For these quotations from Hume and Comte, cf. Mentré (1920)7, pp. 179 f. and 66 ff.
2. The exact titles of all works referred to in this essay can be found in the [references] at the end of the book.
3. Rümelin's attempt seems to be the most scientific; he tried to assess generation periods in various nations, using purely statistical methods and ignoring all problems related to intellectual history. The two decisive factors entering into his calculations were the average age of marriage among men, and half the average period of marital fertility. The generation-period is obtained as the sum of these two quantities (which vary as between both social groups and countries). Germany was computed at $36\frac{1}{2}$, and France at $34\frac{1}{2}$ years.
4. Cf. [Mentré].
5. We shall discuss here in detail only those students of the problem of generations whose contributions appeared after the publication of Mentré's work.
6. Mentré, p. 298.
7. Cf. also the books of Agathon, Bainville, Ageorges, Valois, E. R. Curtius, and Platz, also always take into consideration the factor of generations.

8. For the conservative concept of time, cf. "Conservative Thought," to be published in a later volume. For a repudiation of the concept of progress as used to sum up historical development, cf. for example, Pinder, p. 138.

9. Cf. Dilthey, pp. 36 ff.

10. Heidegger, pp. 384 ff.

11. Pinder, cf. especially ch. 7.

12. Pinder, p. 21. Pinder's italics.

13. *Ibid,* p. 20.

14. Cf. K. Mannheim, "On the Interpretation of Weltanschauung," pp. 33 ff.

15. Pinder, p. 98.

16. Pinder, pp. 159 ff.

17. Pinder, *op. cit.,* p. 154, Pinder's italics.

18. Pinder, *op. cit.,* p. 30.

19. *Ibid.,* p. 60.

20. That is, the "cultural situation" and "social and political conditions." Dilthey, p. 38.

21. See [Joel] in the [references].

22. Lorenz sought to substitute for the century as unit a more rationally deducible unit of three generations. Scherer emphasizes a 600-year rhythm in his History of Literature, pp. 18 ff. We shall have to refer to the work of the modern literary historians Kummers and Petersen, as well as L. von Wiese, in the next part of this investigation.

23. In this connection it would be desirable to work out the exact differences between modern youth movements and the age-groups of men's societies formed amongst primitive peoples, carefully described by H. Schurtz.

24. It is a matter for historical and sociological research to discover at what stage in its development, and under what conditions, a class becomes class-conscious, and similarly, when individual members of a generation become conscious of their common situation and make this consciousness the basis of their group solidarity. Why have generations become so conscious of their unity to-day? This is the first question we have to answer in this context.

25. Since actual experiments are precluded by the nature of the social sciences, such a "mental experiment" can often help to isolate the important factors.

26. Cf. Spranger on "being young" and "becoming old," and the intellectual and spiritual significance of these phenomena. (He also gives references to other literature on the psychology of the adolescent—whereon see also Honigsheim). Further, see A. E. Brinckmann (who proceeds by way of interpretive analysis of works of art), Jacob Grimm, F. Ball, Giese. Literature relating to the youth movement, which constitutes a problem in itself, is not included in the [references] at the end of this book.

27. This is not the place to enumerate all the many forms of social memory. We will therefore deliberately simplify the matter by limiting ourselves to two extreme alternatives. "Consciously recognized models" include, in the wider sense, also the body of global knowledge, stored in libraries. But this sort of knowledge is only effective insofar as it is continually actualized. This can happen in two ways—either intellectually, when it is used as a pattern or guide for action, or spontaneously, when it is "virtually present" as condensed experience. Instinct, as well as repressed and unconscious knowledge, as dealt with in particular by Freud, would need separate treatment.

28. This process of discovery of hidden possibilities inherent in transmitted material alone makes it clear why it is that so many revolutionary and reformist movements are able to graft their new truths on to old ones.

29. That is, if we ignore—as we said we would—the biological factors of physical and psychological ageing.

30. It must be emphasized that this "ability to start afresh" of which we are speaking has nothing to do with "conservative" and "progressive" in the usual sense of these terms. Nothing is more false than the usual assumption uncritically shared by most students of generations, that

the younger generation is "progressive" and the older generation *eo ipso* conservative. Recent experiences have shown well enough that the old liberal generation tends to be more politically progressive than certain sections of the youth (e.g., the German Students Associations— *Burschenschaften*—etc.). "Conservative" and "progressive" are categories of historical sociology, designed to deal with the descriptive contents of the dynamism of a historical period of history, whereas "old" and "young" and the concept of the "fresh contact" of a generation are categories belonging to formal sociology. Whether youth will be conservative, reactionary, or progressive, depends (if not entirely, at least primarily) on whether or not the existing social structure and the position they occupy in it provide opportunities for the promotion of their own social and intellectual ends. Their "being young," the "freshness" of their contact with the world, manifest themselves in the fact that they are able to re-orient any movement they embrace, to adapt it to the total situation. (Thus, for instance, they must seek within Conservatism the particular form of this political and intellectual current best suited to the requirements of the modern situation: or within Socialism, in the same way, an up-to-date formulation.) This lends considerable support to the fundamental thesis of this essay, which will have to be further substantiated later—that biological factors (such as youth and age) do not of themselves involve a definite intellectual or practical orientation (youth cannot be automatically correlated with a progressive attitude and so on); they merely *initiate* certain formal tendencies, the actual manifestations of which will ultimately depend on the prevailing social and cultural context. Any attempt to establish a direct identity or correlation between biological and cultural data leads to a *quid pro quo* which can only confuse the issue.

31. It is difficult to decide just at what point this process is complete in an individual—at what point this unconscious vital inventory (which also contains the national and provincial peculiarities out of which national and provincial entelechies can develop) is stabilized. The process seems to stop once the inventory of a-problematical experience has virtually acquired its final form. The child or adolescent is always open to new influences if placed in a new *milieu*. They readily assimilate new unconscious mental attitudes and habits, and change their language or dialect. The adult, transferred into a new environment, consciously transforms certain aspects of his modes of thought and behaviour, but never acclimatizes himself in so radical and thoroughgoing a fashion. His fundamental attitudes, his vital inventory, and, among external manifestations, his language and dialect, remain for the most part on an earlier level. It appears that language and accent offer an indirect indication as to how far the foundations of a person's consciousness are laid, his basic view of the world stabilized. If the point can be determined at which a man's language and dialect cease to change, there is at least an external criterion for the determination also of the point at which his unconscious inventory of experience ceases to accumulate. According to A. Meillet, the spoken language and dialect does not change in an individual after the age of 25 years. (A. Meillet: *Méthode dans les sciences,* Paris, Alcan, 1911; also his *Introduction à l'étude comparative des langues indo-européennes* 1903, as quoted in Mentré, p. 306 ff.)

32. Spranger also assumes an important turning point about the age of 17 or so (p. 145).

33. This throws some light on the way in which "ideas" appear to precede real social transformation. "Ideas" are understood here in the French rather than in the Platonic sense. This "modern Idea" has a tendency to de-stabilize and set in motion the social structure. It does not exist in static social units—for example, in self-contained peasant communities—which tend to draw on an unconscious, traditional way of life. In such societies, we do not find the younger generation, associated with ideas of this kind, rising against their elders. "Being young" here is a question of biological differentiation. More on this matter later.

34. The following seems to be the sequence in which this process unfolds: first the "conditions" change. Then concrete behavior begins unconsciously to transform itself in the new situation. The individual seeks to react to the new situation, by instinctive, unconscious adjustment. (Even the most fanatical adherent of an orthodoxy constantly indulges in an adaptive change of his behaviour in respects which are not open to conscious observation.) If the dynamic

of the situation results in too quick cultural change and the upheaval is too great, if unconscious adjustment proves inadequate and behaviour adaptations fail to "function" in the sudden new situation, so that an aspect of reality becomes problematic, then that aspect of reality will be made conscious—on the level of either mythology, philosophy, or science, according to the stage of cultural evolution reached. From this point on, the unravelling of the deeper layers proceeds, as required by the situation.

35. L. von Wiese, gives a vivid description of this father-son antagonism. Of considerable importance is the suggestion that the father is more or less forced into the role of representing "Society" to his son (p. 196).

36. It should be noted, on the other hand, as L. von Wiese (*op. cit.,* p. 197) points out, that with the modern trend towards individualism, every individual claims more than before the right to "live his own life."

37. This is a further proof that natural biological factors characteristic of old age can be invalidated by social forces, and that biological data can almost be turned into their opposites by social forces.

38. Up till now we have not differentiated between generation location, generation as actuality, etc. These distinctions will now be made.

39. Cf. the quotation from Heidegger, p. 282, above.

40. Mental data can both bind and differentiate socially. The same concept of Freedom, for example, had totally different meanings for the liberal and the conservative generation-unit. Thus, it is possible to obtain an indication of the extent to which a generation is divided into generation-units by analysing the different meanings given to a current idea. Cf. "Conservative Thought" (to follow in a later volume), where the conservative concept of Freedom is analysed in contrast to the liberal concept current at the same time.

41. In the 40s in Germany, for example, when oppositional ideas were in vogue, young men of the nobility also shared them. Cf. Karl Marx: "Revolution and Counter-revolution in Germany." (German edition, Stuttgart, 1913, pp. 20 f. and 25).

42. For instance, Nietzsche may be considered the forerunner of the present neo-romanticism. An eminent example of the same thing in France is Taine, who under the influence of the events of 1870-71 turned towards patriotism, and so became the forerunner of a nationalistic generation. (Cf. Platz, pp. 43 ff.) In such cases involving forerunners, it would be advisable to make individual case-analyses and establish in what respect the basic structure of experience in the forerunner differs from that of the new generation which actually starts at the point where the forerunner leaves off. In this connection, the history of German Conservatism contains an interesting example, i.e., that of the jurist Hugo, whom we may consider as the founder of the "historical school." Nevertheless, he never thought in *irrationalistic* terms as did the members of the school (e.g., Savigny) in the next generation which lived through the Napoleonic wars.

43. The speed of social change, for its part, is never influenced by the speed of the succession of generations, since this remains constant.

44. We draw on examples deliberately from the history of political ideas, partly to counter-balance the tendency (especially evident in Germany) to study the problem of generations exclusively in the context of the history of literature or art; and partly to show that we believe that *the structural situation of decisive social impulses and also the differentiation between generations is clearest at this point.* The other entelechies and changes of style must of course be studied for their own sake independently, and cannot be derived in any way from political factors, but their reciprocal relations and affinities can best be understood and made clear from this angle. The artist certainly lives in the first instance in his artistic world with its particular traditions, but as a human being he is always linked with the driving forces of his generation even when politically indifferent, and this influence must always transform even purely artistic relations and entelechies. As a point of orientation for a survey of the whole structure, the history of political ideas seems to us to be most important. This matter will be further dealt with below.

45. From our point of view, the "spirit of an age" is thus the outcome of the dynamic interaction of actual generations succeeding one another in a continuous series.

46. Romanticism and Conservatism did not always go together. Romanticism was originally a revolutionary movement in Germany, the same as in France.

47. Petersen, pp. 146 ff.

48. This can also be observed in the modern youth movement, which is constantly in process of social and political polarization. Purely as a social phenomenon, it represents a coherent actual generation entity, but it can only be understood concretely in terms of the "generation units" into which it is socially and intellectually differentiated.

49. Cf. A. Weber: *Prinzipielles zur Kultursoziologie (Archiv für Soz. Wiss. u. Soz. Politik,* 1920).

50. Pinder, p. 156.

CHAPTER THREE

The Cohort as a Concept in the Study of Social Change

NORMAN B. RYDER

Society persists despite the mortality of its individual members, through processes of demographic metabolism and particularly the annual infusion of birth cohorts. These may pose a threat to stability but they also provide the opportunity for societal transformation. Each birth cohort acquires coherence and continuity from the distinctive development of its constituents and from its own persistent macroanalytic features. Successive cohorts are differentiated by the changing content of formal education, by peer-group socialization, and by idiosyncratic historical experience. Young adults are prominent in war, revolution, immigration, urbanization and technological change. Since cohorts are used to achieve structural transformation and since they manifest its consequences in characteristic ways, it is proposed that research be designed to capitalize on the congruence of social change and cohort identification.

◇ SOCIAL CHANGE AND DEMOGRAPHIC METABOLISM

This essay presents a demographic approach to the study of social change. The particular meaning here given to change is structural transformation rather than the network of actions and interactions predicated in the routine operation of the institutional structure. Discussion is restricted to the variations in social organization that are reflected in measurements on individu-

NOTE: Reprinted by permission of the author.

als, summarized in aggregate distributions of performances and characteristics. Changes in an individual throughout his life are distinguishable from changes in the population of which he is a component. The biological ineluctability of the individual life cycle carries no necessary implication for transformation of the population. Every society has pretensions to an immortality beyond the reach of its members. The lives and deaths of individuals are, from the societal standpoint, a massive process of personnel replacement, which may be called "demographic metabolism." This essay is concerned with interdependencies between social change and population process, including in the latter both demographic metabolism and the life cycles of individuals considered in the aggregate.

Society is a functioning collectivity of organic components. It persists as if independent of its membership, continually receiving raw material by fertility and discharging depleted resources by mortality. To survive, it must meet the challenge to persistence implicit in this continual change of membership, and especially the incessant "invasion of barbarians." Every individual arrives on the social scene literally without sociopsychological configuration. As a requisite for effective performance, the society seeks and promotes a minimal degree of stability and predictability, and frequently succeeds. The agencies of socialization and social control are designed to give the new member a shape appropriate to the societal design.

Perhaps stability is a more likely institutional goal than innovation because it is simpler and safer, at least in the short run, but any fixed set of solutions to problems posed by a threatening environment becomes a liability whenever such problems change. The capacity for societal transformation has an indispensable ally in the process of demographic metabolism. Mortality and fertility make flexibility possible just as they make stability problematic. The continual emergence of new participants in the social process and the continual withdrawal of their predecessors compensate the society for limited individual flexibility. For every species the inevitability of death impels the development of reproduction and thus variation and evolution; the same holds for societies. The society whose members were immortal would resemble a stagnant pond.[1] Of course death is no more an unmixed blessing to the society than it is an unmixed curse to the individual. Metabolism may make change likely, or at least possible, but it does not guarantee that the change will be beneficial. As a minimum, mortality permits perennial reappraisal of institutionalized formulae.

The aggregate by which the society counterbalances attrition is the birth cohort, those persons born in the same time interval and aging together. Each new cohort makes fresh contact with the contemporary social heritage and carries the impress of the encounter through life. This confrontation has been called the intersection of the innovative and the conservative forces in history (MacIver, 1963, pp. 110-111). The members of any cohort are entitled to participate in only one slice of life—their unique location in the stream of history. Because it embodies a temporally specific version of the heritage, each cohort is differentiated from all others, despite the minimization of variability by symbolically perpetuated institutions and by hierarchically graduated structures of authority.

To assert that the cause of social change is demographic replacement would be tantamount to explaining a variable by a constant, yet each fresh cohort is a possible intermediary in the transformation process, a vehicle for introducing new postures. The new cohorts provide the opportunity for social change to occur. They do not cause change; they permit it. If change does occur, it differentiates cohorts from one another, and the comparison of their careers becomes a way to study change. The minimal basis for expecting interdependency between intercohort differentiation and social change is that change has variant import for persons of unlike age, and that the consequences of change persist in the subsequent behavior of these individuals and thus of their cohorts.

For the most part, the literature on the cohort approach is divisible into two almost antipodal categories. On the one hand, the cohort concept, under the label "generation," has long been used by historians of the arts—in rebellion against the Procrustean frame of chronological sections favored by conventional historians—as well as by political journalists and other humanistic interpreters of the passing scene (see e.g., Petersen, 1930; Peyre, 1948; Renouard, 1953; and in sociology, Mannheim, 1927/ 1952b, pp. 276-322). The other field of application has been the work of demographers, particularly the recent redirection of the study of fertility time series away from the period-by-period format toward an appraisal of temporal variations from cohort to cohort (Ryder, 1956). Although written by a demographer, the present essay is concerned not with the many contributions to technical demography which utilize the cohort concept, but rather with the sociological arguments underlying it, and the conceptualization of social change it suggests.

⊠ THE COHORT FROM A MACROANALYTIC STANDPOINT

A cohort may be defined as the aggregate of individuals (within some population definition) who experienced the same event within the same time interval. In almost all cohort research to date the defining event has been birth, but this is only a special case of the more general approach. Cohort data are ordinarily assembled sequentially from observations of the time of occurrence of the behavior being studied, and the interval since occurrence of the cohort-defining event. For the birth cohort this interval is age. If t is the time of occurrence and a is the age at that time, then the observations for age a, time t, apply (approximately) to the cohort born in year $t-a$, as do observations for age $a-1$, time $t-1$, and so forth.

The cohort record is not merely a summation of a set of individual histories. Each cohort has a distinctive composition and character reflecting the circumstances of its unique origination and history. The lifetime data for one cohort may be analyzed and compared with those for other cohorts by all the procedures developed for a population in temporal cross-section. The movement of the cohort, within the politico-spatial boundaries defining the society, is a flow of person-years from time of birth to the death of the last survivor. This differs from a synthetic cross-section because time and age change *pari passu* for any cohort. A cohort has an age distribution of its person-years of exposure, provided by its successive sizes age by age. The age distribution varies from cohort to cohort because of mortality and migration. Thus a cohort experiences demographic transformation in ways that have no meaning at the individual level of analysis, because its composition is modified not only by status changes of the components, but also by selective changes of membership.

The most evident manifestation of intercohort differences is variation, and particularly abrupt fluctuation, in cohort size, attributable to changes in the numbers of births from year to year or, less commonly, from brief heavy migration or mortality the impact of which is limited to a narrow age span. A cohort's size relative to the sizes of its neighbors is a persistent and compelling feature of its lifetime environment. As the new cohort reaches each major juncture in the life cycle, the society has the problem of assimilating it. Any extraordinary size deviation is likely to leave an imprint on the cohort as well as on the society. In the United States today the cohorts entering adulthood are much larger than their predecessors. In consequence, they were raised in crowded housing, crammed together in schools, and are now threatening to be a glut on the labor market. Perhaps they will have to delay marriage, because of too few jobs or homes, and have fewer children. It is not entirely coincidental that the American cohorts whose fertility levels appear to be the highest in this century were those with the smallest numbers.

Size is only one characteristic by which the cohort aggregate is differentiated from its temporal neighbors. Many statistical facets of cohort composition, broadly influential as independent variables, differ at age zero from one cohort to the next, and remain approximately unchanged throughout the cohort's history. Consider the various inherited items like race, mother tongue and birthplace. The cohort is not homogeneous in such characteristics, but the distribution of its heterogeneity tends to be fixed throughout its life in a shape which may differ from those of preceding and succeeding cohorts. Other birth and childhood characteristics are differentiating: for example, family structure by age, sex and generation determines the relative frequency of only children, younger and older children of like or unlike sex, and younger or older parents. Intercohort variability in these characteristics may derive from fertility, mortality or migration, to the extent that these are selective for the characteristic concerned and variable through time. Differential migration is the most striking influence in the short run, but differential natural replacement is generally more important in the long run.

Cohort differentiation is not confined to characteristics fixed at birth. Other status changes tend to be highly localized by age, relatively universal in occurrence, and influential in the rest of life (Neugarten, Moore, & Lowe, 1965). Age is not only a general rubric for the consequences, rewards and penalties of experience; it is an important basis for role allocation in every society (Levy, 1952, p. 307). Age ascription is the cross-sectional counterpart of cohort differentiation. Similarities of experience within and differentiation of experience between age groups are observable in every culture. Similar functioning is imposed by society on those sharing an age at a particular time. Any legislation that is age-specific, either *de jure,* or, by virtue of its content, *de facto,* differentiates cohorts. Such norms give a distinctive age pattern to the life cycle of each cohort. If age-specific norms, or the context within which they are being applied, change through time, cohort experiences will be differentiated.

Thus marriage has a high probability of occurring within a narrow age span and is responsive to the exigencies of the moment. The members of a cohort are influenced in the age at which they marry, the persons they choose to marry and even their eventual likelihood of marriage by the particular set of circumstances prevailing at the time they reach marriage age. The outcome is not so individualistic as the romantic love ethos might suggest. The state of the marriage market is an aggregate phenomenon: the probability of marriage depends not only on an individual's personal characteristics, but also on the comparative characteristics of all others of the same sex, and also on the availability of those of the opposite sex who meet the approximate criteria of nubility. Underlying this is the propitiousness of the period for marriage, the relevance of which for cohort delineation depends directly on the age variance of marriage for the cohort. The same is true of any major event in personal history which is concentrated by age.

The time of completing education is also highly age-specific in its location and influential both in personal futures and in societal change. The intimate relation of education to social change is properly emphasized in programs of social and economic development. It is "the modern world's cutting edge." Changes through time in the proportions completing various stages of education are familiar trends in modern life which provide an indelible differentiation of cohort character and behavior (Parsons, 1959). The differentiation encompasses not only mere duration but also the quality of teaching, the nature of instructional materials and the content of the curriculum (Foote, 1958).

The consequences of distinctive educational preparation prevail in the cohort's occupational flow-chart. The experience of the cohort with employment and labor force status begins with the character of the employment market at its time of entry.[2] The cohort is distinctively marked by the career stage it occupies when prosperity or depression, and peace or war, impinge on it. The occupational structure of the cohort is not crystallized upon entry into the labor force, but the configuration imposed on individual economic histories has a high sequential dependence through time (Jaffe & Carleton, 1954). One explanation advanced for the baby boom is that the cohorts responsible had an unprecedented educational advantage when they sought their first jobs (Easterlin, 1961). Projections of labor force participation rates for women have been successfully designed on a cohort basis, because of the observed continuity of differences between cohorts (Durand, 1948).

The attractive simplicity of birth cohort membership as signified by age cannot conceal the ways in which this identification is cross-cut and attenuated by differentiation with respect to education, occupation, marital status, parity status, and so forth. Every birth cohort is heterogeneous. To some extent all cohorts respond to any given period-specific stimulus. Rarely are changes so localized in either age or time that their burden falls exclusively on the shoulders of one cohort. Intercohort analysis is profitably supplemented with cross-classification by relevant compositional variables (Evan, 1959). The meaning of sharing a common historical location is modified and adumbrated by these other identifying characteristics (Ralea, 1962). Different subsets of the cohort have different time patterns of development. Youth of manual and nonmanual origins differ in length of educational preparation and age at marriage. The various members of a cohort follow differently paced occupational lines. This may be especially true of intellectual histories. The differing tempi of careers in literature, music and mathematics yield different productivity modes by age, and therefore responsiveness to different historical circumstances, despite membership in the same birth cohort (Berger, 1960).

As a minimum, the cohort is a structural category with the same kind of analytic utility as a variable like social class (Lipset, Lazarsfeld, Barton, & Linz, 1954). Such structural categories have explanatory power because they are surrogate indices for the common experiences of many persons in each category. Conceptually the cohort resembles most closely the ethnic group: membership is determined at birth, and often has considerable capacity to explain variance, but need not imply that the category is an organized group.

Two research suggestions may be advanced. In the first place, age should be so interpreted in every statistical table as to exploit its dual significance—as a point in the cohort life cycle and as a temporal location. Age is customarily used in statistical analyses merely in the former role, if not as a cross-sectional nuisance to be controlled by procedures like standardization. This implicitly static orientation ignores an important source of variation and inhibits the progress of temporal analysis. In the second place, age-cum-cohort should be used not only as a cross-classification to explain the internal variations of other groups, but as a group-defining variable in its own right, in terms of which distributions by other variables may be compared through time. In this way, research results may be compared in cumulated fashion, linking the outputs of the various studies using the same cohort identifications, just as has been done with other quasi-group categorizations. Each such study can enhance the significance of others for the same cohort. Comparison of such composite cohort biographies would yield the most direct and efficient measurement of the consequences of social change.

The proposed orientation to temporal differentiation of cohorts emphasizes the context prevailing at the time members of the cohort experience critical transitions. The approach can be generalized beyond the birth cohort to cohorts identified by common time of occurrence of any significant and enduring event in life history. Cohorts may be defined in terms of the year in which they completed their schooling, the year they married, the year in which they migrated to the city, or the year in which they entered the labor force full time.[3] Each of these events is important in identifying the kinds of situation to which persons respond differently, and establishing a status to which future experiences are oriented. The research implication of this viewpoint is that more effort should be devoted to collecting items of dated information, to identify not only statuses but times of entry into them. Birth date serves as a surrogate for cohort identification by date of occurrence of other relevant events. It is a satisfactory approximation to the extent that variance in the age at which the event in question occurs is small. Thus the cohort approach may be generalized to consider any class of event in terms of the experience of successive cohorts defined by time of initial exposure to the risk of occurrence of that event.

The strategic focus for research on social change is the context under which each cohort is launched on its own path. The prototype is the cohort of persons entering the labor force each year. The annual meeting of prospective employers and employees produces an occupational distribution which manifests and foretells social change. The process requires macroanalysis because the possibility of an individual finding a particular job, or of an employer securing a needed talent, is a function of the entire set of comparative characteristics of all participants in the market. The educational system has prepared the new labor force entrants for this confrontation. Although the stimulus for innovation is most likely to come from the employers, the feasibility of new directions depends in part on how well they have been anticipated by the educational system. Indeed the conditions determining labor supply go all the way back to the composition of the relevant cohorts at birth. The implicit link between reproduction in one year, and characteristics of the labor market some two decades later, is an important channel for transmission of disturbances through time.

Out of the confrontation of the cohort of any year and the societal structures into which it seeks entry, a shape is forged which influences the directions in which the structures will change. More generally, the proximate indication of direction of change is the movement of personnel from one status to another, as the result of quasi-market activity in one or another role sphere. The market metaphor extends into the consideration of differential rewards, and thus of changing role evaluations, cognate with the Davis-Moore (1945) theory of social differentiation. The importance for social change of the kind of selectivity exercised in forming the cohort is largely obscured in this essay by exclusive attention to the birth cohort, which is more random in composition than any other cohort type. The study of the formation of cohorts defined in terms of specific role markets promises to provide a focused view of the processes that transform the different parts of the social system.

◇ THE IMPACT OF HISTORICAL CHANGE ON COHORTS

The preceding section emphasized several stages in the cohort life cycle at which major transitions occur, and proposed that the temporal context of these transitions would differentiate cohorts. The same point can be made from the opposite direction, by observing types of major change, and the extent to which participation in them is age-specific and therefore cohort-differentiating. All those alive at the same time are contemporaries but they respond and contribute to social history in different ways unless they are also coevals. In particular, the potential for change is concentrated in the cohorts of young adults who are old enough to participate directly in the movements impelled by change, but not old enough to have become committed to an occupation, a residence, a family of procreation or a way of life. Furthermore the fact of change facilitates their development of other orientations than those of their parents and their community.

The most dramatic instance is war. Participation in war is limited in age, and the extent of war is limited in time. The Great War weakened a whole cohort in Europe to the extent that normal succession of personnel in roles, including positions of power, was disturbed. Sometimes the old retained power too long; sometimes the young seized power too soon.[4] The most obvious effect of war is the mortality and morbidity of the participants, but war transforms non-combatants as well. Several novels have utilized the theme of the peculiar poignancy of those who were old enough to comprehend the war but not old enough to participate in it (Brittain, 1949; Gläser, 1928; Hughes, 1963). The intellectual development of Mannheim, who brought the cohort concept into sociology, can be partly explained by the historical location of his cohort.[5] Teenagers in France can now meet easily with German youth groups because they are free of war memories.[6] German youths moving into the labor force are reported to be repudiating the labor discipline of their elders, whom they identify with the Nazi era.[7] The cohort consequences of war extend into the intellectual realm. Following the decimation of some French cohorts in the Great War, a split developed between those following the traditional path in mathematics, and those concerned with creating a new vocabulary. The latter produced the bible of modern mathematics, the *Elements of Bourbaki* (Félix, 1961).

Anyone reading the newspapers of the past decade needs no reminder of the prominence of uncommitted cohorts in the task forces of nationalistic or revolutionary political movements. The persons most active in the Protestant Reformation and in the Revolutions of England, France and America were youthful (Sorokin, 1947, p. 193). The contemporary "Children's Crusade" is too recent to have been investigated carefully, but there are some suggestive analyses of the position of youth in revolutionary change.[8] In his discussion of China, Levy (1949, pp. 297 *et seq.*) places primary emphasis on the role of the "ch'ing-nien" in societal transformation: this term for young adults has been retained by the aging leaders of the Communist movement. Irene

Taeuber (1964) has advocated a research program for China based on the fact that the Communists have now been in power 15 years; change is imminent as these new cohorts are ushered in. Eisenstadt (1956, pp. 98 *et seq.*) has documented the experience of youth movements in Israel and in prewar Germany. Both of these were rebellions against elders and their ideas, viewing youth alone as pure enough to accomplish the task of re-creating society.[9] Perhaps the affiliation of youth with the revolutionary phase of a charismatic movement is linked with the appeal for them of techniques of violence (Gerth, 1940). Rintala (1958) has suggested that people who un- dergo disruptive historical experiences during their formative years may be unusually vulnerable to totalitarian appeals. Young people who are students, or unemployed, in the big cities of developing nations, are likely to be available for demonstrations and have large places in which to congregate.

A popular but unsupportable argument is that the emergence of a new cohort somehow guarantees progress. Mentré (1920) reports approvingly Comte's opinion to this effect; Mannheim (1927/1952, p. 297) reports disapprovingly Cournot's like opinion. The entry of fresh cohorts into the political stream represents a potentiality for change, but without specifica- tion of its content or direction. The prominent role played by youth in the totalitarian movements of this century has been widely noted (Heberle, 1951, chap. 6). A new cohort provides a market for radical ideas and a source of followers, and they are more likely than their elders to criticize the existing order.[10] Replacement of much older by much younger leaders, as Eisenhower by Kennedy, may have a profound symbolic impact. The direction of change may be to the left or to the right, toward democracy or toward totalitarianism, but whatever the trend, it is most manifest in youth. Whether new cohorts are more or less crucial to the implementation of a revolution, they are clearly differentiated by its occurrence (Hinshaw, 1944, p. 69). The case of the Soviet Union is well documented by Bauer, Inkeles, and Kluckhohn (1960). Stalin created a generation of modern technicians to supplant the old Bol- sheviks, because the latter's skills in the dialectic and in conspiratorial politics did not suit the age of machine tools and modern armies. Now the decision system is passing into the hands of cohorts brought up under socialism (Rostow, 1960, pp 134-135) Journalists have recently begun to draw the line between those brought up under Stalin and those whose impressionable years coincided with de-Stalinization (Johnson, 1963). Al- though these latest cohorts are not yet in position of political power, they are beginning to have some influence, particularly through cultural acti- vities.

The adaptive transformation of revolutionary movements has frequently been discussed from a structuralist standpoint (Parsons, 1951, p. 507). The audacity and independence required to overthrow a regime are not the skills requisite for administering a stable government in the sequel. The lions and the foxes must change places. If this comparative statics model is reconsidered in processual terms, it is clear that cohort differentiation will result. Rostow (1960) has suggested naming the process the "Buddenbrooks dynamics." If change occurs, those who are brought up in the new world will differ from those who initiated the change. In consequence, more change will occur, but interest is transferred from wrecking a hated system to the task of constructive continuity. Gradually death claims both winners and losers of the old struggle. Support for the new system becomes broad and stable. Thus the cohort succession serves as cause and effect in the phases of revolutionary transformation.

An experiential chasm between cohorts also occurs when immigration or colonization produces an intersection of two cultures. The European immigrant arriving in the New World identified himself with an ethnic group resembling the culture in which he was raised. His children went to American schools, chose American playmates, and often escaped from the subculture (Herberg, 1960, pp. 27-31). The parents' inadequacy as a basis for orientation toward the new society reinforced the children's resort to peer groups. Similarly, the impact of western culture on primitive peoples is likely to yield disruption of family life, changing mutual evaluation of the generations, and ideological identification of youth with resistance. Kwame Nkrumah recently remarked on the appearance in Ghana of a new cohort without firsthand knowledge of colonial rule and without the habit of obsequiousness to the European. Mannoni (1956) has provided an absorbing account of the structural complexities in a population containing two generations of colonists and two generations of natives.

Traumatic episodes like war and revolution may become the foci of crystallization of the mentality of a cohort. The dramatic impact may mark indelibly the "naive eyes and virgin senses" of the cohort in the vanguard and change them into an entelechy with an explicit mission, a virtual community of thought and action. Yet such vivid experiences are unnecessary to the argument. Cohorts can also be pulled apart gradually by the slow grind of evolutionary change. The nucleus and epitome of social change, as determinant and consequence, is the city. Urbanization is the outstanding manifestation of the world transformation of the past few centuries. Cities have been populated largely by the continual infusion of new cohorts. Rural-urban migration is highly selective of younger persons; changes requiring population transfer will be undertaken only by the more flexible and less burdened members of the society (Bogue, 1961). The young move away from the community that would envelop them in the traditional mold and into a new way of life. America may be less tradition-bound than Europe because fewer young couples establish homes in the same place as their parents.

The principal motor of contemporary social change is technological innovation. It pervades the other substructures of society and forces them into accommodation. The modern society institutionalizes this innovation and accepts it as self-justifying. To the child of such a society, technological change makes the past irrelevant. Its impact on the population is highly differential by age, and is felt most by those who are about to make their lifelong choices. Technological evolution is accomplished less by retraining older cohorts than by recruiting the new one, and the age of an industry tends to be correlated with the age of its workers. Accessions to the labor force flow most strongly into the new and growing industries; separations from the labor force are predominantly out of declining industries (Clark & Dunne, 1955; Hawley, 1950, p. 25).[11] The distinctive age composition of the industrial structure is nowhere more evident than in the rapid industrialization of a previously traditional economy. In effect, it is accomplished not so much by educating the population as a whole as by introducing each new cohort in turn to the modern way of life. In traditional society, age is a valid surrogate for relevant experience, but when the industrial revolution occurs, age comes to signify historical location and degree of disfranchisement by change, rather than the due prerogatives of seniority.

⬦ INDIVIDUAL DEVELOPMENT AND THE FAMILY

Implicit in the foregoing account of the interdependency of social change and cohort differentiation is the assumption that an individual's history is highly stable or at least continuous. If a person's future were molded irrevocably by his earliest experiences, there would be a strong case for assembling data for aggregates of individuals on a cohort-by-cohort basis. The model dominating the literature on human development presents life as a movement from amorphous plasticity through mature competence toward terminal rigidity (Anderson, 1957; Birren, 1959; Child, 1954; Welford, 1958). The preparatory phase, during which individuals are susceptible to influence, is distinguished from the participatory phase, during which their predetermined destiny is unfolded. The central sociopsychological postulate in the spirit of Freud is that the core of personality is laid down at the beginning of life; what may look like changes later are merely minor variants on the established theme. The popularity of this assertion is as indubitable as its irrefutability. Discussion in this vein confuses ineluctable species characteristics and culturally variable designs, and fails to cope with the phenomenon of societal change.

In the conventional development model, the very young organism is presented as fluid, polymorphous, multipotential and perverse, susceptible to suggestion and rudimentary of will. Each interaction between organism and environment modifies the shape the organism takes into the next encounter. The earlier a situation imposes itself, the more likely it is to add an enduring element, partly because early learning is general enough to escape outright contradiction in subsequent particular experience. Gradually capacities are shaped and strengthened by use, with increasing self-regulation and independence of fluctuations. New experience is assimilated on the stratum of first impressions in a way that preserves self-consistency. The self-perception of persistence is ratified by others' recognition.

Thus the organism acquires an adult's efficiency at the price of a child's versatility. New ideas compete on unequal terms with old ones, because the latter have a place in the structure and have been used to direct behavior. Systematization and ritualization of response frees energy for higher-level integration. When a new situation accords with previous experience learning may be rapid, but not when it competes with established responses. The products of earlier education become debris that chokes off later growth. In due course the adult organism rigidifies and deteriorates into senility.

Any model of individual development which postulates early crystallization is embarrassing to the person explaining rapid social change. If personality is viewed as a quasi-hereditary phenomenon, the possibilities of change are reduced, following the biological analogy, to evolution through natural selection—a very slow process—and to mutation. Hagen (1962) finds himself in this box in his attempt to construct a theory of social change concordant with his belief that persons cannot move in later life from psychological stances established in childhood. Hagen's mutation-like proposal is that parents who encounter status frustration cannot change themselves, but their children may perceive the source of parental anxiety and avoid it by retreating. Their children, in turn, by a similar unconscious perception, may become innovators. The tempo of transformation is thus constrained to a generational rhythm.

The complexity of this construction is a direct consequence of two articles of faith: that social change cannot occur without personality change, and that personality change cannot occur once childhood is past. The present writer would propose that the social system rather than the personality system belongs at the center of any model of societal transformation. In this view personality is considered a by-product, at the individual level, of socialization procedures designed to achieve various objectives at the societal level. Socialization is a process of committing an individual to a term of service in a group, by progressively confining his behavioral potentialities within an acceptable range and by preparing him for the types of role he will be expected to play (Sewell, 1963). Far from being monopolized by the parents, socialization is a continuous process throughout life, shared in by every group of which a person may become a member. Even if the family-fostered self were immune to modification, the society could still retain the necessary degrees of freedom by altering the criteria for selection, from among different personality types, to fill the various roles.

Important to the present argument are two propositions: first, that social change implies a transformation of the relative contributions to socialization made by the various possible agencies of socialization; second, that this transformation identifies the cohort as a social reality, reflecting and implementing the social change to which it owes its existence. The principal socialization agency in every society is the family. It is an omnipresent authoritarian component of the child's environment, a primary group satisfying virtually the entire range of needs and furnishing the context within which the concept of self relative to others first arises. Family socialization is adequate to the extent that the structure of relationships portrayed and utilized in family life resembles that of the society into which the young adult must move. When a society breaks out of a static familistic mold, the family no longer suffices for the tasks of socialization.

Most writing about what is here called a cohort employs instead the term "generation," signifying all those within a broad (characteristically unspecified) age span during a particular epoch, and implicitly those with common characteristics because of common experiences. It is also used in synchronic structural analysis concerning relations between persons of markedly differing age, such as institutionalized deference (Cain, 1964). For the sake of conceptual clarity, "generation" should be used solely in its original and unambiguous meaning as the temporal unit of kinship structure, and the first two ideas should be signified by the terms "cohort" and "relative age status" respectively. "Generation" may be a fitting general temporal referent in societies where the dominant mode of role allocation is ascription on the basis of kinship. In such a context cohort identity is often trivial because the bulk of temporal variation coincides with the life cycle, as reproduced in annual cross-section. But societies undergoing cultural revolution must generally break the grip of the family on the individual. In so doing they diminish the social significance of "generation," in both its kinship and relative age connotations, and produce the kind of social milieu in which the cohort is the most appropriate unit of temporal analysis.

A prominent theme in discussions of modern society is intergenerational conflict. Although some of this is probably intrinsic to the family life cycle, current analyses emphasize the exacerbation of the tendency by social change, through intercohort differentiation (Davis, 1940; Elkin & Westley, 1955). As an Arab proverb has it, "Men resemble the times more than they do their fathers." Role differentiation that gives the old power over the young is justified when age is correlated strongly and positively with control of cultural content, but the correlation may even become negative during rapid social change because age differences in one direction signify cohort differences in the opposite direction. This is a familiar literary theme, as in Turgenev's *Fathers and Sons*. For reviews of the literature, see: Mentré (1920), Renouard (1953), and Sorokin (1941, pp. 504 *et seq.*).

Many writers have used the succession of cohorts as the foundation for theories of sociocultural dynamics. This approach has been aptly labeled "generationism," because the writers mistakenly transfer from the generation to the cohort a set of inappropriate associations. Some generationists maintain that there is a periodicity to sociocultural change caused by the biological fact of the succession of generations at 30-year (father-son) intervals.[12] There is no such periodicity. Other generationists develop a conflict theory of change, pitched on the opposition between the younger and the older "generations" in society, as in the family. But a society reproduces itself continuously. The age gap between father and son disappears in the population at large, through the comprehensive overlapping of life cycles. The fact that social change produces intercohort differentiation and thus contributes to inter-generational conflict cannot justify a theory that social change is produced by that conflict. Generationists have leaped from inaccurate demographic observation to inaccurate social conclusion without supplying any intervening causality. All these works suggest arithmetical mysticism, and the worst of them, as Troeltsch said, are *"reine Kabbala."*

◇ CHANGING AGENCIES OF CHILD SOCIALIZATION

With the advent of modern society, changes in the agencies of socialization establish a context favorable to the identification of cohorts. The individual mobility and achievement-based status required of a modern occupational structure seem much more harmonious with the conjugal family than with the traditional web of kinship obligations (Goode, 1962, chap. 1). Revolutionary regimes may adopt specific policies to reduce the importance of the family as an agency of socialization and as a bulwark of the old stratification system. Consider, for example, the Soviet emphasis on early education of the child away from home, the Chinese attempt to shift the locus of authority away from the older generation, and the Israeli use of the kibbutz to communalize child care and restrict parent-child interaction to the affectional realm. Such attempts to place collective identification above family solidarity may not have been completely successful (Talmon-Garber, 1959), but they are consistent with reorientations throughout the modernizing world. The potentially perpetual consanguineal unit is being supplanted by a conjugal family with a limited lifetime, and the institutional scope of family affairs is narrowing.

In particular, the reallocation of responsibility for child socialization away from the family and toward the school on the formal level and the peer group on the informal level gives analytic form to the cohort, just as specific historical changes give it analytic content. Parental capacity to prepare the child for his adult roles depends on the simplicity and stability of life. In a society of specialization and change parents are inadequate models for children and the specialized agency of formal education must be created. The school develops a commitment to the implementation of societal values, teaches the skills needed to perform adult tasks, and contributes to manpower allocation. As the content of education evolves, it differentiates the knowledge of parent and child, and equips successive cohorts with a progressively enlarged culture. To the extent that school instruction differs from what is learned at home, it provokes independent thought. The radical potentiality of education is clearest in the university, which has the function of discovering as well as transmitting knowledge.

By substituting teachers for parents, society symbolizes the difference in historical location between child and parent, and attenuates the bonds between them. Education expands in a modern society to encompass almost all members of each cohort and for a progressively longer age span, not only up into early adulthood but also down into the "formative" period cherished by personality theorists. The long time during which individuals are embedded in the lockstep age-hierarchized school system gives the cohort an ample opportunity to identify itself as a historical entity. The school is a cohort creator.

Socialization in every society is the function not only of institutionalized authorities but also of coevals. An increase in such "self-socialization" is to be expected during social change, because this makes the experiences of the peer group (the cohort) unique, and develops similarities within and differences between cohorts. One of the themes in *The Lonely Crowd* (Riesman, Denney, & Glazer, 1950) is the replacement of the inner-directed type, whose standards are his parents', by the other-directed type, whose standards are his contemporaries'. The congruence with the present position is obvious.

The peer group is a subset of one's cohort. It consists of people of the same age with whom one has attitude-forming relationships, or, to use an old-fashioned but etymologically apt term, one's cronies (Pitts, 1960). It is oriented to its members' needs and interests rather than to the pursuit of goals deemed by external authority. Perhaps when a collectivity rather than an individual is being socialized, it develops a sense of cohort solidarity and alters the outcome of socialization. Although providing nonadult approval, it need not be deviant, and may even give strong support to the conventional moral code (Reiss, 1960).

Peer groups are functional in modern society (Eisenstadt, 1956, 1963). If the principles regulating family life harmonize with those of other institutional spheres, an individual can attain full membership in the society through behavior learned in the family. But modern society is regulated by criteria which contradict those appropriate to kinship. For the individual this poses the problem of transition from one universe of discourse to the other; for the society it poses the problem of developing bases of extra-familial solidarity. The solution is the peer group, which has the primary group characteristics of the family and the achievement orientation of the society.

It is tempting to treat the peer group phenomenon as signaling the creation of a sense of solidarity if not reality as a social group, and thus derive support for the view that a cohort is more than a mere category in statistical tables. Solidarity is encouraged by idealized self-definitions in reaction to ill-specified rights and responsibilities of the status, by sharing anxieties concerning imminent and hazardous transitions, and by explicit associations that encourage the development of attitudes unsanctioned by family or community. The age (and cohort) variance of membership in voluntary associations is smaller in youth than later, because small age differences mean more during development. The mass media aim specifically labeled appeals at these ages. Vocabularies specific to the age and time are invented to serve as communications channels and boundary-maintaining mechanisms.

In an epoch of change, each person is dominated by his birth date. He derives his philosophy from his historical world, the subculture of his cohort. The community of date equips each cohort with its own expanse of time, its own style and its own truth. The ideas, sentiments and values of members of the same cohort converge; their actions become quasi-organized. As social change creates divergence in the experience of successive cohorts, it may transform them from locations into actualities (Mannheim, 1927/1952b). It is possible for most of a society's youth to develop an ideological direction (though probably under adult leadership) but the burden of proof is on those who insist that the cohort acquires the organized characteristics of some kind of temporal community. This may be a fruitful hypothesis in the study of small groups of coevals in artistic or political movements but it scarcely applies to more than a small minority of the cohort in a mass society. Commonality is likely but not community.[13]

Age-homogeneous groupings of children and adolescents are common to all societies. Mostly they remain undeveloped because kinship groups form the basic units of task performance. In some cases the cohort—known to anthropologists as an "age grade"—may function continuously throughout life. In the Hamitic culture of East Africa, for example, the age grade is a system of compulsory association enduring from puberty on, with permanent privileges and obligations. The system cuts across family lines, gives the individual interests in tribal concerns, and may be used for governmental or religious functions (Driberg, 1958). This is very different from the history of a modern adolescent peer group. The features that make it attractive to its members are liabilities for its persistence (cf. Matza, 1964). The peer group has fluid boundaries, with individual members drifting into and out of association. Its numbers are ordinarily small and its functions vague and diffuse. It may provide recruits for radical movements, but it is just as likely to veer toward frivolity or criminality. Its dilemma is that it is terminated by the arrival of adulthood. The peer group has little time to develop effective strength. It faces the common difficulties of any group composed mostly of transients. The members are dispersed by the growth of heterosexual interests, by the formation of families of procreation, and by movement into the labor force and out of the conveniently age-homogeneous arrangements of school.

The peer-group phenomenon provides insufficient support for a cohort approach to social change but it does exemplify the tendency toward cohort identification within the time structure of a changing population. The peer group is a symptom of the strain imposed on modern youth by its location at the fulcrum of change. The schedule of development includes a psychosocial moratorium between preparation and participation (Erikson, 1950, 1963). This is when the youth first gets a chance to temper with reality the rigid precepts implanted in childhood. Lessons too sophisticated for children can now be learned. There are many answers for the questions of the age, from various and often contradictory sources. The imprecision of youth's role definition encourages receptivity to new ideas. Movement out of the equilibrated orientation provided by family and school and into a cognitively unstructured realm leaves them doubtful and uncertain but sometimes creative (Lewin, 1939). The new cohort of young adults lives in a phase of the life cycle when dramatic transitions are occurring in rapid succession. Perhaps the pace of personal change increases sensitivity to the possibilities of social change.

⊠ SOURCES OF INDIVIDUAL STABILITY IN ADULT LIFE

The cohort approach to social analysis derives strong support from the continuity of individual life, from a time-specific and thus historically located initiation. A person's past affects his present, and his present affects his future. Persistence is enhanced by the tendency to structure inputs, so that each will disturb as little as possible the previous cognitive, normative or even esthetic design, and, in the extreme, to reject dissonant items. Although individuals differ in the ingenuity with which they may retain disparate elements or achieve reformulation, the feasibility of extensive transformation is obviously quite limited. Individuals seek coherence, and manifest continuity to the extent that they achieve it. An individual's life is an organic entity, and the successive events that constitute it are not random but patterned.

The initial contribution to the design of a lifetime is made at conception, when the individual is provided not only with a fixed genetic constitution but also, under ordinary circumstances, with the two parents to whom society will assign responsibility for his early socialization. Furthermore, every society seizes upon the circumstances of birth as modes of allocating status, limiting the degrees of freedom for the person's path through life. Virtually every subsequent occurrence will depend on the societal plan for utilizing characteristics present at birth: sex, race, kinship, birthplace, and so forth. Perhaps the most important influence of status ascription on the future of an individual in a modern society is its effect on access to different amounts and kinds of formal education.

Beyond the age of noncommitment, the new adult begins a process of involvement in the various spheres of life, in which his actions and those of others progressively reduce the degrees of freedom left to him in the societal scheme (Becker, 1960). Facing various decisions among alternative roles open to him, an individual generally makes choices somewhat congruent with his value-orientations—unless he is to be credited with pure perversity.

Within each role, once allocated, he forms a growing commitment to a line of activity. Each contract between group and individual contains a relatively determinate description of role requirements, and the contract is strengthened by stabilized interactions between the individual and occupants of interdependent roles. The temporal commitment is perhaps most relevant to the present argument. Thus a company's interest is served by bureaucratic arrangements, such as pensions and seniority rules, which penalize movement out of the system. On the job, the older employee becomes adjusted to his work, gravitating toward tasks that are congenial to him, and learning enough about them to exploit their advantages and minimize their liabilities. His psychological stake in his niche includes a modification of aspirations in consonance with his true abilities and the demands of the system for them. It should be clear that though this example is occupational, similar principles operate in every group of which a person becomes a member.

The apparent rigidity of an older worker in the face of a demand to adapt to a new procedure may flow simply from the circumstance that something valuable is being taken away from him (Tannenbaum, 1961). The difficulties of learning new skills are more formidable for one who has acquired and utilized traditional work practices (Mead, 1953). This may also hold for the domestic technology of contraception (see Hill, Stycos, & Back, 1959). Career continuity is bolstered by investing time and money in a particular kind of vocational preparation. Continuous obsolescence of the individual is a feature of contemporary industrial society. It is to be expected that the old hands will resist innovation; otherwise they may be displaced before they are ready to retire. Resistance may be successful for a while, because the oldest workers are most likely to occupy positions of authority. The term "vested interests" suggests capitalistic profits threatened by change, but it applies equally to the skilled worker standing guard over his way of doing things. Perhaps this is especially true for higher levels of technical skill, where workers are less interchangeable, and the individual and the industry commensurately less flexible (Moore, 1946, p. 60).

Around his job, the individual establishes a network of spatial arrangements linking places where he lives, shops, plays and visits. An older man with a family feels obliged to remain in a situation from which a younger unencumbered person would readily move. The assumption of the parental role makes a person an agent of the society as a teacher of its new members, and the private attitude to which a man once felt himself entitled as a youth must now be subordinated to the more conventional public postures expected of the father (Presley & Kuhlen, 1957, pp. 494 *et seq.*) "Nothing makes a younger generation settle down faster than a still younger generation showing up." Children are powerful instruments in making conformists of parents. They terminate definitively the brief period of "horizontal" freedom between the vertical structure of the family of orientation and the vertical structure of the family of procreation.

In a modern society, most adult roles are located in hierarchized structures. Factories, churches, labor unions and political parties distribute income, prestige and power along an approximately age-graded continuum. Memberships in such structures decrease the probability of individual transformation. In the majority of occupations a steadily upward progression of status occurs throughout most of the age span. Seniority can be viewed as commitment to particular modes of solving particular problems. The personnel of organizations tend to fall into Old Guard and Young Turk positions, emulating generations within a family. Young men must wait a long time for positions of power and responsibility, and may never arrive if they display ideas and attitudes deviating from those of their seniors (Berger, 1960). Conformity to such vertical structures, and acceptance of the rewards and duties defined by superiors, implies resistance to change. To advance in a particular economic order requires support of that order. Success reinforces the way in which success has been achieved; failure is resisted from whatever position of accrued power has been attained. Social change creates continuing conflict between the rewards of seniority and the penalties of membership in older cohorts.

Students of political affiliation have been concerned with the ages at which people's experiences have most influence on their political behavior.[14] The hypothesis that youths acquire a structure of political attitudes from parents and peers, which persists unless disturbed by dissonant events, seems to be contradicted by the conservatism of older voters. Some of the tendency for older Americans to vote Republican may be explained by theories of aging, and by association with preferred statuses accompanying age, but a residual remains to be explained by intercohort differentiation (Crittenden, 1962). Perhaps the stereotype of the older person as a dogmatic conservative fits a person whose education dates back to a time when attitudes now regarded as conservative were more common. Yet persistence and continuity in the political as in the occupational sphere seem to grow with commitment to adult affairs, as exposure to alternatives is reduced, and penalties of change increase (Hinshaw, 1944, p. 69).

As life takes on a steadier tempo, routinization predominates. Routines are barriers to change because they limit confrontation with the unexpected and the disturbing. Older people learn to exercise greater control over a narrower environment, and avoid risks of venturing into unstructured situations. The feasibility of personal transformation is probably limited more by restricted membership than by physiological aging. A persistent research problem is the difficulty of distinguishing between characteristics which are indeed intrinsic to aging, and those which merely appear to be so because of the cohort contribution to the age vector in times of change. Social change ordinarily touches older persons less closely. They lead a more restricted social life, they read less, they attend fewer movies, and their friends, books and movies are more carefully chosen to conform to their biases. Their residences and their friendships become more stable. The longer a person persists in an established mode of conduct, the less likely its comprehensive redefinition, especially if he invests it with normative content. Aging involves disengagement and withdrawal, a restriction on the quantity and intensity of interaction with others, and an approach toward self-centered and idiosyncratic behavior. Consistency through time is achieved by developing a vested interest in forms to which past behavior has again and again been oriented. To change the basic conceptions by which one has learned to assess the propriety of situations would be to make a caricature of one's life.

In later years, the cohort identity is blurred. Age becomes progressively less precise as an index of a person's social characteristics. Individuals experience what Cain (1964) calls asynchronization—they possess different "ages" in the various institutional spheres. People vary physiologically, and also in the extent to which they continue to learn. Adjacent cohorts tend to permeate one another as the pattern of life chances works itself out. Definitions of age become predominantly social rather than biological categories; they change with time, and with the groups one joins and leaves. The intrinsic aging process may be variously accelerated or retarded by many different institutional arrangements.

The research recommendation implicit in the preceding discussion of the sources of continuity in individual lives is longitudinal analysis. The category includes case histories, repeated interviews with the same respondents (of which panel studies are a special case), analyses of diaries and dated letters, and, on a larger scale, continuous work histories or morbidity histories, for insurance purposes.[15] The *raison d'être* of the longitudinal approach is the organization of personal data in temporal sequence, to determine the causal potentiality of otherwise isolated acts. This procedure has dominated behavioral inquiry, particularly under psychoanalytic influence, has become standard operating procedure in social psychology, and has been described as "the perfect type of sociological material" (Blumer, 1939; Thomas & Znaniecki, 1919, p. 6).

The data produced by such inquiries are disjunctive with most statistical analyses of aggregates in two ways. First, the intensive detail of longitudinal analyses proliferates hypotheses but ordinarily lacks that broad evidential basis requisite to generalized verification which is a principal virtue of census tabulations, for instance. In this sense life histories and statistical analyses are complementary approaches (Volkart, 1951, p. 24). But their potential complementarily is prejudiced by the second disjuncture—between the time axes of the two procedures. The life history has been called the long-section and the statistical the cross-section view of culture. The typical emphasis of the latter on simultaneity between corresponding events from different lives implies over-valuation of the existing situation—"the socio-logical error par excellence" (Dollard, 1935). Aggregate analysis destroys individual sequences, and diverts attention from process. By implying that the past is irrelevant, cross-sectional analysis inhibits dynamic inquiry and fosters the illusion of immutable structure (Evan, 1959).

This outcome can be avoided by using the cohort approach. The cohort record, as macrobiography, is the aggregate analogue of the individual life history. It provides the necessary temporal isomorphism for linking small-scale intensive longitudinal analyses with extensive surveys of the society at a point of time. It has the time dimension of the former and the comforting statistical reliability of the latter. In a similar vein, Ortega has rejected both the collectivist and the individualist interpretations of historical reality, in favor of an orientation based on the cohort—"the dynamic compromise between mass and individual—the most important conception in history" (Ortega y Gasset, 1933, pp. 13-15).

⬦ SOURCES OF FLEXIBILITY: INDIVIDUAL AND GROUP

The predominant theme of literature on socialization and development is early crystallization. Perhaps this is because students of child development are most concerned with the personality, the control of primary drives, and the internalization of general value orientations, and not with the learning of specific norms and skills to be demanded of the adult. Clearly childhood socialization cannot prepare a person for all the roles of his later years. Indeed, parents effectively inhibit many types of learning by selectively sheltering their children from and exposing them to the world outside the home. Many types of economic, political and social participation are effec-tively limited to later life, e.g., the problem of support for older parents is not ordinarily encountered by the "child" until he approaches middle age.

Socialization continues throughout the whole of life. Specific socialization occurs every time a person occupies a role in a new group, for every group has and is an agency for socialization and social control (Brim, 1964, pp. 1-5). Although the codes of new groups the individual joins are often limited in content, they may tend to contradict the general precepts of earlier training. That there is considerable flexibility is evident from the experience of social and cultural mobility. For all the resistance of the culturally conditioned personality, individuals do move between cultures, subcultures and classes.

Socialization need not mean rigidification. Normative postures are often acquired imperfectly, incompletely and tentatively. Perhaps it is simpler to indoctrinate entrants with a set of immutable recipes for action in prescribed situations, but room is almost always left for interpretation. The situations to be encountered cannot all be anticipated, and the appropriate prescriptions for them may require improvisation. Experience can strain the sacred formula to the point of forcing reconstruction. The intellectual convenience of the assumption that development ceases once adulthood is attained must be sacrificed in the face of the annoying complexity of reality (Strauss, 1959). Behavior can be modified by increasing rewards for innovation, expanding tolerance of some kinds of deviation and softening penalties for movement. Indoctrination can be designed to encourage experimentation rather than unreflective obedience, and place primary emphasis on adherence to broad principles. Of particular importance are institutionalized procedures that provide legitimate modes of modification, such as debate in political negotiation and disciplined doubt in scientific inquiry. Such procedures impose a burden of doubt and strain on individual participants, but do leave room for social change through individual change.

Although the difficulty of teaching an old dog new tricks may be inherent, it is also possible that this is a myth given approximate reality by training programs based on it. The feasibility of adult change is probably contingent in large part on the character of early training, and on the opportunities provided for retraining. Perhaps older workers are less adaptable because the earlier cohorts of which they are members received a limited general education. Potential obsolescence may in the future be reduced by more general training, so that people will still be able to acquire in their later years the new capacities and skills needed for continuing employment. It is not outside the bounds of speculation to look toward the day when accelerating change will make economic an extension of education throughout the entire life span, as a continual adjunct to the work week, or as a routine sabbatical renovation.

Yet the flexibility of the social system and its components need not rely on the imperfect tentativeness of socialization procedures, nor on the prospects of retraining the individual. Every group has some control over its own demographic metabolism, and over the content of socialization. The society achieves pattern and direction partly through general selection mechanisms. Change can be mediated through modifications of role allocation as well as through flexible socialization. The system of role allocation can be manipulated to achieve stability and continuity for the group and for the individual, and permit the continuing transformation required by a dynamic society.

Like individuals, organizations (including the total society) have characteristics that influence their degrees of freedom with respect to change. In particular, the different system levels vary in the feasibility of transformation by substituting rather than by modifying components. In biology, the capacity for change is greater at the organismic than at the cellular level. The life of a cell is short relative to that of its encompassing organism. In turn, the organism must die but the species persists and changes, through reproduction and selection. Each higher level has greater modifiability through time, based on the feasibility of metabolism of lower-level components. The analogy of society and organism was always somewhat unfortunate, for reasons unnecessary to rehearse, and also because it may have obscured the more fruitful analogy between society and species. The society is a looser and less sharply defined system than the organism because its constituents possess the possibility of independent mobility in space. In turn, the society is a more flexible system than the species, because it has greater possibility of independent mobility in time. It can control not only the physical replacement of members, like the species, but also the replacement of norms through cultural transmission. In a sense, the society has two types of membership: biological, consisting of human organisms, and cultural, consisting of social norms. The replacement of each is of course interdependent with the replacement of the other.

Now the processes of normative replacement and personnel replacement occur at all levels of social organization. The study of the demographic metabolism of specific groups is a relatively uncharted area of great importance to the student of social change. The individual differs from the organization because he is attached to a mortal body, and lacks the capacity for freedom with respect to time which is within the grasp of the organization. Organizations, like individuals, may acquire structural rigidities, but they can modify their course by replacing individuals as well as by transforming them, through their hiring and firing policies. The scope of possibilities for transforming the character and direction of an organization obviously includes succession in crucial leadership roles and the changing criteria for advancement as different talents become more or less valued (Gusfield, 1957).

Indeed, in some respects the subsystems of a society may be even more flexible in this regard than the society itself. They have more scope for applying conditions for remaining and more ways of recruiting new individuals. Enfranchisement and disfranchisement are much more discriminating in their selectivity than natural processes (Simmel, 1956). A society does have some control over the character of its membership, to the extent that differential fertility and mortality are subject to social arrangement, and to the extent that the population is changed by migration, but it is at least common for a society to accept a contractual obligation to all those born within its boundaries (an obligation it has in a sense inherited from its predecessor, the family). But it is perhaps most meaningful from the standpoint of the transmutability of the total society to consider the extent to which its components are groups and organizations rather than individuals. Organizations persist if and because they are successful. New organizations are continually born and old ones die. The replacement of individuals within an organization is paralleled by the replacement of organizations within a society. Once again the opportunities for research are abundant.

◇ CONCLUSION

The case for the cohort as a temporal unit in the analysis of social change rests on a set of primitive notions: persons of age a in time t are those who were age $a-1$ in time $t-1$; transformations of the social world modify people of different ages in different ways; the effects of these transformations are persistent. In this way a cohort meaning is implanted in the age-time specification. Two broad orientations for theory and research flow from this position: first, the study of intracohort temporal development throughout the life cycle; second, the study of comparative cohort careers, i.e., intercohort temporal differentiation in the various parameters that may be used to characterize these aggregate histories.

The purpose of this essay is to direct the attention of sociologists toward the study of time series of parameters for successive cohorts of various types, in contradistinction to conventional period-by-period analyses. There has been a considerable growth of cohort research in recent years, but the predominant emphasis is still on comparative cross-sectional inquiry. Admittedly the new approach shares the vices as well as the virtues of all studies with an extended time dimension. It is cumbersome, inefficient and laborious; data collection is very time-consuming; and the implicit incomparability accumulates as the group changes its composition, and as the data collectors change their definitions (Kessen, 1960). Yet such difficulties are not so much those of the method itself as meaningful reflections of the research investment necessary to study a long-lived species experiencing structural transformation.

Measurement techniques should be designed to provide data that correspond with the theoretical formulations of the phenomena under examination. In the present essay, the purpose has been to present a frame of reference within which theories can be constructed and empirical inquiry prosecuted. Considering the modest results so far achieved in dynamic analysis, sociologists would be well-advised to exploit the congruence of social change and cohort differentiation.

⟨⟩ NOTES

1. Lemuel Gulliver reported that the Luggnaggians solved the problem with their Struldbruggs by desocializing them at 80. Comte hypothesized that progress is maximized by a length of life neither too ephemeral nor too protracted (Martineau, n.d., pp. 152-153).

2. Bracker (1954) noted that the graduates of American universities of the class of 1929 were united by the distinction of being educated for prosperity and then vaulted into depression.

3. As an exotic example, Hyman Enzer has recently completed a study of the cohort of all 118 American authors whose first novels came out in 1958 (see Dempsey, 1963).

4. An extensive bibliography is given in Neumann (1942).

5. Paul Kecskemeti, the preface to Mannheim (1927/1952b). In turn, Mannheim ascribes growing interest in the cohort problem to political discontinuities in the late 19th century.

6. A movie opened in Paris in 1963, called: *Hitler? Never Heard of Him.*

7. Wagner (1956) has discussed the significance for the German labor movement of the absorption of cohorts who grew up under National Socialism.

8. For example, *U.S. News and World Report,* June 6, 1960; *Look,* January 3, 1961. These accounts are more impressive for the frequency than for the detail of instances reported. Somewhat more helpful is Baldwin (1960).

9. Many accounts of the Negro civil rights movement in the United States have contained the assertion that Negro youth provide the initiative for protest, in impatience with the gradualism of their elders.

10. This may not be so if youth is directly affected by the change, as with school desegregation (Hyman & Sheatsley, 1964).

11. On December 1, 1963, a federal arbitration board authorized American railroads to eliminate most of their firemen, by attrition.

12. The Spanish philosopher, Ortega y Gasset, and his disciple, Julian Marias, assert that modern history is punctuated by 15-year caesurae, beginning with 1626, the year Descartes turned 30 (Renouard, 1953).

13. "Belonging to a generation is one of the lowest forms of solidarity." In Rosenberg's (1959, pp. 241-258) opinion, generation identifications are concocted by journalists out of trivial or ephemeral data.

14. For summaries of the literature, see Lipset et al. (1954), and Hyman (1959).

15. For a summary of the technical problems, see Goldfarb (1960).

CHAPTER FOUR

On the Importance of Age

LAWRENCE HAZELRIGG

◇ INTRODUCTION

One of the great debates of Europe's late seventeenth and eighteenth centuries concerned the age of planet Earth. This debate, like others during that fertile period, engaged a still struggling modern science in quarrels with the ancients and with contemporary religious authorities. An official answer to the question of Earth's age had been established through Bishop Ussher's (1658, p. 1) exacting calculations from the *Genesis* account: "the beginning of time . . . fell upon the entrance of the night preceding the twenty third day of *Octob.* in the year of the Julian calendar, 710" (i.e., 4004 BCE). Ussher's verdict had been comfortingly close to Martin Luther's previous estimate (4000 BCE), which in turn had corrected the calculations of earlier scholars such as the third-century Julius Africanus (5500 BCE) and the second-century Theophilus of Antioch (5529 BCE). For many authorities of the day the question of Earth's age was largely settled.

The young interests of a scientific geochronology were sensitive to the importance of getting the number right, of course, and already lessons discerned in nature's text had suggested to some inquirers that the good Bishop's sacred number was either wildly inaccurate or peculiar to a counting system very different from mundane chronology. But the debate as it unfolded *within* the nascent science itself, though still influenced by the account from theology, had less to do with the accuracy of a numerical estimate than with a methodological issue concerning the significance of age (see, e.g., Burchfield, 1975). In brief, this issue can be characterized by a pair of questions: Does one begin with substantive understanding of a process and from that understanding calculate the time budget implied by the dynamics of the process? Or does one begin with a time budget, a temporal gradient extending from an absolute zero-point ("origin") to a "now," and determine how the observed or imagined stages of a process fit between those limits?

That difference manifested what was arguably *the* core issue in a contest of views among those who were attempting a geochronology other than the theological account. Both views were "developmentalist"—that is, concerned to understand the history of Earth's changing face and stratigraphy as an unfolding sequence of stages of formation, governed by an inner logic of geological process. But in one view (commonly called "Neptunist") "age" *as such* had a certain defining significance—for some, a sacred significance—whereas in the other ("Vulcanist") view "age" was simply one of several traits that *followed from* specific causal processes that had governed the geological course of the planet. Indications of age were significant because they reflected major transitional events in that geological course, not because they were its regulative meter.

In retrospect, the debate between Neptunists and Vulcanists can easily seem a quaint page from modern science's early record of efforts to winnow error and error correction in the design of strategies of inquiry. Although we may continue to dispute various means, outcomes, and ramifications of estimating Earth's age, hardly anyone now entertaining such disputes believes that the definitive postulate (or fact) from which all else must follow is a fixed budget of time. And yet, conceptions of "age" as a characteristic of a *person* often do proceed from the significance of a time budget to consequences for various processes. The peculiar tendency to regard time as a commodity—indeed, a commodity subject to increasing scarcity as a function of time—lends a certain gravity to the meaning of personal age and aging.

Unlike the age of Earth, the age of a person is experienced directly and internally, nearly from start to finish. The experience is of a relatively short, relatively fixed interval—the finitude of a "lifetime," experienced within a lifetime. In everyday understanding of that interval, every person begins with zero degree of age, every person ends with a number on a death certificate, and all events and stages of the processes of a lifetime must fit between those limits. Given that experiential matrix, "age" *as such* becomes a definitive initializing characteristic which otherwise seemingly detaches from causal process to such an extent that the question "What is the cause of age?" loses sense. One simply "has" an age, because one "has" a lifetime. The etymology of "age" speaks the connection: the derivation is from the Latin *ævum* ("lifetime") and is akin to the Greek *aion* ("period of existence," "lifetime"). Lexically, "age" is the part of a lifetime extending from the beginning of the lifetime to any given moment within the lifetime. To ask the cause of a living being's age is to ask the cause of an event that has yet to happen, death. Age is integral to the being of a person—so much so that, despite the gathering critique of essentialism in understandings of a wide array of phenomena, age seems an incontrovertibly essential property. Whereas a "social construction-ist" understanding of variations in age-accounting schemes, or in systems of "age status," can be credibly rendered, it nonetheless still seems assured that beneath all such variations any person is essentially, not accidentally, a certain age. One can imagine a person living outside a system of "occupa-tional status," in the sense of having *no* occupational status because they have no occupation whatsoever. Likewise with respect to a system of "educational status," "income status," and so forth. One can imagine a society without ethnic or racial differentiation, every person manifesting a virtually unique genealogical mixture of what were once regarded as ethnic and racial "stocks." One can even imagine a society in which persons have no gender, no "sexual difference," with species reproduction occurring by partheno-genesis (the male of the species thus rendered superfluous). But can one imagine a person having no age?

What is more, age as a property of persons seems to be robustly self-sufficient. Or nearly so; it *is* contingent on survival (though "survival" occurs in more than one register: the age of Buddha or Jesus or an ancestral spirit is still often recorded). One can change jobs, lose or win a fortune, switch allegiances in a system of secular or sacred authority, re-engineer the gen-dered portions of one's body, all without notable effect on one's age. Age is one of the least alienable properties a person "has." Although it often figures in resource-eligibility and allocation rules, age as such cannot be exchanged for something else (despite the tendency to regard time as a commodity). Although accumulating kinds and quantities of resource rarely happens instantaneously after the event of birth, and therefore parallels change in age, an accumulated resource is even more rarely convertible into age as such. Passing behavior can be and is practiced; but the dissimulator is rarely oblivious to the dissimulation. Amnesia may confound the counting of age; but no one, including the amnesiac, doubts that at any given moment a precise part of a lifetime has been lived from its beginning.

Anything so staunchly resistant to alienation, constantly "there" as a property of a person yet constantly changing, must be, one easily imagines, among the most potent of explanatory variables in social science's toolkit. Surely "age" explains a lot.

Or does it? One can argue that age *as such* explains very little, perhaps nothing of abiding interest. To be sure, age is part of the trait *description* of persons. Description by age is one of the small number of operations by which persons have systematically distinguished and categorized themselves in every known society, in every known culture. But even though "explanation" is a sort of description (e.g., a causal account or model of a process is a description of how the process works), description is not necessarily explanation.

Like gender or height or the presence/absence of ear lobes, age itself is not a cause of anything. Rather, it is properly regarded as a classification variable, the title of a set of categories in a particular classification system, just as is an ethnic title or a gender title. This is surely not to say that titles lack social significance, nor even that titles cannot be causally significant. Being "tall" or being "short" is a title that often implies some degree of relative advantage or stigma, as Martel and Biller (1987) have described. Likewise, ethnic titles, gender titles, titles such as "skinny" or "fat," and so on. (On the other hand, the "lobed versus unlobed" difference in ear morphology is not, so far as I know, a similarly significant title in social classifications.) Socially significant titles cover variably complex sociocultural formations, including some which are directly implicated in personal and collective identities. So, for instance, having the title "child" is testamentary of a broad array of correlated traits and normative expectations within a differentiated and stratified field of identities. But the significance of a title generally consists in its informational or signaling capacities in some type of discriminatory or selection process. Actors tend to see, evaluate, and respond to each other differently, in accordance with the signals read from state titles. A title such as "elder" or "woman" will be causally significant insofar as an actor's practical grasp of the implications of that title for the actor's behaviors or actions influence those behaviors or actions. This sort of "internal" causal significance is manifest in motivational and intentional structures—for example, in the discrimination and selection of "appropriate" action repertoires. But the causal force is contributed by the selection process and resulting discriminatory behavior or action, not the state title to which the selection and the resulting behavior or action refer. Moreover, the discriminatory behavior or action may be manifest in one or more other processes (e.g., processes of allocation, succession, maturation, identity formation, etc.), which tend to reproduce the state titles (and more generally the classification system) as signals or markers. Consequently, the titles (and associated traits) tend to be notably correlated with both the discriminatory behaviors or actions and their outcomes. As markers, the titles have descriptive value—for the analyst observing the behaviors and actions, as for the observed actors themselves. But they lack direct explanatory value in a causal framework. For this latter purpose (causal explanation), substantive interest is better directed to the processes of discrimination or selection, as Heckman and Robb (1985) argued.

The same can be said of related titles such as "cohort," "generation" (in its nominative sense), and "historical period." These are shorthand expressions referring to multiple, interrelated processes of various kinds, and here, too, substantive interest (in terms of solving problems of conceptualization, measurement, and model specification) is better directed to the complex processes "covered" by those titles. Shorthand expressions—as in the locution, "the effect of cohort succession on social structure"—are convenient taglines, but they easily mislead into a confusion of compositional effects as causes. Consider the oft-stated claim that as the mean age of a society's population increases the crime rate declines. It is not that population aging *causes* a reduction in the number of observed criminal acts per capita. Rather, the complex causal processes that end in a particular number at one date and different numbers at subsequent dates have been resorted in correlation with the population composition of causally significant characteristics.[1] Or consider Easterlin's thesis regarding effects of the size distributions of successive cohorts (Easterlin, 1980; Pampel & Peters, 1995): to expect that the predicted effects would obtain during different strips of history or in different societies is to ignore the several specific causal processes on which the tagline of Easterlin's thesis utterly depends.

Titles of chapters are also meant to have descriptive value; and these, too, can mislead. In the present instance a bold title announces more than will pass for inspection. The importance of age is roughly the size and complexity of all the reasons that age is a topic. My aim is not to survey those reasons, nor is it to weigh importance throughout all or representative dimensions of the conceptual and methodological text that opens from the question, Why *is* age a topic? Much more modest aims ride on selective forays into that text: first, to use a sequence of states conception of age as a means of clarifying "age" vis-à-vis other processes; second, to review some differences in the semantics of age states, relative to uses of "age" as a classification variable in the field of social status; third, to consider conceptions of temporality in conjunctions of age-state transitions and other processes, with particular reference to notions of "the aging self." In the unlikely event that anything mildly new but nonfoolish is said in these ruminations, it will have been due

to stimulations from a varied set of guides, always welcome when reaching
for hooks and handholds in new territory.

⊠ TRAITS, STATES, AND SEQUENCES

"Age" is one of the commonest entries in social science's typical r x k matrix
of observations. It is one of the "basic demographic facts" we remember to
record of individuals. And not only of individual persons; for "age" is a trait
intelligibly applied in observations of members of many different membership classes—planets, trees, stones, organizations (e.g., a firm or a baseball
club), social movements, relationships (e.g., a contract, a dyadic tie), ideas
or beliefs (e.g., belief in the existence of phlogiston), and so forth. Moreover,
populations of a particular unit of observation (persons, trees, breweries,
etc.) are characterizable by age.

But "age" is also one of the most complicated, and complicating, of data,
in part because it serves as a means of event dating, a metric of experience
at the juncture of biography and history. The accounting problems that arise
when an analyst seeks to disentangle age, cohort, and period effects in a set
of data illustrate one aspect of the complications. Another, closely related,
aspect appears in model specifications that include, along with age, a list of
age-constrained or definitionally dependent variables—for example, years
of schooling, length of work experience, and so on. Difficult, often intractable technical problems of identification arise, as numerous scholars have
described (e.g., Glenn, 1976; Heckman & Robb, 1985; Tuma & Hannan,
1984, pp. 189-193). Moreover, the root of the problems is not merely an
inadequacy of available technique, a limit that can be overcome by the
invention of a new analytic technique. The limit is of analysis itself. Too
many independent units of information are being sought in the same set of
observations. "Age" is complicating as well as complicated because it is
densely implicated in a manifold of processes at both individual and population levels of organization. The chief technical issue is whether, or under
what conditions, specific components or dimensions of the dynamics of those
processes and their intercalations can be modeled with definitional independence of one another.

Although age is conventionally regarded as a trait—a property that one
"has" in the same way that one "has" a height, a gender, an eye color, and so
on—it is useful to think of "age" as a sequence of events, where the event is
"survival." The sequenced events define states in a process of endurance. A
specific age-state, the condition of "being such and such age," is a dis-

criminable membership category of relative stasis within the process of endurance. Thinking of age in terms of states and sequences is a useful exercise because the classificatory and the processual aspects of age are addressed within a single framework, which, in the rather abstract formality of its heuristics, may facilitate clarifications of the semantical and syntactical operations involving and involved in "age." Others have already made good use of this approach (e.g., Campbell & O'Rand, 1988; Featherman, 1986; Featherman & Lerner, 1985; Featherman & Petersen, 1986; Nesselroade, 1988). The following discussion is partly a review and partly an extension of earlier explorations and proposals.

A state is necessarily qualitative; it is a membership category, a state of being in some specified condition, of being describable in some specific way. A state may also be quantitatively defined in one or more characteristics of the membership category. A sequence of states, on the other hand, is necessarily both qualitative and quantitative—qualitative because the component states are discriminable in a classification germane to the entire sequence, and quantitative at least to the extent of the ordinality of "earlier" and "later" in sequence. So, for example, "old" or "85" is both different from and after or later than "young" or "37." The dynamic aspect of the sequentiality consists in state durations and interstate transitions. A state has a specifiable duration—not in the sense that a specific state is defined as a temporal length (as in the "Neptunist" view) but in the sense that being in or "occupying" a specific state implies an interval of duration, the interval during which a particular observational unit fits the description of a specific degree of endurance in the process or processes (the "Vulcanist" view). Durations can be more or less heterogeneous across observational units of a given membership category (i.e., a state need not have a uniform duration for all occupants), and durations can vary across states in a sequence. Transitions also have duration, ranging from the theoretically instantaneous (or imperceptible) to some limit interval that spans the theoretical ambiguity between "transition" and "state." A transition need not be of uniform duration. Both the probability of a transition and the duration of a transition may be variably sensitive to the preceding state duration, as well as to other factors.

Whereas the process of endurance is itself generally repetitive—that is, "occurs" for each new member of a membership class (persons, planets, buildings, etc.)—the sequence of states and transitions *within* the process of endurance may be nonrepetitive. For certain membership classes, such as individual persons or planets, age-states are nonrepetitive. Each member is constrained to occupy a given age-state only once—though the duration of occupancy may vary, depending on the state semantics (see below). When the membership class is defined at a population level, however, age-states may be occupied repeatedly, since at a population level age-states are a function of relative rates of nonsurvival (mortality, out-migration) and generation (fertility, in-migration) among the compositional units. Thus, a population of individuals can be "young," then "old," then "young" again.

Sequencing is usually "memory-endowed," in the sense that a later state in the sequence remembers information of earlier states, which means that the states are not independent (a pronounced serial or auto-correlation).[2] Memory endowment in sequences of age states is generally quite strong. This establishes a "path dependence"—perhaps a new name in social science but hardly a new understanding. Weber's frequent use of the *Eigengesetzlichkeit* concept (roughly, the "inner logic" that is manifested as endurance of an organizational form) captures that meaning, as does Whitehead's (1929/1978) discussion of the process by which "an enduring entity binds any one of its occasions to the line of its ancestry" (p. 104). Any current state reflects cumulative effects of causal events in prior states, which is to say that the experience of a given state and/or transition casts forward a shadow that influences probability distributions of possible experiences of subsequent states and/or transitions. This implies a number of important constraints. For instance, absent a complete structural amnesia, a person cannot have a zero degree of biography (despite the appearance of an "age zero" in the counting system of age) precisely because the initial conditions of a biography are of a generative process that already has a history (see, e.g., Hume, 1777/1985, p. 476; Mannheim, 1927/1952b, p. 277).[3] Second, memory endowment implies strong constraints on state repetition: what may otherwise appear to be a state reoccupied will be a *non*repeated state insofar as it remembers sequencing history. Third, the sequence of age states tends to be consequentialist (at least for persons) insofar as an intentionality of "survival to the next state" implies at any current state an anticipated (projected, imagined) information about subsequent states and transitions, which influences the probability distributions of possible current-state behaviors and actions (which in turn may influence subsequent-state behaviors and actions; see below).

This process of enduring to a next stage in sequence is "the aging process" in its most rudimentary sense, a sense equally applicable to persons, planets, stones, organizations, beliefs, and so forth. Endurance may seem as empty as the abstractness of time. But endurance is not empty. It is empirical—a "lived experience" in the sense of Dilthey's concept of *Erlebnis* (see, e.g., Dilthey, 1883/1989, pp. 381-385, 1927/ 1958, pp. 228-231, 244-245). Endurance is structural, a structure of relations. The experience *of* endurance consists in classification (by which age states are discriminable as nonrandomly different) and order (by which age states are discriminable in sequences of before and after); these structural relations constitute the stability on which a *knowledgeable* experience *of* endurance logically and empirically depends. But endurance also *is* experience, a *lived* experience, and this experience is necessarily lived *within* a classification and order—that is, within a sequence of age states understood rudimentarily as states of survival or endurance. Because of classification and its framing effects, experience of endurance tends strongly to be episodic (an experience of "states of age," under one or another semantic specification), which means that the "pacing" of endurance tends to be uneven. However, the pacing is also characterized by another dimensionality, due to memory endowment in the order of sequencing. To the extent that effects endured in earlier states persist or are reproduced in later states, the process of endurance tends to be hysteretic (Georgescu-Roegon, 1971, p. 205). That is, the dynamics of the process tend to be retarded not just in but *by* the "operation" of the process. Endurance is self-limiting.[4]

Of course, the process of endurance does not come without clothing. It is expressed in various other processes—development, maturation, accumulation (e.g., of memories, performative repertoires, habits, products, risks, acquaintances), allocation and selection regimes, and many others.[5] Indeed, as noted in the preceding section, the counting system inherent in sequences of survival events forms a metrical platform or grid on which the counting systems (or systems of event dating) of other processes can be erected. But the process of endurance—"aging" in that rudimentary sense—is not necessarily identical with any other specified process. Thus, a person survives with probability $p(S_t)$ to state S_t (in a populationist assessment), or survives or not to a state S_t (in an individualist assessment), but in either assessment the transition to state S_t does not necessarily correspond to *any* transition in a maturational, developmental, or any other substantively specified process. Given this conceptual independence, one can intelligibly evaluate the "aging" of empirical instances of many different sorts of substantively specified processes—for example, the age of an empirically specific process of job training or of selecting contest winners. That is, whereas any process necessarily transpires in the midst of, as part of, the ongoingness of history, there is also a historicity *of* process, in the sense that the dynamics of a process are subject to change not only exogenously, as the historical conditions of the process change, but also as a function of characteristics of the process itself (e.g., state duration, memory endowment), and this change of dynamical properties may be treated as an aging.[6]

To repeat, "age" is complicated and complicating because it is implicated in so many other processes—for example, variously specified types of duration-sensitive processes (e.g., socialization or acquisition of attributes and capabilities, such as skills, habits, performative repertoires), density-sensitive processes (e.g., cohort or vintage stratified competitions or allocations), path-sensitive processes (e.g., an endowment inertia of sequences of investments or options), and trait-sensitive selection or sorting processes (e.g., eligibility or risk-distributive criteria of membership). In addition, numerous processes involving complex implications of age-state sequencing (at both individual and population levels of organization) have been collected under an umbrella notion of a "life cycle," in substantive formulations derived from late eighteenth and nineteenth-century accounts of homologies and analogies of evolutionary change.[7] O'Rand and Krecker (1990), reviewing uses and relative advantages of "life cycle" concepts, emphasized three major processes that involve different though interrelated organizations of age-state sequencing: generation ("reproduction of form"), maturation ("irreversible development"), and punctuated succession ("successive forms" or "stages"). Whereas each can be regarded as an irreducible property of a life cycle, each can also be modeled as a composite of processes, all of them age-related. Indeed, the often used locution, "age-related phenomena," covers a plethora of indications. Most if not all compositional dimensions of socially significant classifications are age-related insofar as they manifest sensitivities to processual characteristics.

The basic condition of the implication of age in other processes consists in that rudimentary sense of "aging" described above—aging as process of endurance, with its basic properties of classification, order, and memory endowment. But the extent of implication exceeds that condition, since both a lived experience *in* endurance and an experience *of* endurance typically consist in multiple classifications. Endurance is "filled" with events, different kinds of events. So, whereas the initial condition of the implication of age in another process (such as accumulation or allocation) is the process of endurance, the implication immediately becomes mutual. Properties of the sequence of states and transitions particular to any other process in which age is implicated are transposed to the sequence of age states and transitions. Consequently, "age" and "aging" are polymorphous. The semantics of age states and the syntactics of sequencing tend to vary, in other words, depending on the process(es) in which age is implicated. Aging can be socialization or accumulation or generation or degeneration or any number of other processes, as well as complex combinations thereof. The strongest transposition occurs with "developmental process" (which, on minimal definition, involves a memory-endowed or path-dependent sequence of states, usually called "stages").[8] Indeed, "aging" and "development" are often regarded as synonymous, at least at the level of individual persons and other living beings. Consider, for purposes of general illustration, a theory of development that includes a stage named "adolescence." This stage is typically defined as a complex function of the state sequences of multiple processes— for instance, production of sex hormones and secondary sex characteristics, acquisition of skills of self-direction, expansion of networks of social ties, and so forth—which vary in rate, duration, reversibility, and other properties from individual to individual. These variable, and variably interrelated, sequences can be uniformly dated by means of the simple counting system of aging in its rudimentary sense of endurance; "adolescence" is equated with some range of age states (e.g., 12 to 20 years of survival). But at the same stroke, a new age state is produced, "adolescence," which has the specific properties of a "stage of development." And with that transposition the significance of being 14 years old or 17 years old is primarily the significance of *being an adolescent.* Multiple heterogeneities are subsumed in a title, the name of an age state that has relatively long duration. "The passion of naming," to borrow Bannerji's (1995) use of that phrase, has visited "age" as well as other categories of social status, albeit generally with lessened intensity in recent times.

⬙ DURATION AND STATE SEMANTICS

The stratification approach to the study of age properly regards age as a classification variable of social status (see, e.g., Riley, 1987). In principle, that treatment accords considerable importance to age, even if, like other classification variables of social status, it is the importance of a title. Naming is not a neutral activity and *being* named is not an activity of free agency. The list of available options—internal boundary conditions, centralities, dispersions, marginal spaces—is for any given person largely inherited and reproduced in distributed probabilities ("life chances") within institutionalized structures of opportunity-and-constraint, both "externally" as context and "internally" as consciousness. The very fact of being a classification variable of social status means that age can figure as sorter as well as signal for a host of regulations—often all the more effectively because having a certain age, being in a certain age-state, is not a condition that ordinarily requires either explanation or justification.

Classification, by age or by any other variable, not only *is* regulation, of course; it is regulation with a reflexive cast insofar as the regulation structures consciousness. To ask a person how he or she organizes his or her consciousness anticipates too much, no doubt, if the answer must come from some backstage director who exercises inner mastery of all the knobs and strings of a presentation of consciousness. That notion of a free agency is lost in the incessantly receding spiral of reflexivity. But even though the basic classifications are always inherited, constitutive of the boundary linking interior and exterior, and too obvious typically to be noticed in their effects (much less to be explained in their causes), a person is ineluctably complicit in the organization of her or his consciousness. And the stratification approach is right in emphasizing that age, one of the classification variables in the field of social status, has been and remains important in the organization of consciousness. Indeed, if any classification variable can be persuasively defended as *universally* important (which is not to say of constant or uniform importance) in the organization of consciousness, age surely stands among the top candidates. Surviving—reaching certain milestones of age, such as 13 or 30 or half a century—does have a significance that is not wholly reducible to schedules of childrearing, formal schooling, work, and the like. A recognition at age 50 that the consciousness of a person aged 20 is organized differently from one's own may begin and end as a mostly introspective act (e.g., querying the memory endowment of "being 50," looking for traces of one's own consciousness at 20). But it *is* a socially significant recognition, one that carries an ambiguous weight of history even more than of biography (or of the differences between a longer and a shorter biography), for it signifies what is not shared in the stratification of a collective memory (see Halbwachs, 1925/1992). Much of the recognition is no doubt surplus: being 50 and being 20 are states differentiated in an institutionalized life course that, as Meyer (1986) observed, is so highly standardized and explicitly regulated that large patches of it "would be unconstitutional if it were organized on any other basis than age" (p. 202). The recognition is not entirely surplus, however. Some interactions across age states run against the grain of an institutionalized life course, seeking means to a relationship of personal equality in the midst of the field of status inequalities—for instance, building the solidarity of a social movement or the trust of a friendship. There, of course, the recognition of difference in an organization of consciousness can be especially poignant—perhaps never more so than when the difference is ordered by age, for age is the classification in which one can be incorrigibly "too late" or "too early."

It is often noted that classification by age in a field of social status is distinctive—by comparison to gender or race/ethnicity or even education, occupation, and income—in that most persons hope to pass through all of its categories, all age states. And insofar as the chance to survive is made good, everyone does just that, passes through the succession of age states, whatever the design of those states in an institutionalized life course or life cycle. This "endurance in passage"—warf to the pattern-making woof of events—is the fluency of an imperceptible transmutation wherein the experience of a moment, a lyrical form, vanishes into an epic narration of sequences and durations, the experience of a lifetime (see White, 1992a, pp. 212-215). Age classification contributes signposts in that narrative form, linking memory and anticipation, an iteratively remembered past and an iteratively expected future. Except in very young children, an organization of consciousness *without* age is usually regarded as pathological—a variety of amnesia, for instance, or a dementia.[9]

Since age classification is integral to a "normal" organization of consciousness, encompasses everyone at least by external criterionization (i.e., children too young to be aware of age, amnesiacs, and so on, are still classified by age), *and* orders individuals more or less independently of their ordering by other variables of social status, it might seem to follow that age is one of the most important, even the most central, of all variables or dimensions of status stratification. The fact that modern social science's founding theorists of the realm of status—Max Weber, for example—thought to say so little systematically about age could be attributed simply to myopias of the day, or perhaps to the scale of demand in founding a new discourse.

But it is not at all clear that age matters very importantly as a classification variable in the field of social status. Not today, that is. To be sure, age classification remains important in other ways—for instance, in dating events (age at marriage, age at death of one's parent or child, etc.), as a marker or signal in the regulation of some process (occupational licensing, eligibility to begin formal schooling, or to activate pension receipts, etc.). But as a classification variable in the field of social status, age itself is of little importance today, by comparison to other variables (education, occupation, income) and by comparison to the importance of age states in an earlier era.[10] Granted, recent controversies of a "new politics of age" may seem to belie that judgment, as issues of "generational equity" and the principle of seniority in regulating certain queuing behaviors (e.g., public pension funds, layoffs due to plant closures) have been sometimes heatedly joined in debates of public policy (see, e.g., Hardy, Hazelrigg, & Quadagno, 1996, chap. 6; Quadagno, 1989). A somewhat longer perspective is needed, however; for as Michael Young (1958) cautioned even 40 years ago, "it is [still] difficult for us to realize how strongly entrenched" were the rule of seniority and habits of age deference in the lives of our not-so-distant ancestors:

> Status for age had once been linked with hereditary status, but it [age status] was far less easy to discredit. By the middle of last century it was extremely rare to hear anyone openly defending a hereditary system. Kinship connections were no longer thought to confer merit on a man. But age was. Age was accorded deference for no better reason than that. (pp. 85-86)

The anthropological literature offers many examples of societies or cultures (once called "traditional") in which age figured prominently in the organization of status groupings. Village elders were a repository of great social honor, for example, and often-elaborate rites of passage celebrated transitions from one age state to another. The example of village elders might suggest an explanation of the lessened importance of age in matters of social status today, since elders were in those societies a scarcity and, in that scarcity, a spiritual visitation ("the perfected form of the ancestor"; Baudrillard, 1976/1993, p. 163). For both reasons, "old people" were highly valued not as a social problem but as a resource of symbolic exchange. However, as Young's (1958) description of the equation of seniority and merit in industrial societies of the nineteenth century indicates, the difference marked off by that fund of anthropological description involves more than the scarcity element of exchange relations and pertains to more than age as a classification variable. Status itself is not what it then was.

The general argument is a familiar one. Maine's (1861/1963) version, constructed in a format of legal history, distinguished "status society" (the older) from "contract society" (the newer). Weber's (1919/1946) alternative account—albeit characteristically more nuanced, less content with encapsulation by dichotomy—nonetheless featured a similar contrast, as in the following adumbration in which Weber drew on his reading of Tolstoy:

> Abraham, or some peasant of the past, died "old and satiated with life" because he stood in the organic cycle of life; because his life, in terms of its meaning and on the eve of his days, had given to him what life had to offer; because for him there remained no puzzles he might wish to solve; and therefore he could have had "enough" of life. Whereas civilized man, placed in the midst of the continuous enrichment of culture by ideas, knowledge, and problems, may become "tired of life" but not "satiated with life." He catches only the most minute part of what the life of the spirit brings forth ever anew, and what he seizes is always something provisional and not definitive, and therefore death for him is a meaningless occurrence. (p. 140)

And, to cite a third example, Baudrillard (1976/1993), partly updating but mostly reprising Weber, observed "of the situation today" that "old age is literally being eliminated. In proportion as the living live longer, as they 'win' over death, they cease to be symbolically acknowledged. Condemned to a forever receding death, this age group loses its status and its prerogatives" (p. 163).

It is not that age has disappeared, of course. Rather, the semantics of age states has been remade in accordance with the historical trend toward substitution of the older status system by a newer status system, one in which contractual relations have increasingly displaced organic relations and quality has come increasingly under the rule of quantity. As Fortes (1984) put it, when "the politicojural and the domestic domains of social life" (p. 115) are differentiated, and "a political and legal framework takes precedence over familial and kinship relations for determining citizenship" (p. 115), classifications of age as well as other traits pertinent to the field of status undergo corresponding changes. An organization of age states in terms of organic relations of maturation and generation, for example, which "subsumes the ostensible discontinuities between successive generations in a framework of overall continuity" (p. 114), is subordinated to and increasingly displaced by a more abstract chronology of age, which "operates atomistically and leaves the matter of structural continuity or discontinuity to the nonfamilial institutional order" (p. 109).

Whether one agrees with all aspects of Fortes's account or not (some reservation will be noted below), the general thesis of historical trend has been a standard feature of social science's historiography of modernity and its predecessor. In the older status system, "status," communally anchored in "the social estimation of honor" (Weber, 1919/1946), and "status group" ("estate," "*Stand,*" "station in life") were intensively qualitative. Status was also quantitative, of course, inasmuch as social honor was ordinal and status groups were discriminated hierarchically. But the fundamentally distinctive feature was quality: to be of a certain status was to be a certain *kind* of being. Kind begat kind (though category errors of generation were recognized and often invested with special powers). Just as a "child" was "naturally generated" by a "father" (from the "material vessel" of a "mother"), so a "peasant" was "naturally generated" by a "peasant," a "noble" by a "noble," and so on. Status was integral to membership in a specific community, tied to a specific place, and therefore not easily portable. Age states in this system of status occurred in rather large chunks of duration, primarily marked off as stages in a life-cycle process—birth, weaning, independent play, puberty, and so on to elder, death, and finally (in some versions of the system) ancestral spirit.

The sequence was united in the process of generations, as familial generations.[11] Transitions across age states were regulated by a local calendar.[12] Location on a calendar, the timing of transitions, was decided in terms of organically particular qualities or capabilities of the community member. Thus, for example, it was the onset of a capability for independent play (which, in terms of the modern concept of chronological age, varied from person to person) that determined transition to the next state in sequence.

In the modern status system, by contrast, a relatively abstract gradient of quantity tends to rule over quality. Educational status refers less to a "character formation," a *Bildungsprozess,* and more to the formality of "years of schooling completed." Occupational status refers less to *kind* of skillful practice defining a person's lifetime (e.g., the artisanal stonemason), often in a familial lineage, and more to an abstract gradient of "prestige" (together with income-bearing probabilities and location in a continually revisable network of authority relations). These variables of status are not dependent on membership in a specific community or anchored to a specific place. As for age classification in this status system, one ticks off the years like cogs passing the escapement gear of a clock. Indeed, whereas the calendar function of event dating in the older system was jealously local, the clock function of event dating has succeeded remarkably well in attaining a universalism (e.g., the 1884 International Meridian Conference fixing world time zones so that everyone could/would follow the same timing-dating algorithm). Some ticks do have special significance, usually in a signaling function—for instance, political franchise after the tick to year 18 of age. But beneath that, and in general, one tick of the clock is like any other tick of the clock. Enfranchisement could as easily occur at commencement of year 17. And the ticks, whether special or ordinary, are exactly the same for everyone. Thus, one is enfranchised at year 18, regardless whether one has attained "political maturity" as defined in a qualitative register.[13]

As Hume (1777/1985, p. 476) remarked in his essay on the "original contract" fiction, transitions in human generative processes are always mixed affairs, "the old" continuing to mingle with "the new," rendering any "fresh start" only partly fresh. So it has been with the transformation of social status (Mannheim, 1930/1952a, pp. 266-275; Weber, 1922/1968, pp. 936-938, 1086-1087). The long struggle of the "free" or "liberal professions" to maintain their claims of distinction by traditional standards of social honor, rather than "mere" prestige, and to evade "reductions" to bureaucratic relations of authority and employment systems provides one interesting illustration, especially as the failure of that struggle has become increasingly evident in recent years (see, e.g., Haber, 1991). A number of classifications from the older status system remain highly salient in the midst of the newer: gender, racial, and ethnic titles have certainly not vanished, even though these classifications have also not been immune to influences of the modern system of status. As for age classification, the developmentalist sequence of titles ("infant," "child," "pubescent," "adolescent," etc.) retains considerable significance, despite displacements of organic relations by contractual relations even in familial and generational settings of the institutionalized life course (see, e.g., Glendon, 1989). It is certainly still the case that an actor qualified by any one of those titles—or by "youth" or "middle-aged" or "old"—is distinctively situated in the framing effects of a classification and tends to experience self-and-world, and to be an object of others' experiences, within those framing effects.

However, whereas each of those age states has a rather long duration, one of the hallmarks of the modern status system is an emphasis on finer gradations of discrimination, and relative to that preference the durations of age states such as "child," "adolescent," and "middle-aged" are increasingly regarded as *too* long, in the sense that intrastate heterogeneities have become too great by comparison to between-state heterogeneities. Finer distinctions are wanted. Many observers have argued, for example, that persons classified as "the old" are simply too diverse to be adequately described under a single title, that the tendency to focus on the modal description under that title ("the old") neglects enormous diversity (see, e.g., Dannefer, 1988). The recent invention of a subdivision—"the younger old" and "the older old"—partly responds to that concern, though it was stimulated mainly by the growing number of people surviving beyond age 80. In other arenas finer distinctions are already widely practiced. Advertising agencies no longer target "youth" or even "teenagers" but, instead, consumption groups that are more finely graded by age (e.g., "12- to 14-year-olds") as well as by other traits. Manufacturers of toys and games label the packaging with "recommended ages" (e.g., "6 to 10 years"). Insurers set premiums not by "young adult," "middle-aged," and the like but by narrower intervals of age (increasingly often by single-year intervals, in the case of health insurance as well as life insurance). Indeed, the age classification that now figures most prominently not only in official demographics and in social science's typical data matrix but also in the consumer profiles and dossiers maintained by marketing agencies, credit bureaus, employment bureaus, investment firms, and countless other organizations is nearly as abstract as the integers of number theory: "1 year of age," "2 years of age," . . . , "22 years of age," and so on.

It is with respect to this last sequence of age states that Fortes's (1984, p. 109) remark about the "atomistic" operation of chronological or "clock-time" age is particularly apropos. The age states are of very short and uniform duration; the duration is inelastic under all conditions; transitions are not sensitive to duration. The sequence applies uniformly to everyone (to the extent of survival). Being in/of a particular state implies little that is qualitatively distinctive, as compared with age titles such as "child" or "adolescent" or "elder" (being "14," for example, is the thinnest of titles, too thin to support the semantics of *kind* of being). The states are distinguished increasingly as ciphers in a continuous series: "age differences are leveled out" (Durkheim, 1902/1984, p. 236).

The operation of that sort of age classification may certainly be considered "atomistic." But it is the result of an increasing *individualization* in socially significant classification, as group-based characterizations and identity formations give way to individual traits and identities.[14] To be sure, "gender" still comes in very large chunks (by most accountings, only two). And despite the fact that the enormous acceleration of human migrations has resulted in highly mixed genealogies, many people continue to describe themselves by one or two of the "traditional" ethnic titles and most by a single racial title, instead of inventing new titles that would describe the now enormous number of mixtures. Nevertheless, both the "race" and the "ethnic" chunks are slowly fragmenting, and even "gender" is increasingly subject to individualization.[15]

The process of individualization in age classification is much further along. Thus, the categorical difference between contiguous large-duration age states (such as "adolescent" and "adult"), which lost all clarity at the boundary when formal rites of passage decayed, continues to dissipate into the much smaller quantitative differences of "years of age." Burt's (1991) network analysis of social ties provides good evidence of the classification effects of age in the sorting of social ties, and most of the age-state durations documented by that analysis were no more than 6 or 7 years in length. With increasing individualization the social significance of age classification and of age *as such* lessens. The institutionalized life course continues to use age as a marker or signal for other processes, such as political franchise, because it is a procedurally efficient means of regulating eligibilities, risk distributions, and other sorts of queues in highly standardized, routinized processes. Substantively, the age-linked signal may not be very reliable in any given case.[16] Reaching age 18 and thus the political franchise does not necessarily mean that the person has attained "political maturity," as defined in a qualitative register, just as completion of the fourth year of high school and thus (almost as automatically) a diploma does not necessarily mean that the graduate has attained or exceeded some qualitatively defined competence.

But reaching a particular age state in this status system is simply not the same sort of transitional event as the event of passage into, say, the age state of "weaned" or "eligible to marry" or "village elder." Reaching age 23 or 35 means little more than 23 or 35 years of survival.

This disjuncture may well contribute to an alienation of the individual from the institutionalized order of the life course, as Meyer (1986) has argued: "the modern self is disconnected from the life course (including its subjective elements)" *and* the "disconnection is institutionalized" (p. 201). Modern life is lived in two separate registers at once. On the one hand, most of a life experience is formed directly and indirectly in the highly standardized sequence of sequences (schooling, work, retirement) of an institutionalized life course that emphasizes procedural rules and the stability of routine, thus very predictable, state durations and transitions.[17] On the other hand, those aspects of life experience that are *not* institutionalized and structurally stabilized in life-course sequencings tend to be directed to meaning formations that have little or no connection to status dimensions and structural locations in the life course—meanings of self-image, personal satisfaction, existential aesthetics. The modern self is *expected* "to relativize its stance to the institutional context," to be flexible, transient in commitments and adaptable in interests, to be a personal project under continual revision. It is not surprising, Meyer (1986, pp. 211, 209) avowed, that researchers find little stability in "personal" aspects of selfhood, or that what individuals express in their attitudes and opinions about themselves and their locations in the institutionalized order correlate so weakly with those locations and predict their behaviors so poorly (see also McGuire, 1989).

◈ AGE, PROCESS, AND "THE ELEMENT OF TIME"

Age as a classification variable is causally significant insofar as the dynamics of a given process are sensitive to the age states of persons involved in that process. Empirical determination of that sensitivity can be very difficult to achieve, for reasons previously noted. An apparent sensitivity to age *might* be to age state as such, but it could be instead a sensitivity to some other variable or variables with which age is correlated (perhaps serving as a marker or signal). Consider, for example, two conventionally discriminated types of process: mate selection and political enfranchisement. Both appear to be age-sensitive in some manner and degree. The second of the two is age sensitive by formal-legal definition of eligibility. The same is true of mate selection, inasmuch as the copulative component of mating behavior is proscribed until an age-eligibility threshold has been reached. But the process of mate selection appears to be age-sensitive even beyond that threshold, since in most couples the members' ages are within a few years of each other. Is this an outcome of selection on age as such? Note that a possibly indistinguishable outcome would be observed if potential mates used age-state membership only as a signal in initial screenings on other traits, especially traits not so easily evaluated by superficial inspection (e.g., fecundity, cognitive and emotive compatibility, morbidity chances, probable remaining lifetime). Note too, however, that much of the apparent age sensitivity in mate selection, at least in first marriages, simply manifests sampling effects of propinquity or availability queues in the highly institutionalized sequence of socialization states (formal schooling). The shared variance among these conceptually distinctive queues—age, year in school, and propinquity or availability—is quite substantial. It is also empirically nonpartitionable.

Similar complications are involved in the age sensitivities apparent in many other socially significant processes. By way of another sort of illustration, consider a reversible process such as "skill acquisition." It is a reversible process in the sense that, at some point following a gain in a specified skill, a gradual but accelerating loss of the skill occurs. If one plots the process as in the diagram shown in Figure 4.1a, the trajectory of gains in skill would resemble line (a,b). Note that the reverse trajectory (b,c) does not retrace (a,b) because at any given level of skill the rate of loss consistently lags behind the rate of gain. After some duration of inactivity, for instance, one's skill with a musical instrument will have declined, but it never returns to zero degree of skill (point a). In short, this reversible process displays properties analogous to the hysteresis effect previously described (note 4) in the magnetization example. Now, "skill level" in this reversible process of skill acquisition is necessarily age-related. But "age" cannot be the identity of the unlabeled x-axis in Figure 4.1a, since that would imply that age itself is reversible. We can respond to this problem by replotting the trajectory (as in Figure 4.1b, where the x-axis is labeled "age"): draw an imaginary line through (b) perpendicular to the x-axis, imagine that line is a hinge, and then swing line (b,c) 180 degrees around the hinge. Now we seem to have skill level expressed as an increasing function of age until the inflection point (b), and thereafter as a decreasing function of age, although (as before) at a rate slower than the rate of gain had been. But this is wrong. The inflected line (a,b,c) is *not* a plot of correlated cross-sectional variations in skill level and age. Rather, it is a trajectory of the reversible process of skill acquisition (i.e., the *change* of skill level), plotted for an individual or

(a)

Skill Level

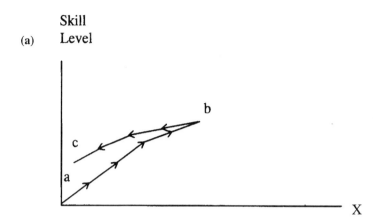

(b)

Skill Level

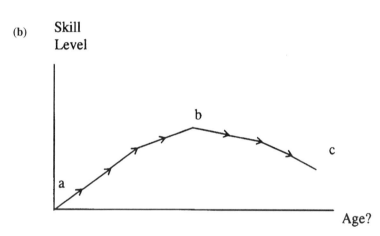

Figure 4.1. Illustration of Hysteresis.

for the average of a population of individuals.[18] Thus, age is not the x-axis (as mislabeled in Figure 4.1b). Age is represented in the trajectory of durations and transitions of states (levels) of skill. The x-axis represents some as yet unnamed causal factor (or, more likely, a complex set of) factors) that "drives" or motivates the process. Treating the gain and then loss of skill as a function of age amounts to little more than treating a sequence of state durations and transitions as a function of nearly the same sequence of state durations and transitions.

The source of the complications illustrated in the foregoing examples lies in the very idea of *process*: whatever adjective is placed in front of it ("developmental," "allocational," etc.), "process" involves a sequencing of states and transitions along some sort of metric; and whereas each substantively specified process may have its own substantively defined counting system for dating and timing state durations and transitions, all are rooted in the same metric of endurance. It is this common root that enables comparison, coordination, and translation across the counting systems of substantively differentiated processes. Thus, in Figure 4.1a, a sequence of state durations and transitions in the driving force represented on the x-axis covaries with a sequence of state durations and transitions in skill acquisition because, by theory, the force causes skill acquisition. When the driving force diminishes to some threshold level—which, necessarily, happens when the given individual occupies some specific age state (though the specific age state may vary across individuals)—the rate of acquisition declines to zero and reverses to a negative rate (loss of skill). This latter phase of the process might be described as a "degeneration," but the degeneration is a function of the diminished driving force, not of age as such. For any given individual, the sequence of age states and transitions implied in one side of the function exactly matches, by necessity, the sequence of age states and transitions implied in the other side of the function. The three sequences—in driving force, in skill level, and in age states—share the same underlying metric of rate of change.

It is tempting to call this metric "time" and intend something other than, sturdier than, more objective than, "endurance." Tempting, but idle.

Alfred Marshall (1961, p. vii) observed in the opening pages of his *Principles of Economics,* first published in 1890, that "The element of Time . . . is the centre of the chief difficulty of almost every economic problem." No less can be said of any process of interest to social science, whether it be qualified as economic or political or whatever. Because timing matters (which means that in some sense of the word "age" must matter, too), "the element of time" and information about "timing" should be *explicitly* treated in our theoretical models and empirical analyses. So Winston (1982, p. 3) has urged; and so it should be, if social science is seriously concerned to explain how processes work in addition to describing states of affairs (conditions, outcomes, etc.) and cross-sectional covariations among them. But what exactly *is* this "element of time"? Winston's own rich treatments are exemplary in demonstrating that it is, at root, experience of (as well as experience in) endurance—that is, state durations and interstate transitions. This understanding is entirely consistent with the dominant heritage within which modern social science resides. Whereas the everyday sense of "time's passage" appears to refer to something external to the act of referencing (e.g., something like a "vessel" through which time flows), there is and can be no empirical referent. Kant's formulation of the argument is still the standard: "Time is not something that exists of itself"; time is "nothing but the form of inner sense," the "formal *a priori* condition of all [phenomena] whatsoever" (Kant, 1787/1952, B49, B52). We cannot know "time itself," nor can we know whether any thing-in-itself is temporal. All we can know is a thing *in* time and space—that is, a thing experienced, which is temporal (inner sense) and spatial (outer sense).

Kant's formulation was part of an elegant theoretical systematization of practical understandings already at work, though in fragmented and often implicit ways. The remarkable insightfulness of his systemization can be appreciated retrospectively by measuring the extent to which the subsequent history of European (and Euro-American) sociocultural formations, including social science, has continued to unfold and develop practical implications of that system, as if Kant himself had designed the history in advance. Increasingly from the eighteenth century onward, for example, the identification of "age" with a local "calendar time" of lunar cycles, cycles of festivals and planting seasons, and the like, has dissipated into the very different schedule of regularities associated with "the universal form of time." In this abstraction of time, the sequence of age states becomes an ever more abstracted manner of "telling time" on a purely quantitative gradient of uniform (and infinitely divisible) intervals, with transitions seemingly occurring at a uniform rate of "one day per day," "one year per year," and so on.[19] It is by virtue of that abstractedness that we can use a common metric[20] in which to relate "timing" (e.g., aging) *as* a particular process with "timing" (aging) *of* any process, distinguish some processes as "time-variant" from other processes as "time-invariant" (and thus strictly iterable), integrate a process such as memory endowment as a characteristic of another, substantively specified process (e.g., "development"), and think coherently the laminations of "historicity." These are, needless to say, useful abilities.

Consider, by way of illustration, the notion that a specified process is iterable, that the self-same process works again and again with each new set of members in some membership class.

To the extent that the dynamics of a process include memory endowment (path dependence) in the sequence of states and transitions, that process itself cannot be strictly time-invariant. Any given "strip" of the process in operation is not a random sampling (with replacement) of all possible strips, because the strips are not independent of each other. The path dependence internal to the dynamics of the process create a path dependence in the process as such. In other words, the process as such has a history. It is not an iterable process, unless historicity is cyclical or otherwise repetitive.

Thus, for example, a process of "human development": if each generational cohort came on the scene all at once and left all at once, as in Hume's (1777/1985, p. 476) thought experiment, its members would be free of any "past" and could (indeed, of necessity *would*) start afresh. But insofar as that is not the case, the process of development among members of any new generational cohort will carry or reproduce information from the developmental process as it worked in the past (i.e., in that cohort's pre-biographical past, which is now integral to the cohort's biography because of the memory endowment). Thus, the iterability of this process of human development is "compromised"; it is not, strictly speaking, iterability of the same (despite the unchanging name of the process). The *process* called "human development" is itself historical—that is, variable as a function of its own operation.

Hume's (1777/1985) thought experiment draws attention to the formal condition under which strict iterability of a process as such can occur even when the dynamics internal to that process evince strong path dependence. To illustrate the point with a very simple example, consider again the magnetization process described earlier (note 4) in conjunction with hysteresis. Path dependence within the dynamics of magnetization is necessary to the occurrence of hysteretic effects; yet it is evident that magnetization can occur repeatedly as exactly the same process. This is possible because (and only insofar as) each chunk of iron newly subjected to the process is strictly independent of any chunk of iron already magnetized.

Mannheim's (1927/1952b) interest in Hume's thought experiment was primarily an interest in that formal condition, coupled with his interest in identifying the organizational properties of a possible "carrier" or "bearer" of what he called "the rhythm of history." The simple physical system of the process of magnetization is easily isolable (within very small limits of tolerance), and the process can be turned on and off by the flip of a switch. But historicity, in at least most of what interests a social scientist, is hardly so simple. Generational cohorts are not independent chunks of iron, the history of generational process does not stop or start with the flip of a switch, and any "initial conditions" of (as well as in) that process are very loosely bounded. Nevertheless, generational cohorts *are* chunks—strips of the history of developmental or life-cycle sequences of (relatively) long-duration age states ("infancy," etc.)—and although these chunks are not strictly independent of each other (i.e., the generational process as such is historical), the dependence might be weak enough that one generational cohort could shake off its ancestry and radically innovate—start afresh, not completely but in some large way. A tradition of studies inherited by Mannheim had identified "generations" (generational cohorts) as organizational units distinguished from each other by and as distinctive packets of commonly experienced age-related events. These packets seemed to manifest a definite "rhythm in the sequence of generations." Perhaps (the conjecture was) this rhythm is a principal, even *the* principal, if not the sole component of history's distinctive rhythm—that is, a rhythmic pattern of history that differed both from the continuous reiteration of a time-invariant process (e.g., exactly the same process of development occurring again and again with each new member) and from the continuous flow of a time-variant process in which memory endowment from the initial conditions ("starting values") of the process regulates all other memory endowments (e.g., a process of development that continuously evolves from some origin according to a uniformly self-regulative inner logic). Waves of generational cohorts, roughly 30 years from crest to crest, carry the rhythmic experience of major social change.

Although the notion of generational transition continues to inform analyses (e.g., Inglehart, 1991; Schuman & Scott, 1989; see also Kertzer, 1983), essays on "the problem of generations" are rarely written today. Mannheim's own diagnosis includes a gloss of an explanation of the diminished salience, and the gloss resonates with experiences of life today probably more than it did for Mannheim or most of his first readers: The "tempo of social and cultural change" has greatly accelerated. In a much earlier era the "rhythms of history" were generally too slow to be carried by waves of generational cohorts. The sequencing of events recognized as indication of "major social change"—transformations of the structural template of "normal states of affairs"—was markedly out of phase with the sequencing of "generations." By the last quarter of the eighteenth century, however, observers apparently saw enough evidence of phase conjunction that Hume (1777/1985) could propose his thought experiment as a reflection on the actual significance of generational phenomena without much doubt of being understood. But 150 years later Mannheim (1927/1952b, p. 310) was surmising that "the tempo of social and cultural change" might become "too greatly accelerated" to correspond with "the rhythm of successive generation locations." In other words, as the meter of temporality itself accelerates (an implication of the experience of increasingly rapid social change), the likelihood that a group identity will coalesce across the heterogeneities of 30 years, or even 20 years, sharply diminishes.

The chief understandings of temporality, including those that have extended well into this century, have shared a number of core features. One is the notion that events have monadic temporal properties—futurity, presentness, and pastness—that inhere in "eventness" regardless of observer. Any event is first "in the future," then becomes momentarily "present" before receding ever further "into the past." A future event or state of affairs does not yet exist; a past event or state of affairs no longer exists. However, a sharply contrasting theory, conventionally dated from a famous paradox drawn by McTaggart (1908), constructs a rather different understanding of temporal properties. The central point of difference is that, according to the post-McTaggart theory, the *only* temporal properties of events or states of affairs are relations of sequencing: "before" or "earlier than," "now" or "simultaneous with," and "after" or "later than." Events or states of affairs are equally real, whether they are described as "future," "present," or "past." These latter descriptors are simply indexical expressions irrevocably tied to the here-and-now of usage.[21]

Another important difference associated with this so-called tenseless theory of temporality concerns the constitution of personal identity or "self," and therefore the central referent of the notion of an "aging process." By the conventions of our "common sense," and behind that a long tradition of formal commentary on morality, "self" is conceived as an essentially constant substantivity that perdures "in time." In its "passage through time," a self successively acquires and sheds particular properties ("accidental properties," in classical vocabulary), but the agent or "active thing" that *does* the acquiring and the shedding is itself a perduring core of "essential properties," something that *can* "pass through time." However, one can also conceive "self" or personal identity rather differently, a sequence of temporal parts— "moments of selfhood," one might call them—a sequence of I at t_1, I at t_2, I at t_3, and so on. This is hardly a novel proposal, to be sure. G. H. Mead's (e.g., 1913, 1938) account of the sociogenesis of self incorporates the understanding that "self" is a sequence of momentary events (or event-defined states and transitions). Dilthey's (1883/1989, 1927/1958) theoretical investigations contain much of the basis for such a conception. And as Mead's account makes abundantly clear, the conception is strongly indebted to formulations by Kant (see Hazelrigg, 1991). More recent contributions such as Goffman's (1959, 1974) studies of "impression management" and framing relations, Ainslie's (1985, 1992) development of some interesting conjunctions of theoretical problems, and White's (1992a) theorizations of processes of identity and control supply further examples.

In general, self-formation is conceived as a continual process in which moments of selfhood are arrayed in a strongly memory-endowed sequence. That is, the moments of selfhood, the moments of lived experience (*Erlebnis*), are integrated as states of self-identity in and as an experience of endurance or temporality. These states are necessarily age states in the rudimentary sense of the aging process: later states of selfhood are anticipated as older selves; earlier states of selfhood are remembered as younger selves. An individual actor, acting in and as the present moment of self, engages *intrabiographically* in intertemporal transactions that are arguably analogous to an actor's transactions with other persons and their perceived biographies at any given moment.[22] One interacts retrospectively with one's younger selves, recalling earlier states of selfhood in the productive functioning of memory, and interacts prospectively with one's older selves, anticipating conditions, actions, goal realizations, and the like, of later states of selfhood.

This conceptualization of "person" as an ensemble of interacting aged states has a number of useful properties. One is that it invites explicit attention to the premises we make in regard to analytic issues of "change and stability." The traditional conception of "self" as built around a stable, self-identical core (often named "the will")—a conception deeply nourished by the egocentric bias that renders for each of us the world just as it is sampled from each's perspective—proposes that the interesting issues are primarily issues of lability and change. So, to recall Meyer's (1986) discussion, attention is drawn to issues of why individual actors are so often inconsistent in their behaviors and actions, inconsistent between their beliefs and attitudes about specific courses of action and the actions they themselves undertake. Lability is assumed to be the exceptional or problematic condition, the primary focus of explanatory effort. But given the inherent temporality of selfhood, a perspective that foregrounds stability rather than lability might be more fruitful (see, e.g., Ainslie, 1992; Gergen, 1980).[23] It is not that an entity exists *and* changes, as if in alternation between two distinct states of being, existence and change. Existence *is* change, the ongoingness of process. The abiding struggle is for control—"control of the process," shaping the ongoingness to suit specific interests. The task of a person is to build and maintain a stable identity—which is to say a stability of relations, enough stability to have at least minimally dependable information concerning today's actions and tomorrow's consequences—all in the face of constantly changing circumstances.[24] A highly institutionalized life course is one very effective response to the problem of control. It arrays the ages of selfhood in a predictable sequence of states and transitions that satisfies many problems of population management on a societal scale, in part because it institutionalizes expectations of lability on a personal scale—lability of commitment, of interests, indeed of identity (Meyer, 1986; White, 1992). As the tempo of temporality itself accelerates, not only does the rhythm of "generational transition" become too slow to serve as a marker, much less as a "carrier," of major social change. The intertemporal agreements that a younger self can negotiate with its older self become increasingly shorter in duration, each more quickly up for renegotiation.

Max Weber's Protestant ascetics, for whom everyday conduct was "rationally raised into a calling" (Weber, 1915/1946, p. 291), were especially concerned to make provisions for their older selves by resisting impatience. Faced with a conflict of interests between the short term and the long term (gratification now or gratification later), they sought to maximize the likelihood of what was for them the *ultimate* gratification, which came at the termination of everyday conduct, and the ethic of a calling encouraged them not to underestimate the effect of younger self's conduct on older self's benefit. In the vocabulary of modern economics, Weber's ascetic sectarian was especially adept at resisting the temptation to devalue the marginal utility of a good merely because realization of that good lay far into the future, a benefit to be reaped by his or her much older (and no longer mundane) self. In other words, the ascetic's ethic featured a very low discount rate.

Recognition of the general phenomenon of discounting was not unique to Weber's studies of the economic ethic of the world religions, of course. Bernoulli's (1738/1954, p. 25) rule of inverse proportionality with respect to marginal rates of utility—namely, that "any increase in wealth, no matter how insignificant, will always result in an increase in utility which is inversely proportionate to the quantity of goods already possessed"— suggests a strongly uniform tendency of present self to discount older self's increments to accumulation. Among the Austrian school of economists a century ago, Böhm-Bawerk (1889/1970, pp. 117, 261, 272) understood savings behavior (deferred gratification) as an exchange between one's present and older selves, which he regarded as one of the motivations that "determine the direction that production shall take." Gratifications are fundamentally comparable "irrespective of whether they belong to the same or different future periods of time" or to the moment of present self, because they are all related in the same emotions of satisfaction and well-being even though they involve transactions ("trade-offs") among a person's imagined older selves relative to present self. But persons are subject to what Tversky and Kahneman (1973) later called "availability bias" in practical sampling behaviors. When sampling one's imaginable future conditions, the wants and satisficing means of older selves tend to be discounted relative to present self's immediate interests, because the "power of imagination," Böhm-Bawerk (1889/1970, p. 269) argued, varies inversely with the remoteness of those older selves. The more remote the older self, the steeper its utilities are discounted (see, e.g., Ainslie, 1992, pp. 56-95; Loewenstein, 1992, pp. 13-14; Winston, 1982, pp. 218-221).

The record of systematic evidence concerning actual practices of discounting (deferred gratification, resistance to impatience) is still rather sparse. Little is known, for instance, about the sensitivity of discounting to variations in persons' situations and conditions of action or about the stability of a person's discount rate across the life course (see, e.g., Mischel, Shoda, & Peake, 1988). Conceptually, however, the internal logic of discounting, or of action in which anticipations of future states affect present dynamics, suggests an answer to a question that has until now been kept in the background: Does "aging," or "the aging process," have any distinctive content of its own, or is it an umbrella term that refers rather loosely to various more specific processes with which age is mutually implicated?

◇ THE CONTENT OF "AGING"

However else one may define it, "aging" is an organization of temporality. Regardless the processes with which it is mutually implicated, or with which one prefers to identify it as synonym (e.g., "maturation," "development"), "aging" refers to the timing and sequencing in some specified process, to the structuring of its tempo in state durations and transitions. As the Vulcanists better appreciated than their Neptunist opponents during the early years of modern geochronology, that structuring is endogenous to the dynamics of the given process. The metric of timing and sequencing should be defined, in other words, as "a functional endogenous interval determined by the particular process" under study (Winston, 1982, p. 24).

This stands in contrast to the usual practice wherein the temporality of each of various processes is viewed through and as the standardized clock-time metric of age. The uniform metric homogenizes differences in the organization of temporality, resulting in an unnecessary and potentially costly loss of information. In addition, whereas a uniform clock-time age is a convenient surrogate for the organization of temporality in a particular process, the cost of that convenience is further delay in the admittedly difficult task of inventing solutions to the conceptual and mensural problems involved in analyzing the *endogenous* structure of timing and sequencing in the given process.[25] It is no doubt true that a highly institutionalized life course does constrain timing and sequencing in a variety of processes to a standardized chronology—not completely but to a high degree, high enough to create problems of simultaneity in analytic strategies. Populations do tend to be internally sorted (or "self-sorted") by a single classification of age-state sequence and that classification has increasingly approached the continuous metric, "years of age." A number of major events—entry to formal schooling, labor-force entry, first marriage, child rearing, retirement—are effectively coordinated in that classification. However, we risk exaggeration of the constraint and coordination when we rely on a single classification and a single metric in investigations of the several processes, as if all in fact observed the same endogenous tempo. Age-linked markers, such as credentials of socialization, reflect a uniform organization of temporality—by definition. But the process of skill acquisition might nonetheless be organized in a more complex, and complexly varied, structure of timing and sequencing. Of course, insofar as subsequent processes (e.g., of selection, discrimination, allocation) are sensitive only to differences of credentials, obscured heterogeneities of the process of skill acquisition would be of little or no consequence. This question is an empirical one, however, not one to be decided as an artifact of an age-linked marker or because age is a convenient surrogate.

Understood in the rudimentary sense of endurance, "aging" can be specified as the organization of temporality that is immanent to any particular process. Insofar as that process is "time variant," it can thus be described as an aging process—a process subject to aging—in terms of a classification and metric that are sensitive to its own intrinsic tempo. This is useful to the analysis of social change, for it allows the inner logic of a process to be instrumental in nonrandom variations and directional ("secular") changes of the process itself. A particular process (e.g., skill acquisition) may therefore be "old" not merely because it has been in operation many years but because it has changed in some describable way as a function, at least in part, of its own internal dynamics (e.g., a path dependence leading into a cul-de-sac of complexity).

But to return to a question previously announced, where does all of this leave the conventional notion of "the aging process"? Since "aging" always refers to the organization of temporality, the conceptual content of "the aging process" is spread across as many different substantively specified processes as are mutually implicated with age. Certainly "aging" can be identified with one of those processes ("development" is a common choice, though that term itself is an umbrella covering various processes and various schedules of timing and sequencing). But to do so renders "the aging process" perfectly redundant. Is there any sense in which one can speak of "the aging process" as conceptually distinctive, nonredundant in its information? One possibility can be found in the fact that certain processes tend to be hysteretic or self-retarding—that is, retarding as a function of their own intrinsic dynamics. In order to explore this possibility, let's return to the process of discounting.

The simple model manifested in arguments such as Bernoulli's (1738/1954) and Böhm-Bawerk's (1970) predicts that the tendency of one's present self to imagine that one's older selves will be wiser, more resistant to impatience, and the like, decays with increasing years of age. That the process of discounting intrinsically tends to hysteresis is hardly surprising. After all, it is present self's anticipation of older selves' experiences and memories that lies at the core of discounting, and the longer the horizon of anticipation the steeper the discount is likely to be. In other words, insofar as the intentional structure of a young present self projects a relatively long horizon of older selves, the intervals of deferral in deferred gratifications will tend to be relatively long, which implies a relatively high discount rate. The record of systematic evidence pertaining to these relationships is still sketchy, but there is some supportive evidence—for example, that a person's rate of discount is a decelerating positive function of the length of delay in deferred gratification (see, e.g., Loewenstein & Prelec, 1992, p. 121). Moreover, a connection can be drawn between the sensitivity of discounting to the relative age of the imagined older self[26] and the observation that timed intervals of lived experience grow shorter, and transitions faster, as a function of prior accumulation of experience. The duration of an additional year of age today is experientially greater than the duration of an additional year of age projected 10 years hence, and greater still, though not by a factor of two, than the duration of an additional year of age projected 20 years hence. As Georgescu-Roegon (1971, p. 138) put it, age-state durations seem to shorten as we grow older, because "the content of our consciousness increases at a decreasing rate."[27]

Thus, the hysteretic effect in discounting, manifested necessarily in a sequence of age states, illustrates the conception of "aging" as a retardation in the dynamics of various processes. Of course, to say that hysteresis is intrinsic to a process (e.g., the process of deferred gratification) is mostly a descriptive statement. In the case of deferred gratification, the fact of hysteresis must be referred back to the processes that drive the disposition of a present self to attribute greater sagacity and patience to his or her older selves. An accumulation of experience, for example, might imply learning, which could account for the central tendency manifested as a hysteretic effect. After all, a person whose discount rate remains persistently higher than the rates of members of his or her comparison group will gradually lose relative standing (*ceteris paribus*), and perception of the loss might trigger an increased resistance to impatience. As Ainslie (1992, pp. 124-125) has argued, discount behavior is almost surely mediated by other processes. Processes of social comparison are one likely candidate.

Hysteresis in age-related processes gives distinctive content, nonredundant information, to the notion of "the aging process." Granted, it focuses on what might be called the "degenerative" aspects of process, neglecting the "generative" aspects. But these latter aspects are already sufficiently covered by conceptualizations of "maturation," "development," "socialization," and the like. Defining "the aging process" in terms of hysteretic effects in those and other processes fills it with nonredundant information—all in all, not a bad attribute.

◇ NOTES

1. A simple illustration of what I mean by the sorting of a population composition in terms of specific causal processes is given by Lee (1994, pp. 15-16). Imagine that because of an improvement of sanitation engineering initial life expectancy has increased by one year; otherwise the causal process of mortality has not changed. If the population in question is characterized by a relatively fast mortality regime (e.g., initial life expectancy of 40), most of the one-year gain will be distributed among young and middle-aged adults. If, on the other hand, the mortality regime is relatively stingy (e.g., initial life expectancy of 75), most of the one-year gain will be distributed among older persons. Effects of the improved engineering are differently sorted across the two populations "because" of the different age compositions, but one would not properly regard that composition as a *cause* of the different effects.

2. Note that memory endowment exceeds the bounds of any conventionally defined "individual consciousness" not only in the important sense explored by Halbwachs (1925/1992) as "collective memory." For instance, the Eiffel Tower "remembers" its configuration, a materialization of a memory endowment. A mechanical device such as a typewriter is similarly an instrument of a "canned" intelligence. More complexly, "a career embeds identities from different chunks of time" (White, 1992a, p. 221), and "any living cell carries with it the experiences of a billion years of experimentation by its ancestors" (Delbrück, 1949, p. 173; Mayr, 1976, p. 362).

3. This is not to say that memory endowment or path dependence consists in a sensitivity *only* to initial conditions; quite the contrary. Indeed, specifying "initial conditions" can be extraordinarily difficult. Born into a definite set of circumstances, a person assumes the history (or, more carefully, a history) of those circumstances.

4. Georgescu-Roegon drew attention to the hysteretic character of endurance—that it tends to a condition of greater probability—when he (1971, p. 205) noted that "Aging is to grow more and deeper 'wrinkles' as the organism is continuously exposed to accidents. . . . Aging is nothing but the cumulative effect of causes acting in Time; in other words, it is a hysteresis process." This issue of "time" will be dealt with in a later section, again in connection to hysteretic effects and aging. Meanwhile, a couple of textbook illustrations of the significance of hysteretic effects may be useful. The first concerns magnetism. Imagine a small iron bar. Because of the motion of its electrons, each atom of iron is already a tiny magnet; but because the atoms strongly tend

to be arranged in randomly oriented domains, the set of effects is neutral. Place the bar in the midst of an electrical coil. Some portion of the atoms were already aligned with the current; others fall into line as well; eventually the bar as such is magnetized. But the pace of this alignment process (or the transitions between states of alignment) is not monotonic, and it does not keep pace with the strength of the magnetizing field (i.e., the force of the electric current). This lag is one aspect of magnetic hysteresis. Another aspect occurs when the field strength is reduced. Assume that all atoms in the iron bar have been identically aligned. Reduce the field strength. The bar retains a memory of the field even after the field strength has been reduced to zero. The memory gradually decays, but the rate of decay is significantly lower than the rate at which the bar had been magnetized (hence, a "permanent" magnet). The second illustration concerns water from a spigot. Assume a constant water pressure. Turn the spigot's handle to some intermediate position so that water flows, and mark the handle's position so that you can exactly reproduce it later; make a mental picture (or photograph or whatever) of the flow of water. Now turn the handle to the full "on" position; then turn the handle back to the position you previously marked. You will see that the flow of water differs from the flow you noted earlier, even though the dimensions of the spigot opening are exactly the same and the water pressure remained unchanged. In this as in the preceding illustration of even a simple physical system, "history" makes a difference; that is, different sequences of states and transitions entail different memory endowments of succeeding states.

5. I do not mean that these various "types" of processes are unambiguously distinctive or mutually exclusive. For example, "maturation" can be regarded as a developmental process and, at least by one set of theories (e.g., Changeux, 1983/1985; Edelman, 1987), as a selection process. Likewise, the distinctions among allocation, selection, and sorting processes are fuzzy. To speak of these (and other) analytic models as "types" of processes is simply a useful convenience.

6. Some processes are regarded as "time-invariant"; their dynamics are not historically sensitive (at least not sensitive within some very long temporal frame). Other processes are "time-variant"; the sensitivity is not merely at the level of scalar values (i.e., "starting values" of specific variables) but at the level of the form of the process (e.g., sensitivity of vector parameters, of functional form, etc.). Time-variant processes are subject to aging.

7. Not that those accounts were all that novel in their definitions of age-related "stages of development." The seven-days-of-creation sequence in the *Genesis* account has been a sturdy feature of "ontogenic" counting systems: from Augustine's (388/1991) seven ages of human life (in *On Genesis against the Manicheans,* I.23), to the *Etymologiae* (V.39, XI.2) of Isidore of Seville (1911), to Shakespeare's seven ages (in *As You Like It,* 2.7.138), to modern versions. Isidore's description of the sequence is remarkably exacting: following the first stage from birth to age 7 (infantia), a person enters childhood (7-13), then adolescence (14-27), youth (28-49), maturity (50-69), and finally old age (70+), the last part of which is senescence.

8. See, e.g., Dilthey's (1927/1958, pp. 244-245) definition of "development," that stipulates memory endowment—or in his terms an "inner logic" (that is his use of the concept *Wesen*)—as the necessary third property added to classification (states) and ordering (sequence). One might stipulate duration dependence as another necessary property of a minimally defined "developmental process," in the sense discussed by Featherman and Lerner (1986; also see Dilthey, 1927/1958, pp. 229-231; Featherman, 1986; Featherman & Petersen, 1985). That is, only if the rate of change in the outcome of some specified process is sensitive to duration or "waiting time" in a given state of that process will the change (and the process) be counted as "developmental." This stipulation does have some advantages. But it also seems unduly restrictive. Consider this illustration of a negative case: "if it is just as likely for [persons] with different periods of exposure to a given regimen of [potentially acquirable skill] to gain or lose equivalent [degrees of that skill], then the relationship is not developmental" (Featherman & Lerner 1985, p. 667). The governing expectation would thus seem to require that persons respond to a given stimulus situation uniformly, that variations in exposure (state duration) must translate into at least

roughly equivalent variations in outcome. State duration, doubtless an important property of sequential experiences, is a rather insensitive criterion by which to winnow "developmental change" (process) from other sorts of change (process).

9. Self-report of age is often one of the elements of a physician's test of dementia among older persons, even though the boundary condition is ambiguous. When I momentarily forget my "age" (until subtracting birth year from current year), the lapse is by my accounting a performance error; and performance error alone is insufficient indication of failure of competence. But at some point on the age gradient, expectations about the distinction between performance and competence weaken.

10. Two simple indications: First, a person who passes as younger or older than his or her official age usually does not, when detected, arouse the degree of disapproval that is aroused by someone who is caught passing in terms of educational credential or occupational license or gender or race. The exceptions occur when a particular age is significant as a signal—for example, signaling eligibility to purchase an alcoholic beverage or operate a piece of equipment such as a motor vehicle. Second, survey researchers (e.g., Stark & Roberts, 1996, p. 144, note 2) have reported that the once-strong tendency of self-reported ages to clump at certain numbers (29, 39, 49, etc.) has largely disappeared, which suggests a reduction not only in the significance of decade-turning ages but also in the importance of age classification generally.

11. Thus, for example, aristocracy was an intrafamilial "generational" contract of the living with the dead and the not-yet-born members of a family. Primogeniture was an efficient regulative principle of the intertemporal contract.

12. By "local" I mean specific to a culture. Until the late 1600s a calendar was a dynastic property; it marked durations such as Year II of the Reign of Edward the First or Year VII of the Reign of Pope Urban the Second. Calendars were increasingly "democratized," detached from iterative cycles of sovereignty, after the seventeenth century.

13. Standardization by/in clock time tends to entail an anonymization of relationships (e.g., everyone fits anonymously in the age-marked category "politically enfranchised"), which inhibits particularistic information or signaling about maturation.

14. Judging from recent research, our auditory skills in identifying the age of an unseen speaker are remarkably good when tested not only by the criterion of broad titles ("child," "adult," etc.) but also by the criterion of "year of age." Auditors succeed within a small margin of error (e.g., 5 years) at a rate significantly greater than chance. The most salient cues appear to be speaking rate, total speaking time, and "fundamental frequency," which is a function of structural changes of the larynx and vocal folds (see Hollein, 1987; Pittam, 1994).

15. A shift from a primarily qualitative definition of gender states (i.e., *kind* of being) to an increasingly quantitative definition that converts "gender" into correlated gradients of small differences can be discerned in some recent literatures in biological and in social science (see, e.g., Zihlman, 1985; and for a general discussion, Hazelrigg, 1995, pp. 274-290).

16. As Arrow (1973, pp. 25-26) pointed out, the level of signal reliability often needs to be "sufficiently high" only on average. When a particular organization such as a firm can externalize much of the total cost of prejudicial discrimination onto its larger environment ("society as a whole"), the organization might well conclude that it is internally cost efficient to use membership criteria (e.g., educational credential, a range of ages) that reflect a difference of average values in the distributions of relevant individual characteristics (e.g., a specific skill, probable tenure length). If the cost to a firm of acquiring information that is sensitive to individual-level variation in the characteristic exceeds the sum of the cost of using cruder signals and the cost of signal error, the firm might choose to rely on the cruder signals in its hiring decisions, even knowing full well that it is reproducing prejudicial stereotypes.

17. Note that "highly standardized" does not mean "without variation." Rindfuss, Swicegood, and Rosenfeld (1987) examined the sequencing of five "activity states"—schooling, work, homemaking, military service, and miscellaneous "other activities"—among a national sample of young men and women who were observed yearly during the first 8 years following

high-school graduation. Finding considerable heterogeneity in the sequencing, the authors rightly cautioned against the assumption that a single modal pattern of significant states and transitions is descriptively adequate. Life is "messier" than might be construed from a phrase such as "*the* life course." On the other hand, however, most of the heterogeneity was due to individuals who, after having engaged in paid employment or other activities following high-school graduation, returned to the formal educational process. Moreover, of the very large number of possible sequences involving five activity states and eight observation points (5^8 = 390,625), fewer than 0.5 percent were actually descriptive of at least one individual. Burt's (1991) analysis similarly indicates that a very small set of age-stratified life-course activities strongly regulate the sorting of social ties.

18. Note that information on heterogeneity in the population could be easily plotted as a "band width," potentially variable in width, along the line of trajectory.

19. *Seemingly,* because (despite H. G. Wells's time traveler, who must have been "moving" at an accelerated rate, something faster than one second per second) a phrase such as "a rate of one second per second" is infinitely regressive: a rate of t per t' implies a rate of t' per t'', ad infinitum.

20. This is not to deny the relativistic character of the metric. In Kantian construction the form of time is universal, an a priori condition necessary to any experience whatsoever. But it is perfectly consistent with that construction to argue (though Kant did not) that time is culturally relative.

21. Georgescu-Roegon (1971, pp. 131-134) gives a brief account of McTaggart's paradox. For some recent discussions of competing understandings of temporality, see Oaklander and Smith (1994).

22. The presumption of a strong analogy is at least as old as Hume's theorizations (see Elster & Loewenstein, 1992, p. 218). There is some evidence, however, that persons give greater weight to intrabiographic comparisons than to interpersonal "relative standing" comparisons (see, e.g., van de Stadt, Kapteya, & van de Geer, 1985). Note that intrabiographic comparison inherently involves intertemporal transactions among moments of selfhood—as in the stylized questions, "How well am I doing now, as compared to earlier times?" and "How well am I doing, relative to the person I hope to be when I am older?" (see Brickman & Campbell, 1971; Ross, 1989). Tuma and Hannan's (1984, p. 193) notion of "person-specific investments" readily translates from interpersonal transactions to intrabiographic-intertemporal transactions.

23. Note, however, that the "stability vs. change" issue is obscurant when posed so broadly, as if it were indifferent to scale, context, and analytic framing. For an organization such as a firm the chief task may well be to achieve and maintain a stability of organizational integrity in the face of continually shifting environmental factors; but to a new management team intent on reforming the organization from within, the task of achieving and maintaining desired change, of reforming path dependencies or memory endowments in specific ways, is often rather daunting.

24. The conception is suggestive of a "fractured identity" (though that can be read as reproducing the notion of a selfsame identity as "normal" condition that then becomes fractured), and it does accord with psychiatry's "split" or "multiple personality" (Putnam, 1989). But it also accords with the notion that each person is a bundle of selves or identities, more or less well integrated, and that a condition marginalized on the gradient of "integration" as "disorderly" (e.g., "split personality") is a social transaction of policing the boundary between "normality" and "pathology." A present self is strongly disposed to expect that a sequence of aged selves is well integrated, so that the experience of "self-awareness" inheres as an enduring self-identical processor of differing experiences through time. There are some strong tendencies that support and reinforce that disposition, tendencies of path dependence. An actor is a classification-and-measurement instrument with memory. Memory, even were it not reconstitutive or revisionist in operation, implies a strong tendency of each successive act of classification-and-measurement to reproduce something of the actor's previous acts of classification-and-measurement (serial

correlation). That alone establishes an integrative function, a sense of continuity and stability across the aged moments of selfhood. But memory is continually revisionist, persistently productive of "pasts," with a general preference for coherence over incoherence. This reinforces the integrative function. Then, too, an individual actor is inherently social, an "ensemble of social relations"—or to borrow White's (1992a, p. 198) elaboration of the point, "a more-or-less rickety ensemble, . . . firm and whole only temporarily"—which means that others' actions are always implicated.

25. Burt (1991, p. 3) made much the same point when he said that "the most consequential decisions in much of social science research involve assigning units of analysis"—that is, defining classificatory and mensural units—yet these are typically among the researcher's most negligently made decisions.

26. In other words, the temporal distance between present and imagined older self, an interval constrained by the age of present self. Slemrod's (1984, 1986) studies indicate that discounting may be sensitive to differences in remaining life expectancy (though his results could also be indicative of a historical-period effect).

27. Experimental evidence has demonstrated that perceived duration is nonlinear relative to the uniform intervals of clock time. A simple power function best fit Ekman and Lundberg's (1971) observations, for instance: $t = T^c$, where t and T are perceived and clock-time durations, respectively, and $0 < c < 1$. (Thus, if $c = 0.5$, the T series 1, 2, 3, 4, 5 corresponds to the t series 1, 1.4, 1.7, 2.0, 2.2.) But one should expect the magnitude of c to be systematically sensitive to situational, biographical, and historical factors. Here, the expectation is that c diminishes with increasing age.

CHAPTER FIVE

Beyond Trajectories

Multiple Concepts for Analyzing
Long-Term Process

ELIZA K. PAVALKO

Empirical study of individual aging and social change presents a variety of research challenges. Broader theoretical questions about stability and change (Dannefer, 1988; Hazelrigg, this volume; Wells & Stryker, 1988) coincide with difficulties in connecting multiple events across the life course. Data availability often poses an obstacle in these analytic efforts. Despite the growth of longitudinal studies since the 1960s, information on the events between surveys, such as work or marital history, is less common. In addition, surveys of individuals rarely include information that allow researchers to make convincing connections between those subjects and macrolevel changes. For example, the rare longitudinal surveys that span the Great Depression and World War II largely neglect pre-war and wartime events even though those events may be directly related to other issues that are included in the survey, such as occupational changes (Elder, Pavalko, & Clipp, 1993). A second dilemma is that the most widely used techniques for quantitative analyses make assumptions about time that greatly limit our ability to analyze process (Abbott, 1992, 1995; Aminzade, 1992). A final but less frequently addressed problem is that, when quantitative research does attempt to capture process across the lifespan, there may be little or no consideration of different types of processes or the conceptualization of process tends to vary across studies. However, closer attention to different types of processes can provide a broader range of information about social change and individual lives, and it is these issues that provide the focus for this paper.

Understanding process is central to life course research. The life course is often defined as a series of pathways marked by sequences of transitions (Elder, 1992; Elder & O'Rand, 1995; Hagestad, 1990), and both concepts and methods in this area are designed to better explicate the dynamics of these pathways. One way to address these processes has been to conceptualize them in terms of short and long-term dynamics. *Transitions* refer to a change in status—a shift from one state to another —and thus focus on short-term dynamics. Examples of analyses of transitions made by individuals include studies of marriage and divorce, job changes or retirement. Long-term process has been conceptualized in terms of *trajectories* or *careers* that define the broader patterns of events across the life course. Whereas trajectories are often marked by a series of transitions, understanding this longer-term pattern is critical for providing information about the context of any single transition (Elder, 1985, 1992; Hagestad, 1990; Moen, 1985).

The ways short and long-term process can inform our understanding of lives and historical change is illustrated by research on the transition to adulthood (e.g., Hogan, 1981; Hogan & Astone, 1986; Modell, 1989; Modell, Furstenberg, & Hershberg, 1976; Rindfuss, Swicegood, & Rosenfeld, 1987). This "transition" is not defined by any single event but by the relationship between several events that serve as benchmarks of adult life, such as leaving school, starting employment, marrying and having children. The movement from adolescence to adulthood is a process that is best understood by how the events connect to one another. These connections can be examined in a number of different ways, including their timing, spread, and order. Each of these different concepts provides unique information about the process through which one becomes an adult. Relationships between these events have also changed over time (Modell, 1989; Modell et al., 1976), suggesting variations in the ways that the "life course" is defined within and across particular locations of time and space.

Despite considerable discussion of life course dynamics (Elder, 1985; George, 1993; Hagestad, 1990) recent research has focused most heavily on the analysis of transitions. Fueled by the introduction of methods for the analysis of event histories to sociology (e.g., Mayer & Tuma, 1990; Petersen, 1991; Tuma & Hannan, 1984), our understanding of variations in when individuals experience life transitions has grown dramatically (Elder & O'Rand, 1995; George, 1993; Hagestad, 1990). These methods have improved our understanding of the dynamics, not only of the individual life course but also broader issues such as the degree of institutionalization or fluidity of the life course over time and across societies (Meyer, 1986).

Analysis of longer-term processes has been less common, but a variety of innovative methods are being used to capture particular dimensions of long-term process. For example, analyses of repeated events (e.g., Petersen, 1991) provide clues about the spacing between multiple transitions, whereas analyses of career lines (Althauser, 1989; Althauser & van Veen, 1994; Otto, Spenner, & Call, 1980a, 1980b; Rosenbaum, 1984) examine connections between jobs that serve as the structural pathways patterning individual mobility. Optimal matching methods supply tools for analyzing sequences of events (Abbott, 1992, 1995; Abbott & Hrycak, 1990) and descriptive methods (Clipp, Pavalko, & Elder, 1992; Elder & Pavalko, 1993; Moen, 1985; Rindfuss et al., 1987; Verbrugge, Reoma, & Gruber-Baldini, 1994) allow the analysis of variation in general patterns of events, such as women's career types or long-term patterns of health.

Whereas all of these methods provide powerful techniques for the analysis of long-term process, use of them has been scattered. For example, research on career lines has examined branching structures, but application of these techniques has not been extended to other areas where they might be equally useful, such as health, social roles or criminal careers. In addition, many concepts related to long-term process have not been clearly defined (Hagestad, 1990). In life course research, concepts relating to long-term process, such as trajectory, pathway, career, and sequence may be used interchangeably or with little explication of how one concept may differ from the other. References to trajectories may refer to broad connections across the life course whereas at other times may refer to a more specific series of events. The concept may be used descriptively with no implication of direction, sequence or pace (Elder, 1985) or it may refer more specifically to a pathway that, once begun, is largely unidirectional, as in Glaser and Strauss's (1968) discussion of a dying trajectory. Finally, there has been little comparison between different concepts of long-term process to consider how each may provide different information about the process under consideration.

The purpose of this chapter is to examine several different dimensions of long-term process to better understand what each can tell us about life trajectories. The first and most general dimension of long-term process is *pattern,* which focuses on broad descriptions of long-term process and makes no assumptions about direction, pace or order of events within the pattern. A second dimension, *sequence,* highlights the order of events within a given pattern or time frame, and a third, *pace,* addresses the timing of repeated events. The final dimension, *reversibility*, concentrates on turning points and the degree of switching between paths. Whereas this list of dimensions is not exhaustive (see also Aminzade, 1992), these concepts are relevant to life course research and provide a starting point for discussion of different dimensions of long-term process. I begin with a review of how each dimension is currently used in the literature and then turn to the specific example of mental illness careers to consider how each dimension might provide different types of information about these careers.

◇ THREE CONCEPTS OF LONG-TERM PROCESS

Pattern

The pattern concept provides a general tool for analyzing long-term process. Most commonly, a finite number of categories, such as ones reflecting intermittent change, gradual change, and stability are defined and then cases are placed into one of these categories. Patterns have been the most frequently used method of examining long-term process, whether they are patterns of health (e.g., Clipp et al., 1992; Harding, 1988; Verbrugge et al., 1994), career lines (Otto et al., 1980a, 1980b), retirement processes (Elder & Pavalko, 1993) or women's labor force participation (Moen, 1985; Pienta, Burr, & Mutchler, 1994).

Patterns provide a valuable research tool for contrasting variation in temporal processes such as stability versus change. General contrasts between stability and change can be made with broad pattern types. These typologies can then serve as a basis for examining factors that predict whether people will follow a stable pattern versus one characterized by change. Patterns can also serve as the basis for examining later consequences of following one or another pattern type. Women's patterns of labor force participation provide a case in point. Many researchers have shown the relevance of information on women's longer-term patterns of labor force participation. Theories of women's labor force participation can be broadened to examine whether similar factors predict current and longer-term patterns of labor force participation (e.g., Avioli & Kaplan, 1992; Gerson, 1985; Rexroat, 1992) or whether women experience different effects of employment depending on whether they have been employed continuously or have had earlier interruptions in their paid employment (Moen, 1985; Moen, Dempster-McClain, & Williams, 1992; O'Rand & Henretta, 1982;

Pienta et al., 1994; Van Velsor & O'Rand, 1984). In this case, more specific distinctions such as the order of specific jobs within a pattern are less theoretically relevant than the overall distinction between stability and change in labor force participation.

Patterns can also be very important in the early stages of exploring many dimensions of long-term processes. In some cases, more precise questions about the nature of the process are of theoretical interest, but so little is known about the general patterns that these must be explored before turning to more detailed questions about the process. For example, ongoing research by Pescosolido (1991, 1992) on network ties and utilization of mental health services establishes a strong theoretical framework and rationale for understanding the processes through which people enter mental health care. These hypothesized processes raise questions about stages of the process, turning points, and the degree to which earlier decisions shape later options (Pescosolido, 1991). However, because there has been so little prior empirical work on these processes, an important first step involves the identification and description of the different pathways that people take into treatment (see Pescosolido, 1992).

There is no single method for creating patterns but a number of different techniques have been used. The applicability of any single technique depends on the level of detail in the data, sample size, and the complexity of patterns. One technique used with panel data is to group cases by their statuses across each time point. For example, Moen (1985) uses several waves of panel data to define women's patterns of labor force participation. Patterns are defined by mapping out all possible combinations of labor force participation across the survey waves and then aggregating similar patterns to create a smaller number of meaningful patterns. Other measures of women's worklife patterns have been constructed using a combination of quantitative indicators of women's worklives, such as number of years working, the timing of exits in conjunction with the birth of children and reasons for any labor force changes (Moen et al., 1992; Pienta et al., 1994; Rexroat, 1992; Van Velsor & O'Rand, 1984). Other statistical techniques may also be used to identify patterns. Pescosolido (1992) employs clustering techniques to examine whether strategies of seeking help for health care, such as through physicians, friends, family, or home remedies, are combined with one another in common ways.

Other patterns may be more complex and require inspection of the available information for each case before placement into the appropriate category. This type of coding is often necessary when data include multiple dimensions and multiple time points for each individual. Even small increases in the number of time points or the number of dimensions being considered can dramatically increase the amount of data, and visual inspection of the trends for each individual can provide valuable clues about pattern differences. For example, Verbrugge et al. (1994) examined the dynamics of individual disability on the basis of eight different dimensions of disability. Patterns were identified by examining individual stability or change in disability levels across nine time points. For each of the 165 cases, the disability dimensions were plotted over time and then each plot was visually examined for themes. Other examples in which multiple dimensions have been plotted for each individual over time and then grouped into similar patterns include analyses of functioning for persons with schizophrenia (Harding, 1988) or career progression or orderliness (Pavalko, Elder, & Clipp, 1993; Wilensky, 1961). Because placement into patterns is made on a case-by-case basis, this method requires a substantial investment in the coding process. In addition, to assure coding reliability, multiple raters and appropriate checks for inter-rater reliability are necessary (Elder, Pavalko, & Clipp, 1993).

Pattern analysis provides important information about long-term stability and change but there may be other dimensions of long-term change that cannot be captured in this type of analysis. Although most analyses to date have tended to focus on one dimension, such as pattern, exploration of multiple components are likely to provide a broader understanding of any given process. Additional analyses might examine the pace, sequence, reversibility, or cyclical nature of a process (see also Aminzade, 1992). The following two sections focus on three of these dimensions, sequence, pace, and reversibility, because each has particular relevance to life course concepts.

Sequence

Many life course processes can be conceptualized as a series of events over time. When there is a series of identifiable events one question of interest is whether the order or sequence of those events provides information about how the life course is structured. Is the order of these events fairly regular or random? Are there common or identifiable sequences? Do these sequences vary in systematic ways? And finally, are there different consequences of following one sequence or another?

A number of examples demonstrate the relevance of order in life course research. Research on the transition to adulthood examines historical changes in the order of events, whether or not there is a dominant or normative order and the changing consequences of deviating from the most common sequence (Hogan, 1981; Hogan & Astone, 1986; Jackson, 1993; Rindfuss et al., 1987). Attention to order provides information on work careers (Abbott & Hrycak, 1990) or can be used to define the complexity of movement between social roles in a given day to better understand the mental health effects of multiple roles (Hecht, 1996). In addition, numerous studies have suggested that the effect of an event varies depending on when it occurs in the life course, a process Elder refers to as the life stage principle (Elder, 1974, 1992; Elder & O'Rand, 1995). Attention to sequencing would allow further exploration of why this principle holds. It may be that the effect varies by life stage because of the developmental age at which it occurs, but an alternative explanation might be that the effect holds because life stage is a rough proxy for when the event occurs relative to other life course events (e.g., finishing school, moving out of the parental household, or beginning a full-time job). Separating the effect of the age of an event from its position in a broader sequence of events could improve our understanding of this principle.

Attention to the sequence of events is also a valuable tool for analyzing connections between events in different domains, such as work and family. Life course researchers often call attention to interlocking and competing careers (e.g., Elder, 1985), but analyses of the dynamics of multiple careers as well as the intersections between them are complex. Because a sequence of events is defined by the order of some events relative to others it provides a unique way of analyzing competing careers. For example, the intersection between employment and family can be conceptualized in terms of varying sequences of events from both arenas. Sequences between people who have relatively few family events (e.g., one marriage, no children) could be contrasted to those who have many. More subtle differences, such as between those who have most family events early in relation to their worklives, those who intersperse family events throughout their worklives, and those who have them later in the work career, can also be differentiated when we conceptualize these events in terms of their relative order to one another.

The use of the sequence concept has been limited by the analytic complexity involved in defining and analyzing sequences. Difficulties in making sense of data across multiple time points and for large numbers of respondents become even more complex when the order of events is considered. Even a small number of events can produce an astonishing number of possible sequences. For example, the five events over 8 years in the transition to adulthood considered by Rindfuss et al. (1987) produce 390,625 possible sequences. Even when some of these sequences are more common than others, researchers are faced with the task of systematically grouping all possible sequences into a smaller number of meaningful sequence types.

Optimal matching techniques, first developed for DNA sequencing and recently adapted to the social sciences, provide one valuable tool for identifying various sequence types (Abbott, 1992, 1995; Abbott & Hrycak, 1990). Like pattern analyses, optimal matching techniques provide tools to group cases that have similar sequences. Because sequences are treated as a single unit, transitions or turning points within a sequence are only relevant if they distinguish one pattern as different from another. But, the use of sequencing techniques (see also Corsaro & Heise, 1990; Griffin, 1993; Heise, 1991 for an alternative approach to sequencing) allows us to consider far more complex series of events and to incorporate more types of information than is possible with the types of methods often used in pattern analyses.

Optimal matching techniques estimate the difference between each sequence, creating a matrix of distance scores that shows the distance between each sequence and all others (see Abbott, 1992, 1995 for a more detailed description). The distance scores represent the changes (additions, deletions, or substitutions) that would be required to make one sequence identical to another. The "cost" of each change is defined by the researcher. For example, in an analysis of the complexity of the sequence of activities in a woman's day, Hecht (1996) defines some activities as relatively similar to each other, whereas others are more dissimilar. Leisure and sleep are similar activities because both require few role demands and allow greater choice in whether or not one does them. Leisure and childcare are defined as dissimilar. Thus, if three women have the same sequence of activities, but the first woman's sequence includes more time for sleep, the second includes more leisure time and the third woman's sequence includes more time in childcare, the distance between the first two sequences would be less than the distance between the first and third sequence. After distance scores are calculated, clustering methods are used to group similar sequences together, with the end result being a small set of sequence types. Sequence coding can also be adapted to incorporate other concepts such as the pace of events and subsequences as well as the general order. However, the methods become cumbersome with large sample sizes and more complex sequences. Nevertheless, new developments suggest future potential for flexibility in conducting these analyses (Abbott, 1995).

Pace

In recent years, sociologists have raised numerous questions about the timing of key events. Event history techniques have played an important role in addressing these questions because they provide the analytical tools for analyzing the time until an event occurs. However, the majority of these analyses have focused on the timing of a single event, such as time until retirement, first birth, or a job change (see George, 1993, for a review). The concept of pace extends this interest in timing beyond single events, calling attention to the spacing between repeated events. Attention to pace thus provides an important tool for linking the analysis of transitions to longer term processes.

Many events of interest to sociologists, such as marriage, birth, job changes, or hospitalizations are repeatable events, but there has been relatively little attention to variations in the pacing of these events. One notable exception is the literature on child spacing. Developments in this literature are instructive for several reasons. First, questions about the spacing between births are conceptually distinct from those that focus on the timing of the first birth. The timing of the first birth is important because it is one marker of the transition to adulthood and informs policy concerns about teen parenting (e.g., Rindfuss, Morgan, & Swicegood, 1988) whereas the spacing between births is more informative of overall fertility, family size, and family structure (Powell & Steelman, 1990, 1993, 1995; Teachman & Schollaert, 1989; Wineberg & McCarthy, 1989). Second, much of the literature on child spacing demonstrates the connections between transitions and subsequent processes. Factors influencing the timing of first birth differ from those affecting subsequent spacing, but the timing of the first birth becomes an important predictor of timing in later births (Bumpass, Rindfuss, & Janosik, 1978; Wineberg & McCarthy, 1989). Finally, the literature on child spacing demonstrates multiple ways of conceptualizing pace. Birth spacing has been conceptualized as a series of discrete events, with timing between the first and second births analyzed separately from the timing between second and third (e.g., Teachman & Schollaert, 1989) and also as a single process that can be captured by measures such as the proportion of siblings that are closely spaced (Powell & Steelman, 1990, 1993, 1995).

Different ways of conceptualizing and measuring the pace of repeated events depend in part on whether the pace of events is the dependent or independent variable in an analysis. When the pace of repeated events is the dependent variable, analyses are often complicated by variation in the total number of events and the necessity of observing spacing before all families will have completed their family formation (censoring). In these cases, event history techniques can be used to successively analyze the timing between each event and the next occurrence of that event (e.g., Teachman & Schollaert, 1989; Wineberg & McCarthy, 1989) and allow investigation of whether different factors influence the timing between earlier versus later intervals.

An alternative approach also uses event history techniques but analyzes repeated events in the same model (e.g., Petersen & Spilerman, 1990). Single estimates of factors influencing the spacing between all events can be produced, but models can also be specified to explore whether particular intervals, such as those that occur earlier in the process differ systematically from later intervals (Petersen, 1991; Petersen & Spilerman, 1990). Event history models, whether specified as successive models for each event or as a single model incorporating repeated events, analyze each interval as a separate unit. Thus, they provide an incremental analysis of the pace of repeated events.

An alternative approach is to conceptualize pace in a more holistic fashion by constructing measures to capture the timing between all events over a specified period of time. This type of measure is often more appropriate when looking at the effect of the pace of events on other outcomes, such as the effect of child spacing on parental investment in children (Powell & Steelman, 1995). The simplest measure of this type would average the time between all events, created by dividing a specified period of time by the number of times the event in question occurred in the interval (Aminzade, 1992). This type of measure assumes that events are evenly spaced, which is an assumption that is not likely to be valid for most events. However, more specific holistic measures can be created to capture theoretically relevant variations in spacing. For example, a series of articles by Powell and Steelman (1990, 1993, 1995) explore a variety of measures to capture close spacing between children, such as the proportion of children that are closely spaced and a dummy variable contrasting closely spaced siblings to less closely spaced ones. Depending on the types of events being analyzed, other measures of pace might contrast the variation in a given event sequence, comparing sequences that are evenly spaced to those that have more variation in their spacing between events.

Reversibility

Concepts of trajectory, turning point and pathway are often used in life course research. These concepts invoke images of points in people's lives when they start on a particular course that, once started, becomes increasingly difficult to reverse. This image is striking for thinking about different pathways of human lives but also raises questions about the relative power of human agency, events, and institutions to shape the course of one's life. Are there events or institutions (e.g., prisons, mental hospitals, schools) that when structured in certain ways make changing paths increasingly difficult?

If there are such paths, when or how are they started? What can such a process tell us about the relationship between human agency and social institutions?

One way to address these questions is to focus specifically on the degree of reversibility in a given process. Once a path is initiated, how likely are individuals to change to alternate paths? For those who continue on their initial course, does the likelihood of change decrease over time? To what extent do people build up "inertia" once on a given pathway? For example, once one enters medical school, what is the likelihood of change to a different type of work or training? Does the probability of change to an alternate career decrease as medical school and further training are completed? Although the process is never fully determined, the overall pattern is likely to be one of decreasing variation as one's time on the path continues. Alternatively, once such a pattern of decreasing variation has been identified, we could also examine whether other events increase the likelihood of change to alternate paths. Similar processes could be examined for contact with other institutions such as the criminal justice system to gain an even better understanding of processes underlying "criminal careers" (Sampson & Laub, 1993).

The analysis of reversibility differs fundamentally from prior concepts discussed because reversibility focuses on change *within* a given process. Pattern and sequence in particular are designed to examine the process as a whole so that comparisons can be made between different types. Reversibility addresses mechanisms of change within any single typology.

The concept of reversibility has been analyzed in a variety of ways, but most of the methods used are designed for analyzing single or small numbers of cases. For example, Glaser and Strauss's (1968) concept of dying trajectory elaborates many of the key elements such as directionality that distinguish trajectories from more general processes. Similarly, Aminzade (1992) discusses the concept of path dependency for understanding macro historical processes, and event structure analysis provides detailed conceptualization and analysis of branching processes in an event (Corsaro & Heise, 1990; Griffin, 1993; Heise, 1991). When paths for large numbers of people are to be examined, methods used to analyze career lines and branching structures (Althauser & van Veen, 1994; Rosenbaum, 1984; Spilerman, 1977) could be adapted to examine a wide variety of person/institution processes.

Each of these concepts taps different components of long-term process. Whereas few analyses address multiple dimensions in a given process, comparisons across different concepts will provide a broader understanding than focusing on any single one. To further illustrate possible uses of these different concepts, each is used to elaborate different components of long-term mental illness careers.

⬨ LONG-TERM PROCESS IN MENTAL ILLNESS: POSSIBLE USES OF PATTERN, SEQUENCE, AND REVERSIBILITY

Sociologists studying mental illness have long been interested in the concept of illness career. In the late 1950s and early 1960s Clausen and Yarrow (1955), Goffman (1961) and others discussed the process of becoming a mental patient in terms of a series of stages and key decision points; a process they refer to as the "illness career." Thirty-five years later the illness career concept continues to be salient, but the majority of empirical research that follows persons with a severe and persistent mental illness continues to be cross-sectional or only follows subjects over a short time period in their broader illness careers.

Recently there has been renewed interest in conceptualizing and measuring various dimensions of the illness career. Pescosolido (1991, 1992) has proposed a model of pathways to care that incorporates the interactive dynamics of the illness career and social networks. In addition, a number of data collections from the United States and Switzerland that follow persons with severe mental illness for long periods of time are now becoming available (see Harding, 1988). These studies indicate that the long-term prognosis is far more optimistic and variable than had previously been assumed and that the condition of many with severe mental illness improves as they age. The availability of detailed life history data has also raised new questions about processes of illness episodes and recovery that are missed in analyses of change across two time points (Harding, 1988; Strauss, Hafez, Lieberman, & Harding, 1985).

Despite this renewed interest in the conceptualization of illness careers and the availability of rich, longitudinal data that would allow the empirical examination of these careers, the complexities of empirically analyzing a large number of illness careers have raised the same problems as we have seen in life course research (for example, see Harding, McCormick, Strauss, Ashikaga, & Brooks, 1989). Although a number of innovative strategies have been used to summarize patterns of illness (Harding et al., 1989; Pescosolido, 1992), further dimensions such as sequence and trajectory that are likely to be relevant for understanding illness careers have not been explored.

Although the illness career has primarily been discussed as a way of understanding the long-term dynamics of mental illness for individuals, the role of institutions and historical changes in the mental health system are embedded in the shape of these careers. Early uses of the term "illness career" specified it as a pathway shaped by the intersection between the individual and the institution (Goffman, 1961), and the illness careers of persons with severe and persistent mental illness continue to be defined by their institutional contacts. Since the 1950s the mental health system in the United States has undergone massive change, shifting from a system primarily comprised of inpatient treatment in state hospitals to a wide and complex network of inpatient, outpatient, and community care (Brown, 1985; Gronfein, 1985; Wegner, 1990). Changes in rates of inpatient hospitalization, number of patients in mental hospitals, and length of stay all suggest that illness careers of those entering the mental health system today look very different from the careers of those who entered the system in the 1940s or 1950s. Furthermore, whereas the importance of inpatient hospitalization for defining the course of mental illness has lessened, the range of institutions shaping mental illness careers has increased dramatically.

Overall rates of hospital or community service utilization provide a clear picture of institutional change, but understanding changes in how individuals experience the system is more complicated. Current cohorts not only enter a different mental health system, the cohorts themselves are also different (Mechanic, 1989), oftentimes complicating illnesses like schizophrenia or bipolar disorder with drug or alcohol use. The separation of age and period effects also becomes important for understanding observed changes in mental illness across either individuals' lives or in institutions over time. For example, although research suggests that there may be a corrective mechanism with severe mental illness as people age (DeSisto, Harding, & Brooks, 1995), the relationship of that aging process to period effects such as institutional change is not well understood. Thus, examination of illness careers across multiple cohorts can provide a means to better understand these interactive processes of change for individuals and the mental health system.

Further complications come from multiple ways of conceptualizing an illness career. Previous work has defined it in terms of stability and change in the self, general levels of well-being or functioning, presence of specific symptoms, or relationships with others (e.g., Harding, 1988; Perrucci & Targ, 1982; Pescosolido, 1992; Strauss et al., 1985). However, for exploring connections between institutional change and the course of illness (Goffman, 1961), patterns of institutional contact are a critical component of illness careers. The range of relevant institutions has broadened over time but the hospital remains an important component of the mental health system. Furthermore, because the hospital has historically been such an important institution in the treatment of severe mental illness, patterns of hospitalization provide an important marker of changes in the system. Finally, because the event of hospitalization tends to be recorded in official records, this type of information is more likely to be available, particularly over long periods of time, than are other possible markers of the illness career.

What can analyses of pattern, sequence, pace, and reversibility tell us about long-term illness careers? Patterns of hospitalization provide an important starting point for answering basic questions about these processes. If we define patterns in terms of degree of stability or change, we can then contrast more stable patterns to those of change. This type of analysis allows us to assess the variation in illness careers in a given sample and to determine those that are the most common. Identification of patterns also provides a tool for determining whether the broad shape of illness careers varies systematically by gender, race, or birth cohort.

Figure 5.1 depicts several possible ways of conceptualizing hospitalization patterns. The figure is divided by the critical event of first hospitalization. This is a necessary step in defining an illness career but there are many possible pathways leading to and from this event. The left hand side of the figure represents patterns leading into hospitalization. Patterns leading into care could be identified by several ideal types, such as those contrasting direct entry through the medical system with more indirect paths via other support systems (Pescosolido, 1991, 1992). For this type of question stability and change are not as relevant as other criteria, and thus, the lines leading into hospitalization are straight.

Patterns on the right side of the figure represent pathways leading from the first hospitalization and are organized along dimensions of stability versus change. The top and bottom pathways are defined as stable but are distinguished by very different outcomes. The bottom path represents recovery and independent living, which would apply to all persons who experience one hospitalization and then recover. The top path indicates chronic and relatively stable residential care. In earlier decades this would most likely be defined by hospitalization but in more recent times might be broadened to include other types of residential programs. The two middle paths represent change, in which the person alternates between residential care and independent living. As indicated there may be very different patterns of change, some with very frequent intervals of change and others with a more stable pattern marked by a few episodes of residential care. Identifying these paths can provide a wide range of information about the variety of ways people interact with the mental health system as well as predictors or consequences of different patterns.

Attention to the sequence of events within an illness career allows us to consider multiple sources of institutional contact rather than just focusing

Pathways to Care   Pathways from Care

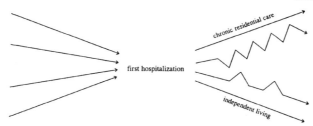

Figure 5.1. Illness career: Pattern.

on patterns of hospitalization. For example, we might contrast sequences that include a small range of institutional contacts, such as movement between hospitalization and independent living with outpatient care, to those that incorporate a broader range of institutions, such as group homes, hospitals, jails, and independent living. Do the types of sequences vary over time? Are non-medical characteristics of the patient, such as gender or race, more likely to be associated with some types of sequences rather than others? Finally, are some sequences more preferable than others in terms of restrictiveness or effects on client's health and well-being?

In Figure 5.2 several hypothetical sequences are shown. For simple sequences such as these, movement from the hospital to a group home to independent living could be contrasted with alternate sequences such as movement from independent living to jail. Even in this example, sequences might be elaborated to take into account variations in length, type of institution, as well as the order of contact. Simple sequences with relatively few events, like those represented in Figure 5.2, might be able to be identified by visual examination of the data. Optimal matching techniques would become necessary for the differentiation of more complex sequences, such as those that include a wide range of institutional settings or incorporate additional information such as length of time in any one setting.

Pace could also be incorporated within a sequence analysis to take into account the space between institutional changes, but questions about the pace of a single event like hospitalization can also provide valuable clues about illness careers. Analyses of the pace of hospitalization might first examine whether factors predicting the timing of the first hospitalization differ from

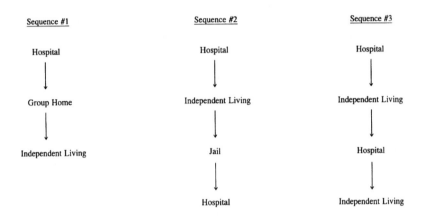

Figure 5.2. Illness career: Sequence.

those predicting the timing of subsequent ones. Regularities in timing, such as whether the timing between the second and third hospitalization tends to be shorter than that between first and second could then be explored. Attention to pace might also raise questions about the extent of variability in the pace of multiple hospitalizations. For example, among those with several admittances into the hospital, do some people have episodes that are more evenly spaced, whereas others have a more uneven pace? If so, it suggests that even for persons with multiple hospitalizations there may be varying pathways, and attention to this variability might raise new questions about the effects of hospitalization on the illness career.

Figure 5.3 illustrates these different ways pace may help to identify variations in illness careers. For this example, we include paths that all consist of four hospitalizations. Attention to regularities in the pace of hospitalizations is illustrated by the first two paths. These paths show differences in the timing before the first and second hospitalization but greater similarity in timing after the second hospitalization. Such a process would suggest that there may be a wide range of factors influencing the timing of earlier hospitalizations, but after a particular point in the illness

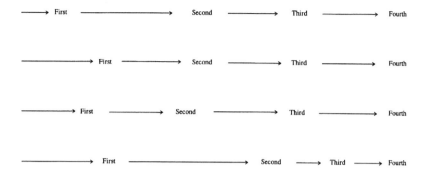

Figure 5.3. Illness career: Pace.
NOTE: Length of arrow indicates elapsed time.

career (e.g., the second hospitalization), timing is less variable. The bottom two paths illustrate the concept of variability in spacing, contrasting a pattern that is evenly spaced to one that mixes a long interval with a series of short intervals. If this type of variation was found among persons with multiple hospitalizations, it would suggest the need to further explore differential causes and consequences of these types of pathways.

Finally, the concept of reversibility can be used to explore the stabilization of mental illness. A number of sociological theories suggest that social processes such as labeling or institutionalization can create stable mental illness (Goffman, 1961; Scheff, 1966) but there are relatively few studies examining this process. Unlike analyses of pattern and sequence, which contrast different types of illness careers, reversibility focuses on a single pathway and thus is ideal for examining processes of stabilization. Is there a trajectory of mental illness that is marked by increasing hospitalization or residential care? If so, are there turning points that increase people's likelihood of entering such a trajectory? Where are they? Conversely, are there other events, such as establishing a new program, that increase people's chances of changing to an alternate path?

Figure 5.4 illustrates one approach to answering these questions. To simplify interpretation, the illness career is defined solely in terms of hospitalization, and stable mental illness is a state in which one has a very low probability of changing to an alternate path, such as independent living. The process begins with the first hospitalization since this is a necessary event in stable hospitalization. An initial question is whether there is a path that is

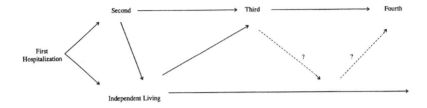

Figure 5.4. Illness career: Reversibility.

increasingly difficult to reverse. For example, with each hospitalization, does one's chance of changing to an alternate path decrease? As one experiences three or four hospitalizations, we would expect that the chances of moving to an alternate path such as long-term independent living would become rare to non-existent. If so, this suggests a process that is increasingly difficult to reverse.

A second step in analyzing reversibility is to identify key turning points that lead people toward or away from stable mental illness. For example, first hospitalization is an initial turning point that increases one's chances of stable mental illness but at this point there are still many alternate pathways. With each subsequent hospitalization we would expect the likelihood of alternate pathways to decrease, but it may be that this process is not linear. A second hospitalization may still leave many paths open but with a third hospitalization this range may narrow dramatically. If such a pattern was found it would suggest that the third hospitalization serves as an important turning point for a pathway of stable mental illness. Other events might also be incorporated to determine whether they serve as turning points either toward or away from a path of stable mental illness.

Existing methods for the analysis of transitions (e.g., event history methods) and especially those for the analysis of repeated events (Petersen, 1991) are directly applicable to these types of questions. Analyses of reversibility and turning points differ from single transition analyses because reversibility connects transition analyses to the broader process in which they are embedded. To achieve this, an analysis of reversibility might combine descriptive analyses of patterns or sequences with transition analyses of specific turning points within those patterns. Similar methodologies developed for the analysis of career lines and branching structures could also be adapted to analyze a wider range of trajectory processes (Althauser & van Veen, 1994; Rosenbaum, 1984; Spilerman, 1977).

◈ CONCLUSIONS

The life course perspective provides a framework for understanding aging and social change. Concepts like transition, trajectory, and cohort focus our attention on processes across individual lives and the ways those processes are defined by history, culture, and social institutions. However, empirical investigations of these issues have only begun to explore linkages and pathways across the life course. Analyses of relationships between events at different points across the life course and general descriptions of patterns provide important first steps in this direction. But, further investigation of particular dimensions, such as sequence, pace, and reversibility are important for examining which elements are most relevant for a given process. Comparison between multiple concepts can also provide different types of information. As a first step in this direction, this paper reviews four concepts of long-term process and discusses how each could be applied to questions about individual aging and social change.

Whereas these concepts are not a solution to broader dilemmas presented by the intersection of individual aging and social change, they provide a wider range of conceptual tools for examining these processes in different ways. For example, although many of the methods used to capture long-term process stem from challenges to long-standing methodological traditions that ignore process and narrative (Abbott, 1992, 1995), they can be used within traditional methodological frameworks. Assumptions about the importance of sequence contrast sharply with Markovian methods that assume that prior history is not relevant because it will be expressed through more recent events. But, in many cases the construction of sequences will ultimately serve as a way to create a new variable (sequence) that is used as a dependent or independent variable in more standard regression methods. Similarly, attention to these concepts cannot step outside of assumptions about stability, change, individual, and society that frame which questions are asked and how they are asked, but they can move us toward more dynamic conceptualization of these relationships. If we are to meet the challenge of moving past the reduction of social contexts to backdrops for the unfolding process of aging or a view of lives as fully determined by social structure, we must continue to develop concepts that capture dynamics in a variety of ways.

CHAPTER SIX

Using Repeated Surveys to Study Aging and Social Change

GLENN FIREBAUGH
DANA L. HAYNIE

Repeated surveys ask the same questions to *different* samples of people. Well-known examples include the General Social Survey and the National Election Study. Because a new sample is selected at each measurement period, specific individuals cannot be followed over time. In repeated surveys, cohorts of individuals born at the same time (birth cohorts)—*not* the individuals themselves—are followed as they age. This feature has important implications for how repeated surveys can and cannot be used in the study of aging and social change.

We begin then by noting that repeated surveys are ill-suited for studying specific individuals as they age. That said, we will not dwell on the point; as the title of the paper suggests we will focus on appropriate uses of repeated surveys in the study of aging and social change. Three things that repeated survey data, as opposed to panel data, do very well are: (a) allowing the estimation of net change in Y for some target population; (b) allowing the estimation of cohort replacement's contribution to that net change—so repeated surveys can be used to assess the implications, for change in some population, of cohorts' "aging out of" and "aging into" that population; (c) allowing the study of changes in individual-level *relationships*—that is, changes in the effects of X on Y over time (one meaning of the term "social change"). Changes in the effects of X on Y can be studied using either fixed-effect or random-effect models. In this chapter, we describe a simple fixed-effect model as well as a more sophisticated random-effect multilevel model for studying changes in individual-level relationships.

The objective of this chapter is to elaborate and illustrate the three uses of repeated surveys: the study of net change at the macrolevel, the study of cohort replacement effects, the study of changing individual-level parameters. Though many of the points we make will not be new to experts in survey research design, this paper provides the opportunity for reflection about the nature of the questions we might ask of repeated survey data and about the nature of the analyses one would need to address those questions.

◇ NET CHANGE

Repeated surveys maintain up-to-date samples of the target population at each measurement period because a fresh sample is drawn for each survey. This refreshment of the sample is in contrast to panel surveys, where the same individuals are reinterviewed; so without some sort of modification (for example, rotating panels: see Duncan & Kalton, 1987), panel surveys do not maintain up-to-date samples of changing target populations such as "adults in the United States" or "the U.S. electorate."

By "net change" we mean change in some characteristic of a population (e.g., change in percent living in poverty). Net change in a discernible direction is called a trend. Net change is to be distinguished from "gross change," which refers to volume of change at the individual level. If 18 % of U.S. households are below the poverty threshold in two consecutive years, then we can say that there has been no net change in poverty; but we cannot rule out gross change, since the stability in the aggregate figure most likely reflects the offsetting forces of some households moving above the poverty threshold and others falling below the threshold (Duncan, Coe, Corcoran, Hill, & Morgan, 1984). Or, to use another example, if the percentage who identify themselves politically as Democrats remains constant over the 1990s, it does not necessarily follow that no one switched political parties during the 1990s. It is possible to have zero net change in the face of substantial gross change. Interestingly, the converse is also possible—net change in the absence of gross change. For example, suppose "once a Democrat, always a Democrat," and similarly for Republican and Independent—then there would be no party-switching, yet there could be change in percentage Democrat due to cohort replacement, as (for example) older more Democratic "New Deal" cohorts die off and are replaced by younger more Republican Yuppie cohorts. In any case, it is important to distinguish net change from gross change and to keep in mind that repeated surveys are designed to study net change, not gross change (Duncan & Kalton, 1987).

Repeated surveys are well suited for estimating net change in a population precisely because they allow for the infusion of new cohorts and the winnowing of old cohorts by maintaining updated samples of the population. In contrast, by failing to include new cohorts, the samples in unmodified panel designs become, over time, less and less representative of a changing population. So panel surveys with a fixed sample are ill-suited for studying social change, if by "social change" we mean change in aggregate characteristics such as "percentage Democrat" or "percentage below the poverty threshold."

Figure 6.1 depicts an example of social change in the sense of aggregate change. Figure 6.1 is a (smoothed) graph of the odds of women voting divided by the odds of men voting in the United States, based on the National Election Study (NES). As the graph indicates, the relative propensities of men and women to vote in national elections has changed substantially in the United States over the past four decades. Four decades ago there was a substantial gender gap in voting, with women's odds of voting being about 60% of men's odds of voting. Today men and women vote at virtually the same rates.

It is important to stress that the National Election Study is a repeated survey. As we will demonstrate later, had we used fixed-sample panel data based on a 1950 sample, we would have concluded that the gender gap in voting participation has remained stable over time—a conclusion that would be incorrect.

Since Figure 6.1 is about gender gaps in voting, why should Figure 6.1 be of interest to those who study aging? The answer lies in the *reason* for the gender gap and for the closing of the gender gap. It turns out that sex differences in voting in the United States (for whites, anyway) are restricted to the Nineteenth Amendment cohorts, that is, to those men and women who came of age in the United States during or just after the era when women could not vote (Firebaugh & Chen, 1995). Recall that with repeated survey data we can follow cohorts as they age. When we follow the Nineteenth Amendment cohorts from elections in the 1950s through elections in the 1980s, what is notable is what did not happen: voting rates did not converge for men and women. Nineteenth Amendment women continued to vote at lower rates than their male contemporaries for 30, 40, and 50 years after the passage of the Nineteenth Amendment, which enfranchised women. In this case, then, *aging did not notably diminish the effects of adolescent imprinting*—all the more remarkable in light of the *absence* of a gender gap for post-Nineteenth Amendment cohorts. The data show that the daughters and

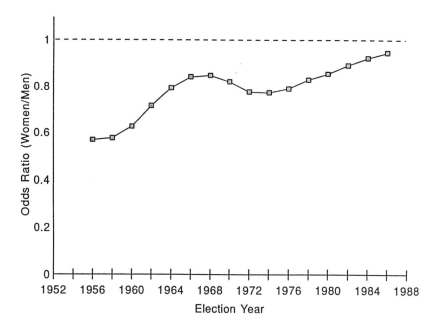

Figure 6.1. Odds of voting, women versus men, over three decades of U.S. national elections (five-year moving averages used to smooth trend).

granddaughters of Nineteenth Amendment women vote at the same rate as their male contemporaries (Table 6.1—adapted from Firebaugh & Chen, 1995, Table 2).

If the daughters and granddaughters of Nineteenth Amendment women vote at the same rate as their male contemporaries, then we expect the gender gap to diminish as the Nineteenth Amendment cohorts "age out" of the population. That is exactly what happened in the United States, as noted earlier (Figure 6.1). Upon closer inspection we find that gender gaps are relatively stable over time within birth cohorts (Firebaugh & Chen, 1995, Table 4). Hence, had we used the usual panel design that follows the same sample of individuals over time, we would have missed the key point that the gender gap is disappearing.

◇ **COHORT REPLACEMENT EFFECTS**

The narrowing of the gender gap in voting in U.S. national elections is due to cohort replacement. Since the gender gap is restricted to the Nineteenth

Table 6.1. Cohort-Specific Sex Differences in Voting in National Elections, 1952-1988.[a]

Independent Variable	Logit[b]	p-value
Sex differences by cohort category:		
born before 1896	−0.76	<.0001
born 1896-1905	−0.68	<.0001
born 1906-1915	−0.36	.0001
born 1916-1925	−0.25	.002
born 1926-1935	−0.04	.61
born 1936-1945	0.06	.47
born 1946-1955	−0.03	.68
born after 1955	−0.06	.61

SOURCE: Adapted from Firebaugh and Davis (1995, Table 2).
a. Coefficients estimated using logistic regression (n=23,973 whites). Results for covariates suppressed to save space.
b. A negative sign indicates that women are less likely to vote than men.

Amendment cohorts, the gap narrows as the Nineteenth Amendment cohorts gradually disappear and are replaced by cohorts that display no gender gap. This observation brings us to our second major point: unlike fixed-sample panel data, repeated survey data permit the estimation of cohort replacement's contribution to net change.

Because repeated surveys follow birth cohorts as they age and add cohorts as they are added to the target population (e.g., become old enough to vote), repeated surveys permit us to estimate the contributions of within-cohort change and population turnover to social change (net change for the population). Such methods are described elsewhere (Firebaugh, 1989, 1992, 1997; Firebaugh & Davis, 1988). Here we want to make the point that—by maintaining an up-to-date sample of the target population as it changes—repeated surveys permit us to estimate the population turnover component of net change in some variable Y. With regard to the gender gap in voting, for example, we could estimate (a) how much of the overall convergence in voting is due to within-cohort convergence as cohorts age and (b) how much of the convergence is due to cohort replacement, as the Nineteenth Amendment cohorts die off and are replaced in the electorate by their daughters, sons, granddaughters, and grandsons.

Panel data designs based on a fixed sample do not permit such a decomposition. To be sure, not all panels are based on fixed samples; panels can be designed with a view to adding cohorts, so that up-to-date samples of the population are maintained. But in doing so we are in effect incorporating the defining feature of repeated surveys: we are selecting a different sample at different points in time. The difference is that with a panel design a significant subset of the new sample overlaps with prior samples, whereas in repeated surveys we expect little or no overlap in the samples. Of course, it is also possible to create a hybrid design by adding a panel component to repeated surveys—a design that Kish (1983) calls a "split panel."

⊗ CHANGE IN INDIVIDUAL-LEVEL EFFECTS

Third, repeated surveys permit us to study social change in the sense of changing individual-level parameters. This is an obvious but underutilized application for repeated surveys. Two strategies immediately come to mind. One strategy is to use interaction terms to capture change (if any) in the effect of X on Y over time. This strategy is essentially descriptive, in the sense that it addresses the question of whether or not effects have remained constant over time; if an effect has changed, there is no attempt to model the causes for the change.

The second strategy attempts to account for the causes of changing X-effects in terms of changing environmental conditions. To locate causes, individual-level parameters are expressed as functions of macrolevel characteristics that vary over time. So the second strategy is a multilevel strategy, using data at both the individual and aggregate levels. The distinguishing feature of this multilevel model is that *time* is the context; most social science applications of the multilevel model have defined contexts by schools or regions.

Observe that the number of contexts equals the number of surveys in repeated survey data (separate surveys taken at different times). In the past this feature limited the utility of a multilevel strategy for analyzing repeated survey data, since there were not enough cases to permit reliable estimation of aggregate-level effects. The multilevel strategy becomes increasingly appropriate, however, as repeated surveys continue to cumulate. Currently there are 20 General Social Surveys (GSS) and somewhat more National Election Studies (NES), and in both data sets new surveys are being added every other year (the GSS has recently changed from an annual to biennial design).

The remainder of this chapter is devoted to an exegesis of the two strategies for using repeated surveys to examine changing individual-level effects. Both can be described as employing "varying-parameter" models since both strategies model change in the effect of X on Y (change in the effect of X on Y *over time,* so the term "changing-parameter" model is also apt). The first strategy adds interaction terms to the individual-level equations, whereas the multilevel strategy begins by adding equations that model the individual-level parameters themselves as functions of macrovariables and a disturbance term. The first strategy is a fixed-effect approach, whereas the multilevel strategy is a random-effects approach. Depending on the nature of the dependent variable, the interaction models often can be estimated with ordinary least squares, whereas the multilevel models require more sophisticated estimation methods.

◇ DETECTING CHANGE IN INDIVIDUAL-LEVEL EFFECTS: THE INTERACTION MODEL

With repeated survey data, it is a straightforward task to use interaction terms in fixed-effect models to test the null hypothesis that the effects of predictor variables are constant from survey 1 to survey 2. Following Firebaugh (1997), the general model for two surveys can be expressed in vector notation as follows:

$$E(Y) = \alpha + \gamma D_{YR} + X\beta + XD_{YR}\,\delta \qquad (1)$$

The D_{YR} is a dummy variable for one of the surveys, X is a vector of predictor variables other than D_{YR}, and β and δ are vectors of parameters. If there are q variables in vector X, then X and XD_{YR} each has dimension lxq, and β and δ each has dimension qxl.

The interaction terms, X times D_{YR}, model the changing X-effects. The D_{YR} is a dummy variable coded 1 for a given year (or month, or week, depending on the frequency of measurement). The X can be either continuous or categorical.

To show the range of the model, Equation 1 states it in general form, with changing-parameter interaction terms for each of the regressors. In applying the model, researchers most often will want to restrict the interaction terms to some *subset* of Xs, especially if the list of regressors is long. The principle for including an interaction term in a model is the same as the principle for including any variable in a model: There must be some good reason (theory, prior evidence, or sensible argument) to believe that the variable has an effect. The greatest danger for abuse of the changing-parameter models lies with researchers on fishing expeditions for time-dependent effects. Interaction terms of this sort should be added only if there is reason to believe that a regressor's effect has changed over time. If interaction terms are added willy-nilly in a model with many regressors, some change in sample coefficients is likely to be statistically significant due solely to chance, and real change in parameters is likely to be missed as standard errors are inflated by multicollinearity.

Suppose we want to study the changing effect of class position on party identification in the United States. Is it the case that professionals and managers are moving in opposite directions, with professionals increasingly identified as Democrats and managers increasingly as Republicans (Hout, Brooks, & Manza, 1995)? Based on two General Social Surveys a number of years apart (say the 1974 and 1994 surveys), we could do two parallel analyses—one for 1974 data and one for 1994 data—and compare the coefficients. Yet with that approach it would not be immediately obvious which differences are statistically significant and which are not. To determine whether or not *differences* between sample coefficients in separate samples (here, separate years) are statistically significant, we must perform the appropriate significance tests. One strategy is to perform separate regression analyses for each of the samples and use the formulas given in Graybill and Iyer (1994, pp. 436-447) to calculate *t*-tests for the differences of interest. With repeated survey data, however, that strategy is seldom necessary, because data collectors most often combine new samples with prior samples to form merged data sets for distribution. With such merged data sets, it is generally easier to test for changing parameters by estimating a single model with interaction terms, and that is the strategy of Equation 1.

Because the model expressed in Equation 1 uses just two surveys, it exploits only a fraction of the data available in the GSS on class and political party. How do we extend the varying-parameter model for two surveys to multiple surveys? As noted, the GSS currently comprises some 20 separate surveys. Consistent with Equation 1, we could include interaction terms for each of the predictors for each of 19 years (20 minus the reference year). If we had five predictors to test for varying effects, we would have 95 regression coefficients to examine. To summarize those 95 coefficients, one might correlate them with macrolevel variables—a step toward multilevel analysis.

Multilevel analysis provides an alternative to such inelegance. DiPrete and Grusky (1990a, 1990b) have applied multilevel methods to 14 annual surveys in the General Social Survey (1972-1987) to estimate a varying-parameter model of socioeconomic status (SES). More specifically, they examine change in the effects of education, race, and father's SES on respondent's SES over the 1970s and 1980s. They estimate separate models for men and women. And they do something that cannot be done in a two-survey analysis: they model change in the effect of education, race, and father's SES as a function of change in macrolevel variables (e.g., government policy, labor supply and demand). They conclude that the effects of ascriptive characteristics such as race and father's SES continued to erode in the 1970s and 1980s (albeit at a slower rate in the latter years) and that the erosion of the importance of such ascriptive characteristics is in fact affected by macrolevel characteristics such as government policy.

The DiPrete-Grusky analyses nicely illustrate how researchers can study social change through the application of multilevel methods to repeated survey data. The next section elaborates the point by offering a brief introduction to multilevel methodology, with an eye toward its application to repeated surveys.

◌ Modeling Change in Individual-Level Effects: The Multilevel Model Applied to Repeated Survey Data

The changing-parameter model with interaction terms represented by Equation 1 (above) is designed to detect—not explain—change in individual-level relationships. To explain change in the X-Y relationship, we can think about time as a context and ask: What are the telling macrochanges over time, that is, what are the key differences between the time contexts that bear on the X-Y relationship?

This sort of thinking leads naturally to a multilevel model with time-varying aggregate-level variables as the contextual variables (as the regressors in a model predicting the individual-level *coefficients*). In other words, we employ a model where the individual-level relationships are themselves expressed as a function of aggregate characteristics that change over time. Social scientists understand how to estimate such models much better now than they did a decade ago, due in large part to the interest in models to estimate school effects (for example Bryk & Raudenbush, 1992; Goldstein, 1987; Willms & Raudenbush, 1989). The multilevel approach inspired by the school effects literature can—with modification (DiPrete & Grusky, 1990a, 1990b)—be applied to the changing-parameter situation where it is time, not school, that forms the context.

The multilevel approach extends and complicates the changing-parameter model of Equation 1 (above) in three important ways. First and most obvious, it adds aggregate-level regressors to the model. The aggregate variables are added to account for change in the slopes *and intercepts* of the individual-level relationships.

Second, the multilevel approach mandates multiple surveys (that is, multiple contexts) and uses them all. Since each survey is one case in the aggregate equation, multilevel models for changing-parameter analysis highlight the importance of continued data series such as the GSS. As noted above, and also by DiPrete and Grusky (1990a, p. 339), multilevel models for repeated surveys should become increasingly important as the GSS, the NES, and other repeated surveys continue to cumulate. Reliable estimation of such models would have been impossible in earlier decades, when re-peated surveys did not have sufficient measurement points for the aggregate-level variables.

Third, estimation of multilevel models generally is more complex. Ordi-nary least squares is inappropriate when the error terms in the macro equation are nonzero (Bryk & Raudenbush, 1992; DiPrete & Forristal, 1994). And estimating multilevel models of repeated surveys is further complicated by the likely serial correlation of the contexts. As noted earlier, the distinguish-ing feature of the type of multilevel analysis proposed here is that the context is *time,* not school or region. This feature presents estimation complications arising from the likely serial correlation of the disturbances at the aggregate level (DiPrete & Grusky, 1990a, 1990b).

To appreciate the complications added by a multilevel strategy, it is useful to consider examples. Multilevel models are distinguished by the presence of regressors at two or more levels of aggregation, which Bryk and Rauden-bush (1992) denote as "level 1" for the microlevel and "level 2" for the first macrolevel. It is convenient to begin by representing the model with separate equations for the level-1 and level-2 relations. To fix basic concepts, consider the simple case where there is one level 1 regressor (X) and two level 2 regressors (Z_1 and Z_2).

The level-1 equation is:

$$Y_{ij} = \beta_{0j} + \beta_{1j} (X_{ij} - \overline{X}_j) + e_{ij}, \qquad (2)$$

where "i" indexes individual and "j" indexes group (in the case of modeling change in individual-level relationships, "group" refers to survey). So X_{ij} is the value of X for the ith individual in the jth survey, and $\overline{X}_j$ is the mean of X for the jth survey. Thus $(X_{ij} - \overline{X}_j)$ is the deviation score on X, that is, it is the deviation of individual i's score on X from the average score on X at the time i was surveyed.

Why do multilevel models use deviation scores for the Xs? The answer centers on the intercept. Note the subscript "j" attached to the intercept term in Equation 2. In multilevel models, the intercept is not assumed to be constant for all surveys but, rather, is assumed to be a function of macrolevel characteristics. By using deviation scores, the intercepts have a substantive interpretation: They are Y-means. Thus β_{01} is the mean of Y for the first survey, β_{02} is the mean of Y for the second survey, and so on.

As Bryk and Raudenbush (1992) argue, an unambiguous interpretation for the level-1 intercepts is important in multilevel analysis because these intercepts are—along with the level-1 slopes—modeled as functions of macrolevel characteristics. Assuming two Zs, the level-2 equations are:

$$\beta_{0j} = \gamma_{00} + \gamma_{01}Z_{1j} + \gamma_{02}Z_{2j} + u_{0j} \tag{3a}$$
$$\beta_{1j} = \gamma_{10} + \gamma_{11}Z_{1j} + \gamma_{12}Z_{2j} + u_{1j} \tag{3b}$$

Observe that the dependent variables in the level-2 equations are *parameters* from the level-1 equations. In Equation 3a, the level-1 intercepts are expressed as functions of Z_1 and Z_2; in Equation 3b, the level-1 *slopes* are expressed as functions of Z_1 and Z_2. To prevent the confusion of the level-2 parameters, we use the notation of Bryk and Raudenbush (1992), where the first subscript for gamma identifies the level-1 parameter that is being used as the dependent variable (coded 0 for the intercept, 1 for the regression coefficient for X_1, and so on). The second subscript for gamma is the conventional notation of 0 for the intercept *in that equation,* 1 for the parameter for the first regressor (Z_1), 2 for the parameter for Z_2, and so on. Substantively, then, γ_{01} is the effect of contextual variable Z_1 on the group means and γ_{11} is its effect on the slope, that is, γ_{11} is Z_1's effect on the *effect* of X on Y.

The level-2 equations imply an error term that violates key ordinary least squares (OLS) assumptions. This becomes apparent when we substitute Equations 3a and 3b into Equation 2:

$$
\begin{aligned}
Y_{ij} &= \beta_{0j} + \beta_{1j}(X_{ij}-\bar{X}_j) + e_{ij} \\
&= (\gamma_{00} + \gamma_{01}Z_{1j} + \gamma_{02}Z_{2j} + u_{0j}) + \\
&\quad (\gamma_{10} + \gamma_{11}Z_{1j} + \gamma_{12}Z_{2j} + u_{1j})(X_{ij}-\bar{X}_j) + e_{ij} \\
&= \gamma_{00} + \gamma_{01}Z_{1j} + \gamma_{02}Z_{2j} + \gamma_{10}(X_{ij}-\bar{X}_j) + \gamma_{11}Z_{1j}(X_{ij}-\bar{X}_j) \\
&\quad + \gamma_{12}Z_{2j}(X_{ij}-\bar{X}_j) + \{u_{1j}(X_{ij}-\bar{X}_j) + u_{0j} + e_{ij}\}
\end{aligned}
\tag{4}
$$

The error term in Equation 4—$u_{1j}(X_{ij}-\bar{X}_j) + u_{0j} + e_{ij}$—implies that the errors will be heteroscedastic and correlated across level-1 units. As a result, OLS applied to Equation 4 will produce biased significance tests, even if conventional assumptions are met for u_{1j}, u_{0j}, and e_{ij}.

Because the problem results from the presence of the macrolevel errors (u_{1j} and u_{0j}) in the microlevel equation, the problem would disappear if we could assume that the macrolevel errors were zero. As DiPrete and Forristal (1994) note, the multilevel or "contextual" analysis of the 1970s and early 1980s (see the literature reviews in Blalock, 1984; Boyd & Iversen, 1979; and Firebaugh, 1978) in effect assumed zero errors in the macrolevel equations. OLS, then, was the estimator of choice in that first generation of multilevel analyses. The model represented by Equation 4 belongs to a second generation of models that has been referred to variously as "multi-level" or "multilevel linear" (DiPrete & Forristal, 1994; Mason, Wong, & Entwisle, 1983), "random-effects" (Laird & Ware, 1982), "covariance components" (Dempster, Rubin, & Tsutakawa, 1981) and "hierarchical linear" (Bryk & Raudenbush, 1992).

Whatever the term for them, the second generation of micro-macro models calls for more sophisticated estimation methods. Those methods have been well-developed for the conventional case where j indexes groups (e.g., schools), and software is now readily available for researchers wanting to analyze the conventional micro-macro case (stand-alone programs include GENMOD, HLM, ML2, and VARCL: see Kreft, de Leeuw, & Kim, 1990, for a review). Unfortunately, methods are not as well developed for the case where j indexes survey (the repeated surveys case). The problem is that the surveys are lined up in time, so errors in the level-2 equations most likely are serially correlated, resulting in biased estimates of standard errors.

DiPrete and Grusky (1990a, 1990b) were faced with that estimation problem in their use of repeated-survey data to examine change in the individual-level determinants of socioeconomic status for men and women in the United States. They hypothesized that macrolevel changes in the United States during the 1970s and 1980s—specifically government policy and the labor market—led to palpable changes in the effects of education, race, and father's SES on respondent's SES. To test that hypothesis, they applied generation-2 multilevel analysis to 14 surveys in the GSS (spanning 1972-1987) to model change in the effects of education, race, and father's SES as a function of change in macrolevel variables. To measure the key macrolevel changes, DiPrete and Grusky (1990a) used indicators of government policy and of the bureaucratic structure of the labor force, and DiPrete and Grusky (1990b) extended the model by adding indicators of labor supply and demand.

It is important to review how the DiPrete-Grusky approach differs from the changing-parameter approach described in the previous section. The interaction models focus on just two surveys and aim only to determine if individual-level relationships have changed. The DiPrete-Grusky studies, by contrast, attempt to model the change as a function of change in macrolevel variables. As such, they attempt something that could not be done with just two surveys, since $N = 2$ is insufficient for estimating the macroequations.

The DiPrete-Grusky studies conclude that the effect of ascriptive characteristics such as race and father's SES eroded over the 1970s and 1980s in the United States. To arrive at that conclusion, DiPrete and Grusky (1990a) developed a generalized least-squares (GLS) estimator for dealing with the serial correlation problem in multilevel analyses of repeated surveys and applied it to their stratification model (DiPrete & Grusky, 1990a, 1990b). To illustrate the application of multilevel analysis to repeated surveys, we summarize their (1990a) results here and compare them to results we obtained by a replication using HLM2. Though we employ the same data and estimate the same models, HLM2 does not adjust for serial correlation in the macroequations. So we know our results will differ from those of DiPrete and Grusky; the question is, by how much.

Because this example is intended only to introduce readers to the models employed and output generated by multilevel analysis, we do not dwell on the question of which results most accurately represent stratification processes in the United States. Nor do we attempt to tie our results to grander themes in the stratification literature. We present this example for heuristic purposes only.

The DiPrete and Grusky (1990a) microlevel equation contains one dependent variable and three independent variables. Hence their multilevel model comprises one microequation and four macroequations (one macroequation for each of the parameters in the micromodel). The dependent variable is respondent's SES (as measured by the Duncan SEI score for respondent's occupation). The independent variables are race (coded white = 1), education (years of schooling completed, truncated at 17), and father's SES (Duncan SEI score). Thus there are four βs in the model: β_{0j}, the intercept; β_{1j}, the effect of race; β_{2j}, the effect of father's SES; and β_{3j}, the effect of education. Here j indexes survey. Each of the βs is assumed to be a function of either government policy (measured by annual expenditures of the EEOC—denoted Z_1) or bureaucratic personnel policies (measured by percentage of the labor force employed as personnel specialists—denoted Z_2), or both.

Table 6.2 reports the results. For the sake of comparison we repeat the OLS and EGLS (estimated GLS) estimates of DiPrete and Grusky (1990a) in the first two columns. Then we report our own results in the column labeled HLM. Estimates are reported separately for men ($n = 5,232$) and women (n = 4,011). Table 6.2 compares only the t-ratios for the three estimators. We do not report the slopes because we were not confident that we had successfully reproduced the metric for SES employed by DiPrete and Grusky. In this instance the more critical comparison centers on the t-ratios, since failure to adjust for serial correlation leads to biased estimates of standard errors, not slopes.

Aside from γ_{00} for men, results are relatively consistent for the three estimation methods. All three estimators indicate that EEOC (Z_1) lowers the intercept for men and raises the intercept for women (line 1b of Table 6.2) and that EEOC expenditures lower the socioeconomic advantage of whites (note the negative t-ratios in line 2b of Table 6.2). The EEOC expenditures also appear to affect SES returns to education, but the effect is erratic and in unexpected directions: expenditures have a positive effect on returns to education for men but no effect for women (line 4b). Coefficients for Z_2—number of personnel specialists—approach significance only in the case of the effect of father's SES on daughter's SES (line 3b). The results indicate that increase in personnel specialists reduces the intergenerational transmission of SES but only for women.

◇ **SUMMARY AND CONCLUSION**

In keeping with the book's theme, this chapter has examined how repeated survey data can be used for the study of aging and social change. We argued that repeated surveys are especially well-suited for the study of net change or trends; for the estimation of cohort replacement's contribution to net change (aging is key here, since cohort replacement occurs as cohorts age into and out of the target population); and for the study of changing individual-level effects.

First, repeated surveys can be used to study net change, or trends. Trend analysis asks whether the average value of Y is changing over time for some group. Hence in trend analysis the expected value of Y is expressed as a function of time. Because these are trends for groups, not individuals, trend analysis as described here is macrolevel. Repeated surveys are especially well-suited for trend analysis because they maintain an up-to-date sample of the target population.

Trend analyses typically employ a limited number of variables, so trend models tend to be fairly simple. In the simplest case, trend analysis is bivariate: a variable Y and time. Very often, though, the purpose of trend analysis is to determine if trends differ for population subgroups. In that case,

Table 6.2. Estimates of t-ratios for a Multilevel Model of the Stratification Process[a]

Parameter[b,c]	Estimates for Men (n = 5,232)			Estimates for Women (n = 4,011)		
	OLS	EGLS	HLM	OLS	EGLS	HLM
1. Level-1 Intercept (β_{0j})						
a. Level-2 Intercept (γ_{00})	−2.29	−1.97	2.63	−5.11	−4.64	−3.22
b. Slope for Z_1 (γ_{01})	−2.82	−2.17	−2.42	1.70	1.57	1.53
2. Effect of Race (β_{1j})						
a. Level-2 Intercept (γ_{10})	3.25	3.41	3.60	3.01	2.81	3.45
b. Slope for Z_1 (γ_{11})	−1.70	−1.87	−2.14	−1.19	−1.21	−2.04
3. Effect of Father's SES (β_{2j})						
a. Level-2 Intercept (γ_{20})	1.53	1.63	1.66	2.18	2.21	2.18
b. Slope for Z_2 (γ_{22})	−0.86	−0.99	−1.19	−1.86	−1.89	−1.96
4. Effect of Education (β_{3j})						
a. Level-2 Intercept (γ_{30})	3.73	0.88	1.61	3.99	1.37	2.43
b. Slope for Z_1 (γ_{31})	3.04	1.08	2.73	−0.79	−0.64	−0.14
c. Slope for Z_2 (γ_{32})	0.38	0.02	0.73	1.07	0.59	1.45

SOURCES:
(1) 1972-1987 GSS (Davis & Smith, 1994) for microlevel variables.
(2) DiPrete and Grusky (1990a, Table 2) for macrolevel variables.
a. Estimates using OLS (ordinary least squares), EGLS (feasible generalized least squares), and HLM2, respectively. OLS estimates and GLS estimates are taken from DiPrete and Grusky (1990a, Table 3 and Appendix Table B). HLM estimates are from HLM2.
b. Variables are coded as follows:
SES - occupation, coded as Duncan SEI score;
Race - 1=white, 0=nonwhite;
Education - completed years of schooling, truncated at 17 years.
c. Macrolevel variables: Z_1 is employment policy (annual expenditures of the EEOC); Z_2 is bureaucracy (personnel specialists).

there are at least three variables: Y, time, and a variable defining the subgroups.

Second, repeated surveys can be used to estimate the cohort replacement component of net change. By following cohorts over time, and by adding cohorts as they age into the target population, repeated survey data can be used to estimate the separate contributions of cohort succession and within-cohort change to an observed trend.

Third, repeated surveys can be used to study changing individual-level effects. This application of repeated surveys is illustrated by the DiPrete-Grusky multilevel analysis of social stratification in the United States. In general, repeated surveys estimate the time-dependence of individual-level relationships by employing some form of a varying-parameter model. In one form interaction terms are used to capture change in the effects of X on Y over time. In another form of the varying-parameter model—multilevel analysis—individual-level parameters are expressed as functions of macro-level variables. The latter application of the varying-parameter model to repeated survey data sets is likely to become more commonplace as those data sets continue to add surveys.

CHAPTER SEVEN

Aging, Social Change, and Conservatism

*The Link Between Historical and
Biographical Time in the Study
of Political Identities*

DUANE F. ALWIN

◈ INTRODUCTION

Few other generalizations about human behavior are as time-worn as the idea
that people become more conservative as they age. Glenn (1974, p. 177)
noted that this view was "prevalent among social scientists, as well as the
lay public." However, he argued that, although "there are theoretical reasons
to believe that certain dimensions of . . . aging contribute to some kinds of
conservatism," there was little in the way of scientific evidence to back it up.
Rather than lead people to develop conservative views on social issues or
adopt a conservative political ideology, if anything, aging contributes to
conservatism only in the sense that attitudes probably become somewhat less
susceptible to change, regardless of the political stance they reflect. How-

AUTHOR'S NOTE: The research reported here is based on a project titled "Aging, Personality
and Social Change," supported by a series of grants from the National Institute on Aging
(R01-AG04743-06). Data used here were made available through the facilities of the Inter-
University Consortium of Social & Political Research, University of Michigan. The author
acknowledges the research assistance of David Klingel and Becky Bahlibi.

ever, because of "intransigent methodological problems that plague the study of aging effects," we may never be able to replace the "conventional wisdom" with "scientific truth" (Glenn, 1974, p. 176-177).

In this chapter, I re-examine the link between aging and conservatism, within a set of more broadly construed issues concerning the linkage between aging and social change. Specifically, I am interested in how *the study of stability in human lives,* the second kind of conservatism to which Glenn (1974) alludes, can help inform the study of social change and vice versa. In my past work on this topic I have, like others, assumed that social change occurs via one or both of two major mechanisms—those factors that influence cohort differences in experiences, and that therefore have the potential of influencing social change via cohort replacement, and those factors that affect individual change within cohorts, due either to processes linked to aging, or to period influences (Alwin, 1994a, 1995, 1996; Firebaugh, 1989). One aspect of social change, thus, is linked to the stable aspects of individuals and another to their unstable tendencies. The fact is, however, that despite our ability to conceptualize social change in terms of this partitioning into within- and between-cohort components of variation, it is very difficult, if not impossible, to identify what is going on from the data themselves (Rodgers, 1990). This is, of course, the classic problem of not being able to design research that permits us to separate age, period, and cohort effects (Mason & Fienberg, 1985).

⬦ AGING AND SOCIAL CHANGE

Students of aging are increasingly concerned with the extent and nature of change that occurs in individuals' lives over the entire life span and not just those features of change associated with the mature years (Riley, 1987). This is a positive sign because human development during one phase of the life cycle is undoubtedly best viewed against the broader landscape of life span development and change. Although there are important gaps in our current knowledge, research focusing on the broader question of human constancy and change suggests that human characteristics vary considerably in their potential for alteration and change. Research also suggests that the potential for change is fundamentally linked to the dynamics of events in both historic and biographic time. That is, there are periods in the life cycle in which people are most malleable and susceptible to change, and there are historical periods in which change is endemic, regardless of where people are in their individual biographies (Alwin, 1994a).

Although it may be safe to argue that individual change and social change are linked, to suggest that we understand the nature of this linkage is probably premature. At an abstract level we can certainly agree that individuals change because of changes in technology, or due to fundamental structural shifts at the societal level, or due to social movements and culture change, and there is a vast research base that supports such a presumption. We can also undoubtedly agree on the obverse, that society changes as a function of the changes in individuals, that is, individual change contributes to social change. It is therefore the case that the nature of human stability not only has implications for the study of aging, it also has implications for the study of social change.

⊠ COHORT REPLACEMENT AND SOCIAL CHANGE

The idea that social change occurs, at least in part, by processes of cohort succession, with each new cohort being exposed to a unique climate of ideas and eventually replacing older ones in the overall composition of society, is an extremely valuable one (Lesthaeghe & Surkyn, 1988; Mannheim, 1927/1952b; Ryder, 1965). A *cohort effect* in this context is a term that is used to refer to differences in the formative experiences of members of different cohorts/generations, which endure throughout the life span. Thus, if particular periods in history have distinct effects on members of cohorts undergoing formative experiences that will shape them for life, it is then possible to imagine that social change comes in part from the succession of cohorts. The alternative to this model of social change is that societal-level changes are reflections, not of cohort differences but of individual-level changes occurring within cohorts. Two classes of factors influence individuals, causing them (and their cohorts) to change: factors tied to life cycle or aging and factors tied to historical or "period" influences.

With respect to the historical process and social change, the concept of *cohort replacement* is useful in conjunction with some notion of *the formative years*, a period in biographical time during which socialization experiences are thought to be critical in shaping the nature of lives in ways that may affect the nature of society. This assumption, that there are unique influences within historical time that help shape the early lives of sets of cohorts, which leave an indelible mark on their characteristic modes of thought and experience, forms the basis for theorizing about "generations" (Mannheim, 1927/1952b). According to White (1992b), cohorts only become "actors" when they cohere enough around historical events, in both their own and others' eyes, to be called "generations." In this sense, we would distinguish between "cohorts" and "generations," in that the former refers simply to *year of birth,* whereas a generation is a "joint interpretive construction which insists upon and builds among tangible cohorts in defining a style recognized from outside and from within" (White, 1992b, p. 31). Through such mechanisms "cohort effects" are given life through these interpretive and behavioral aspects.

The plausibility of the cohort replacement interpretation of social change, thus, rests on two things: (a) the potency of unique historical influences upon each cohort or set of cohorts, such that cohort differences can be said to exist, and (b) a set of assumptions about the nature of individual stability over the life course. The latter poses a particularly interesting set of issues, as the assumption about the stability of individuals over most of their life span is critical. Thus, distinct historical experiences may exist and distinguish cohorts for a time, but if individuals are not stable after some early point in their life cycle, such intercohort differences may perish with time. Humans are often thought to be susceptible to change in their early lives but to become increasingly stable in important respects with age, remaining relatively resistant to change throughout most of adult life. But this may not be the case, and there is an emergent *aleatoric* view of the adult life course as essentially "open-ended," in which human life is characterized to reflect a lifelong openness to change, rather than one of growing stability and resistance to change (e.g., Gergen, 1980).

The Identification Problem

Social scientists often turn to repeated cross-sectional surveys for purposes of identifying cohort effects (see Firebaugh, 1989; Glenn, 1977). However, because cohort membership is highly confounded with age even in these designs, it is impossible to identify such effects in any purely exploratory fashion. One needs to turn to supplementary types of data and invoke theory and common sense to produce what Philip Converse (1976) called "side information," assumptions about the nature of certain historical and generational processes. Ordinarily the types of data available to social scientists to distinguish cohort effects from the effects of aging are not adequate and other steps must be taken. If one can make strong theoretical assumptions about the nature of certain influences (e.g., setting either cohort, aging, or period effects to zero), it is possible to creatively interpret survey data in service of the goal of identifying cohort phenomena when they exist. But, replicated cross-sectional surveys can only estimate net changes in the aggregate and at the level of the cohort. Panel data are necessary to ascertain information on gross rates of constancy and change and to ultimately assay levels of human stability (Alwin, 1995; Duncan & Kalton, 1987).

To illustrate the seriousness of this problem, we assume that variables representing three main sets of factors can be thought of as affecting the mean levels of variables: aging (A), birth cohort (B), and chronological time (C). These are conceptual categories of variables representing rich and complex sets of influences that operate primarily through (a) processes of aging and life cycle changes, (b) processes influencing specific cohorts or generations, and (c) those effects due to the distinctiveness of the time of measurement.[1] The problem is, however, that within a given survey, A (age) and B (birth cohort) are perfectly correlated. And in a series of repeated cross-sections, within cohorts, A (age) and C (chronological time) are perfectly correlated (Mason & Fienberg, 1985). Because Age = Time – Birth Date (A = C – B), there can never be a way of separating the influences of "aging," "cohorts" and "social change" using cross-sectional data alone. One needs to be able to impose a strong set of assumptions about the nature of one of these three sources of variation—aging, cohorts, and social change. Short of such strong assumptions, it is not possible to cleanly disentangle these processes empirically from such data.

Due to the confounding of A, B, and C in a series of replicate surveys, it is never possible to separate the effects of aging, cohorts, and time by simply analyzing the linear additive effects of age, birth year, and time of survey. Without some assumptions, which are often lacking, there is apparently no straightforward solution to the identification problem. However, one can decompose trend data reflecting social change into two orthogonal components: one representing the between-cohort versus within-cohort part of the trend. The between-cohort component can be interpreted as generational replacement if one is willing to assume that the age compositional differences between the cohorts are not actually producing the effect. The within-cohort component, as mentioned above, can be interpreted either in terms of aging or life cycle effects or in terms of historic or period effects (see Firebaugh, 1989). Again, if one assumes that the effects of aging do not operate on the means but on the amount of regression to it (them), then this component is likely to represent period effects. The problems of doing this are discussed by Firebaugh (1989) and Rodgers (1990). What I propose here is that some theoretical insight into the role of aging in producing differences in repeated cross-sectional data can be gained by analyzing the extent of change in individual differences in panel designs, that is, to assess the extent of stability over the life span.

Human Stability
and Change

How stable are individuals? When in the life cycle is stability highest? And, when, if ever, does stability emerge as a predominant form, characteristic of most individuals of a given age? There are undoubtedly a number of different answers to these questions, depending on the qualities under consideration and the period of the life cycle of interest. Few contemporary behavioral scientists would endorse the once popular view of psychoanalytic theory that one can predict most of subsequent behavior by knowing critical features of the nature of development in the first few years, or even months of life (e.g., Thomas & Chess, 1977). But even if this extreme view is rejected, there does exist a widely-held cultural belief that individuals stabilize in many, if not most, of their characteristics by early adulthood.

Personality

Psychologists generally approach the question of human stability through the concept of *personality,* that is, as regularities in behavior that are more or less stable over time and across situations. To some, "the very concept of personality implies a differentiated and organized hierarchy of psychological sets and behavioral dispositions that are manifested as consistent and enduring patterns in denoting the uniqueness of the individual" (Moss & Susman, 1980, p. 73). Although there is superficial agreement among psychologists on the interpretation of the concept of "personality," a closer inspection reveals some disagreement. A key issue is whether to include *all* individual differences, regardless of their origins and regardless of their degree of stability.[2] Strelau (1987), for example, pointed out that some traditions of thought distinguish personality from the concept of *temperament.* In psychology the latter term has come to refer to those relatively stable differences in human behavior that might be explained by biological mechanisms, whereas the term *personality* is reserved for those traits originating primarily from environmental differences. Strelau (1987, p. 109) pointed out that in biologically-oriented theories of personality, the terms *temperament* and *personality* are often used interchangeably (the work of the trait psychologists, phrenologists, and morphologists), whereas other theorists include *temperament,* along with additional traits, such as *intelligence,* within the more global concept of personality as a set of dispositions. In still other theories, the concept of *temperament* is distinguished from *personality,* as a distinct concept, and the two are thought to interact in the production of behavior, as embodiments of the biological and the social, respectively. Strelau (1987), for example, suggests the two concepts be distinguished along the following dimensions (temperament vs. personality): (a) behavior is determined by biology versus determined by social factors, (b) behavior is shaped during childhood versus developed in adulthood, (c) traits applied to both man and animals versus applied only to man, (d) absence versus presence of content-saturated behavior, and (e) the extent to which the construct refers to a central regulating function of humans.

Sociologists, on the other hand, see structural patterning of environments as being largely behind the regularities in behavior, with the possibility that changes in the environment also make it possible that individuals can be quite malleable. Clearly, the origin and maintenance of personality is to some extent dependent on the social environment; thus, most modern developmental theories of personality emphasize the nature of *processes of socialization* through which social environments influence behavioral tendencies and through which individual differences develop. The concept of socialization lacks precision; to quote Musgrove (1977): "the distinction between socialization and maturation is as treacherous as the distinction between nurture and nature (and equally unhelpful if too rigidly drawn)" (p. 214). Nonetheless, to many psychologists and sociologists, the social environment is generally thought to be responsible not only for the development of regularities in behavior but also for the medium through which individuals acquire a range of stable behavioral dispositions, involving language and other symbolic systems, identities, values and goal priorities, beliefs, social norms and ways of behaving, skills, and knowledge.

The sociological literature is actually quite diverse with respect to its views on matters of human stability. On the one hand, to the social constructionists, human personality is all openness and flux, and there is a remarkable avoidance of any association with notions of individual differences that have such permanence in human lives (e.g., Berger & Luckmann, 1971). Some aspects of human differences are "endlessly fugitive . . . always fragile and precarious, and modern man is a chameleon" (Musgrove, 1977, p. 1). The social environment is where change is lodged, according to many sociological views, and some even define constancies in personality in terms of the stability of the person's interpersonal environment (Sullivan, 1953). Thus, although personality may have some constancies, it is also inherently flexible and able to take on a variety of different forms over the span of life, and from this point of view it is undoubtedly a mistake to reserve the term "personality" for just those aspects of individual functioning that are highly stable. On the other hand, recognizing that there must be some ontological constancies at some level of human existence, there are often pleas to make biological assumptions explicit. For example, in what has become a classic of social psychology, Dennis Wrong's "over-socialized conception of man" was such a plea—wherein Wrong (1961) suggested that sociologists accord more attention to biological factors and make clear their assumptions about such biological givens. Wrong is certainly not the first to make such a plea. For example, Freud wrestled with these matters in *Civilization and Its Discontents.*

Symbolic interactionist conceptions of the "self" and "identities" have suggested that constancies in the self over the life span create a set of organizing principles that endure in behavioral orientations. Wells and Stryker (1988) suggested that *identity theory,* as derived from "structural symbolic interactionism," may be used to help understand the subjective changes in age-linked identities attendant to age-linked transitions between social roles and statuses. Identity theory argues that constancies and/or change in the self reflects patterns in social relationships linked to a person's social locations, and changes in individual selves and biographies are viewed as reflecting general sequences of identity transitions over the life span. At the same time, this theory argues that "salient identities" lead to perceptual and other selective cognitive processes that reinforce stability of the self. These self-sustaining components of the self promote stability, in the form of constancies in identities.

Although sociological discussions point to the great potential for change, the realities of various socially structured constraints impede and may largely prevent (or make highly improbable) actual change. I argue that it is the central theoretical role of the "identity" construct that largely mediates the effects of these structural elements on the stability of the self. Naturally the potential for change varies over the life cycle. There may be considerably less stability in identities in young adulthood than in midlife and old age. As Norman Ryder (1965) put it:

> [T]he potential for change is concentrated in the cohorts of young adults who are old enough to participate directly in the movements impelled by change, but not old enough to have become committed to an occupation, a residence, a family of procreation, or a way of life. (p. 848)

The relevance of the concept of identity, along with the concept of commitment—the two important aspects of the self—to issues of consistency in behavioral orientations is clear, and identity theory can assist in understanding tendencies toward both stability and instability.

Traits vs. States

Most social scientists, including both the "social constructionists" and those persuaded by the aleatoric view of life span development, would undoubtedly agree that there are some human characteristics, for example, intellectual skills and personality attributes, which are highly stable—in the sense of stabilities in individual differences—over people's lives. However, in sorting out which types of characteristics fall into this category, I would put much less emphasis on distinguishing among traits according to whether they were primarily biologically- or socially-driven. It is advantageous to study the stabilities of identities and attributes as reflecting dispositional aspects of behavior underlying such phenotypic characteristics, regardless of their origins. In fact, it is no doubt impossible to disentangle the extent of biological versus social influence on behavior; thus, into the domain of personality I would essentially bring potentially *all* human dispositions and behavioral orientations, including concepts such as *temperament,* which are thought to develop early and are closely tied to biological givens.

Developmental psychologists have taken these issues much more seriously than have sociologists. Nesselroade's (1988, 1990) work, for example, has done much to clarify the nature of the distinctions between *trait* and *state,* which helps anticipate conceptually the possibility that some characteristics of individuals may be more stable than others across situations and across time. This distinction is rooted in psychometric approaches to the conceptualization of personality, aimed at distinguishing the stable, interindividual components of behavior (traits) from their intraindividual cross-situational components (states). Behavior is a function of both trait and state components. According to Nesselroade (1988)

> State, in the sense we are using the term, connotes a "dynamic" quality in that people are, at any particular time, located at some level or value on the state dimension but are poised for movement or change to another level. They are variably distributed across a range of possible values on each of a number of state dimensions. . . . From a measurement point of view, a person is many values at the same time, some of which can be quite temporary. (p. 166)

Thus, traits are conceptualized in much the same way that "personality" is normally conceived, namely as relatively enduring or stable characteristics of the individual, which are trans-situationally stable and stable for long periods of time. States, on the other hand, are due to changes in the environment, or experience-based changes in individual characteristics. This joint focus on traits and states enriches the understanding of human behavior and behavior change. One application of these notions (e.g., Steyer & Schmitt,

1990) illustrates how cross-temporal and within-time components of stability can be separated and interpreted in terms of trait and state variation.

One of the purposes of this research is to question which dimensions of human behavior and orientation operate as traits and which operate as states. Or, put more precisely, where on the continuum between these extremes do various dimensions of human orientation fall with respect to issues of stability? For example, if a political disposition has a strong trait component, say in the case of political party identification, it would presumably be highly stable. If there were also a state component, as in the intensity of support for either major political party, it would tend to be less stable. Differences in stability can be viewed in terms of the relative balance of the trait and state components to a behavior. By recasting the issues of development and socialization within a dynamic framework, that is, one that incorporates time, it is possible to focus on the dual questions of (a) how stable are individuals over their lives? and (b) what are the relative contributions of human stability to levels of aggregate societal development and change (Alwin, 1995)?

◻ INDIVIDUAL STABILITY IN POLITICAL IDENTITIES

Theoretical conceptions of human development differ in their specification of the nature of the individual, the influences of the social environment on the individual, the timing of those influences, and the persistence of their effects. The perspective that the early influences of the social environment are the most important is among the most salient. David Sears (1981) recounts the story told about the Jesuits, who believed that they could control a person's thinking for life if they were able to control his or her education up to the age of 5 years. And Frank Musgrove (1977) mentions the views of Bertrand Russell in his book *Education,* published in 1926, in which

> Russell declared that education of character "ought to be nearly complete by the age of six." Courage was an important virtue, but there was nothing that schools could do about this—it had already been done in the home and "One generation of fearless women could transform the world . . . " (p. 215)

These views are compatible with theoretical perspectives that assume there are "critical" stages in which the environment has an impact on the individual and that the "earliest" experiences are the most powerful in terms of their lasting influences on human tendencies. Other perspectives also stress critical stages, but place the molding of human tendencies to be later in life, yet still relatively early. William James observed that many aspects of human personality do not establish themselves until age 30 or 35 years, but then it is thought to be "set like plaster" throughout the remainder of the life span (see James, 1890/1950, p. 121). This view is echoed by Converse (1976) with respect to the development of political partisanship.

As an aspect of personality, political identities may not become a stably differentiated and organized hierarchy of psychological sets and behavioral dispositions manifested as consistent and enduring patterns until early adulthood. Indeed, strong support exists for the view that youth is an "impressionable" time, with political identities remaining in considerable flux, until roughly age 35, when a high degree of stability in orientations crystallizes through midlife. Hardly any support exists for the notion that people remain inherently flexible and able to take on a variety of points of view over the life span, although there does seem to be a slight decline in stability in old age (see Alwin, 1994a, 1995; Alwin, Cohen, & Newcomb, 1991; Alwin & Krosnick, 1991a).

Aging and Conservatism

As I noted at the beginning of the paper, there has been considerable speculation about the tendency for people to become more conservative with age. For example, Crittenden (1962) tried to argue that "the aging process has an impact on party affiliation . . . independent of any such generational factors" (p. 648). He examined national survey data for the years 1946, 1950, 1954, and 1958, concluding that "aging seems to produce a shift toward Republicanism in the period 1946 to 1958" (p. 654). Further research into this issue generally does not support Crittenden's conclusion (e.g., Abramson, 1983; Converse, 1976; Glenn, 1974; Glenn & Grimes, 1968; Glenn & Hefner, 1972). After reviewing the area, Glenn (1974) concluded that "although the evidence suggests that attitudes probably become somewhat less susceptible to change as people grow older, there is scant evidence for any other contribution of aging to (political) conservatism" (p. 176). Rather than people becoming ideologically conservative with age and hence more likely to identify with the Republican party, Glenn argued that people of different ages reacted differently to the liberalizing (or Democratic) influences of the 1930s—a thesis consistent with other types of theorizing (see Alwin, Cohen, & Newcomb, 1991; Sears, 1981, 1983). Thus, one can argue that the effects of "aging" on political identities are minimal (see Glenn, 1980). By contrast, the major ways in which aging and life cycle processes take their toll is to make one more or less open to change across the life span. Old age is likely to strengthen identification with political symbols, political movements, and political issues and actors, although it may not affect the basic direction of party loyalty.

There has been considerable debate about the most plausible interpretation of age-period-cohort patterns in political identities in the National Election Study (NES). In *The American Voter,* on the basis of the 1952 and 1956 election surveys, Campbell, Converse, Miller, and Stokes (1960) found that younger cohorts had weaker party loyalties than older ones. This has since become one of the best documented findings on political identities (see Abramson, 1983, p. 106). Campbell et al. (1960) further proposed that the relationship between age and partisanship had two different but compatible interpretations. They argued that the directional changes in political identities in the U.S., that is, historic shifts in Democratic-Republican-Independent preferences, should be interpreted in cohort terms, akin to Mannheim's notion of generations. At the same time, identities were seen to grow in intensity as a function of aging and life cycle changes, rather than being influenced by cohort differences. The thesis was further investigated by Converse (1969, 1976) and supported by data for the period from 1952 to 1964, a period of relative stability in American politics. While acknowledging the fundamental dilemma of interpretation in cohort analysis, Converse's independent examination of this issue supported Campbell et al. (1960). This two-ply argument was essentially that (a) age differences in the directional component are traceable primarily to cohort experiences, unrelated to aging per se; whereas (b) aging (or life cycle processes) are responsible for the age-intensity relationship. Analyzing long-term U.S. and international data sets (29 samples of the adult national U.S. population conducted at Michigan between 1952 and 1975, among others), Converse found some support for the growing intensity of party affiliations for the period 1952-64, net of cohort differences.

However, looking at the NES data from 1952 through 1980, Abramson (1983) drew the opposite general conclusion. He concluded that when "cohorts are tracked over time, there is virtually no increase in partisan strength as cohorts age, although there is some support for the life cycle thesis if we restrict the analysis to the years between 1952 and 1964" (p. 130). He further asserts that Converse mistook purely generational differences between age groups for life cycle effects. Abramson (1983) claims that Converse's evidence for life cycle effects in the NES data is weak and that the main decline in party loyalty reflects a succession-of-cohorts phenomenon. Converse (1979) responded that "under the simplifying assumptions (necessary for his argument) the test for the pure-generational hypothesis is negative and life cycle gains account for roughly all of the age-strength relationship" (p. 100).

The problem with drawing *any* conclusions from the NES series used by Converse, Abramson, as well as others, is that, given the identification problem noted above, conclusions are contingent on assumptions; different assumptions lead to different conclusions. There is no direct solution to this problem, although some considerable light can be shed on the problem by addressing the question within a quantitative framework that permits a decomposition of the aggregate trends into those components of change due to *cohort replacement* and *intracohort change.* Subsequently we examine such a decomposition, and whereas this approach does not solve the identification problem either, it has the great advantage of bringing the broad features of the data into improved resolution. In addition, although there is an implication in the above discussion of "party strength" as an aspect of political identity, this is more appropriately referred to as "intensity" of party attachment. I have here used the term "strength" to refer to the relative resilience or durability of individual differences, so these two meanings need to be kept distinct. In this regard, it is worth noting, in anticipation of the following results, that *party identification* has many of the features associated with "trait-like" characteristics, whereas the degree of attachment, or intensity (the "strength" component) behaves much more like the "state" component of behavior. We examine this more completely in evaluating the *molar stability* estimates for these two components of political identity.

Research Methods

This paper re-examines these issues, using 36 national probability samples, beginning in 1952 through 1994, of the English-speaking continental U.S. from the Michigan American National Election Studies and the NORC (National Opinion Research Center) General Social Survey. The NES has, since 1952, tracked national political participation in national election years using cross-sectional representative samples of the U.S. household population. On the years of presidential elections, a sample is interviewed before and after the election and in non-presidential election years only postelection surveys are conducted. Data are obtained from face-to-face interviews with national full-probability samples of all citizens of voting age in the continental U.S., exclusive of military reservations, using the Survey Research Center's multistage area sample (see Center for Political Studies, 1990). The samples typically range between 1,500 and 2,000 in each election year. The source of the data for this analysis comes from the National Election Studies 1952-1994 cumulative data file (Center for Political Studies, n.d.). The General Social Survey (GSS) is an annual cross-sectional survey of the noninstitutionalized household population of the continental U.S. aged 18 and over (National Opinion Research Center, 1994). It has been conducted nearly every year since 1972 on approximately 1,500 respondents per year. Surveys were not conducted in 1979, 1981, or 1992. The purpose of the GSS has been to monitor social trends in attitudes and behaviors. During the first few years the samples were either entirely or in part non-probability samples, but since 1977 a full-probability household sample has been employed. Since 1983 the GSS and NES have cooperated in the development of a national sample, so the sampling frames for the NES and GSS are the same since the early 1980s.

In the following analysis I first decompose the trends in political party identification using a linear decomposition technique proposed by Firebaugh (1989). This permits us to examine the potential for changes in party identification due to shifts in cohort representation, or to intracohort change. After demonstrating the ambiguity of these results, I make use of the available panel data in this series to examine the issue of life span stability of political party identification. The assumption is that by examining the nature of individual-level changes in political identities, we can bring some information to bear on the assumptions required to draw interpretations from the decomposition into "cohort replacement" and "intracohort change."

Measurement

One of the most salient ideological differences among Americans (and across generations) is the application of the term "liberal" versus "conservative" to political thought and action. This dimension to a large extent helps distinguish political events, actors, and issues, and it is useful in the present context because whereas political issues and actors (including parties) change, the ideological contrast between "liberal" and "conservative" has considerable historical durability. The NES has measured this dimension in the context of political party identification since the early 1950s and both the NES and GSS have measured this trend since the early 1970s, so there is some purchase on ideological change in the U.S. electorate. Table 7.1 provides a description of the measures used in the following analysis. These two measures are exactly replicated across the GSS and NES surveys. The

Table 7.1. Measurement of Variables in the General Social Survey and National Election Studies.

Measure	Source	Time Period	Question Wording
Party choice	NES GSS	1952-94 1972-94	Generally speaking, do you usually think of yourself as a Republican, Democrat, Independent, or what? IF REPUBLICAN OR DEMOCRAT: Would you call yourself a strong (Republican/Democrat) or not a very strong (Republican/Democrat). IF INDEPENDENT, NO PREFERENCE, OR OTHER: Do you think of yourself as closer to the Republican or Democratic Party?
Liberal/ Conservatism	NES GSS	1972-94 1972-94	We hear a lot of talk these days about liberals and conservatives. Here is a 7-point scale on which the political views that people hold are arranged from extremely liberal to extremely conservative. [SHOW CARD displaying the categories: Extremely liberal, Liberal, Slightly liberal, Moderate (middle of the road), Slightly conservative, Conservative, Extremely conservative]

self-reported party choice questions permit the construction of a 7-point party identification variable (7 = Strong Republican, 6 = Weak Republican, 5 = Independent Leaning Republican, 4 = Independent, 3 = Independent Leaning Democrat, 2 = Weak Democrat, 1 = Strong Democrat). This parallels the 7-point scale of liberal versus conservative self-assessment (7 = Extremely Conservative, 6 = Conservative, 5 = Slightly Conservative, 4 = Moderate, Middle-of-the-Road, 3 = Slightly Liberal, 2 = Liberal, 1 = Extremely Liberal). The NES party identification series begins in 1952 and is available at two-year intervals (except in 1954 inadequate data were provided on birth year, so that survey is excluded).

The GSS contributes to this series beginning in 1972. The NES and GSS liberal-conservative self-rating began in 1972—the NES contributing data every two years and the GSS annually (except 1979, 1981, and 1992). The liberal-conservative rating and the directional component of the party self-identification measure both allow us to capture cohort trends in ideological direction of public political orientations. The party self-identification variable additionally allows us to distinguish between the direction of party identification (3 = Republican, 2 = Independent, 1 = Democrat) and a measure of the intensity or "strength" of attachment to either of the two major political parties (3 = Strong Republican or Democrat, 2 = Weak Republican or Democrat, 1 = Neither Republican nor Democrat). This intensity measure can be interpreted in several ways, among which is the extent of alienation with the institutionalized two-party system in the U.S.

Cohort Replacement or Intracohort Change?

Certainly the distinctiveness of some political eras and the tendencies toward domination of political movements and political parties during particular periods provide a basis for the notion that birth cohorts achieving political awareness during the ascendency of one particular political movement or party will be differentially affected by the popularity of candidates and parties (see Converse, 1969, 1976). It could be that the intensity of involvement in political matters or the degree of political alienation may be determined by these historical factors affecting the young—such that an entire cohort of persons may be more or less inclined to participate in elections and political affairs or may be more or less alienated from the main centers of the electorate (see Abramson, 1976, 1979, 1983; Kahn & Mason, 1987). And finally, it can be argued that the salience of certain social and political issues and priorities during particular historical periods (e.g., periods of economic scarcity or security) can produce unique differences among cohorts in certain economic and political goals that are linked to the major political parties. The question is whether there are indeed generational residues and cohort differences that cannot be attributed to aging or life cycle factors.

Components of Change

The model for describing social change involves a simple linear decomposition of change into a component representing cohort replacement and a component that represents intracohort change. The approach, due to Firebaugh (1989, p. 253), is to first regress the variable of interest on survey year and cohort (birth year), as follows:

$$y = b_0 + b_1 \text{ Year} + b_2 \text{ Cohort} + e$$

The slopes from the estimation of this equation are then used to estimate the cohort replacement and intracohort change components, defined as:

$$\text{intracohort change} = b_1 (t_T - t_1), \text{ and}$$
$$\text{cohort replacement} = b_2 (C_T - C_1),$$

where t_T-t_1 represents the amount of historical time passing between time 1 and time T, C_T is the mean birth year at time T, and C_1 is the mean birth year at time 1. As Firebaugh (1989) notes, due to the fact that the model is often mis-specified in positing linearity and additivity of year and cohort, the two components rarely sum to Y_T-Y_1. But, "the discrepancy should not be large; a large discrepancy suggests that the effects of year (intracohort, the period-age effect) and cohort (intercohort, the cohort-age effect) are not linear-additive" (p. 253) After comparing this method with other techniques that decompose differences of means across time, Firebaugh (1989) concluded that the linear decomposition method expressed above provides reasonably good estimates of cohort turnover (generational replacement) and intracohort influences on means.

These estimates are given in Table 7.2. For both measures of party choice (the 3-point and 7-point scales) there is a significant conservative trend from the early 1950s to the early 1990s.[3] In both cases there seem to be significant patterns of intracohort change; and whereas the cohort replacement contribution to social change is in the more liberal direction, the cohort replacement effect is nonsignificant. Given the sample size, this component must surely be near zero. The 7-point Liberal/Conservatism scale reveals essentially the same pattern—a significant conservative trend with a conservative intracohort shift; however, there is a significant liberal cohort-replacement effect. In the case of the degree of party attachment, or the "strength" component of party identity, there is a significant aggregate change in the direction of disaffection with either major political party over this 40-year period. This change reveals a significant negative cohort replacement effect, suggesting the more recent cohorts are systematically less attached to the political parties than earlier-born cohorts. At the same time, there is a significantly positive intracohort effect on this measure, indicating that, despite the overall trend toward alienation from the major political parties, there is a growth in attachment over time. This intracohort growth in party loyalty is not strong enough to counterbalance the generally stronger cohort replacement component of the trend toward greater conservatism.

These results do not appear to offer support for the hypothesis that the political views of the country are moving in a more liberal direction, as has been argued by others. Analyzing racial attitudes in the GSS, for example, Firebaugh and Davis (1988; see also Firebaugh, 1989) conclude that anti-Black prejudice in the U.S. has declined due to the dual processes of intracohort change and the replacement of older more prejudiced cohorts with more liberal ones. Analyzing gender-role attitudes, Mason and Lu

Table 7.2. Decomposition of Change in Political Self-Identification in the National Election Studies and General Social Surveys, 1952-1994.

			Component of Change			
Dependent Variable	Time Period	N	Social Change	Intra Cohort	Cohort Replacement	Residual
Party choice (7-pt.)	52-94	71,923	.344*	.413*	.018	−.088
Party choice (3-pt.)	52-94	71,923	.135*	.163*	.004	−.032
Party attachment	52-94	71,923	−.199*	.272*	−.439*	−.031
Liberal/ Conservatism	72-94	43,402	.222*	.326*	−.178*	.074

*$p<.001$

(1988), and Alwin, Scott, and Braun (1996) report similar findings, both intracohort and intercohort transitions in a more liberal direction. Tracking trends in 42 different GSS attitude measures from the early 1970s to late 1980s, a period of nearly 20 years, Davis (1991) analyzed aggregate change primarily in terms of the liberal/conservative dimension. Davis's (1991) analysis was an extension of previous readings on these aggregate shifts by Smith (1989) and Davis (1980). Davis found a general trend in the liberal direction across cohorts—a broad shift he calls the "great 'liberal' shift since World War II"—but that the aggregate level shift "hides" the dynamics of the generational phenomena. Within cohorts Davis (1991) finds a "conservative trend between the early and late 1970s and a liberal 'rebound' in the 1980s" (p. 2). The cohort succession results in Davis's (1991) analysis point in the direction of a cumulative liberal generational contribution to the aggregate shift, which in his data is decidedly liberal.

These results differ from those described above in two important respects. The GSS time-span is much shorter, going back only to the early 1970s—and this may in part account for the apparent liberal shift in Davis's analysis. Moreover, the central measures I use from the GSS and NES are different. The GSS has focused since the early 1970s on a set of issues on which there has been a liberal shift: race, religion, and women's issues. For the measures used in Davis's analysis there has been a liberal shift, but even within the GSS series the measures of party attachment and liberal-conservative self-ratings show the same conservative sweep that is evident in the much longer NES series. It is important to note, however, that despite different assessments of the direction of aggregate change in Davis's (1991) study and mine, the intracohort changes addressed in the two studies are essentially the same, namely a within-cohort shift in the conservative direction. The present results diverge, however, in the present finding of little evidence of a cohort replacement effect in the liberal direction.

With respect to party attachment, one could read these results as providing support for Abramson (1976, 1979, 1983) and Converse (1976, 1979), in that there is clear evidence in support of both cohort replacement effects and positive intracohort effects consistent with the aging hypothesis. The problem is, however, that the cohort replacement effect also contains the compositional effects of aging, and the intracohort component contains both aging and period effects. Because of the identification problem, it is still not possible to determine what is going on. Throughout the table, the intracohort component contains both linear aging and period effects and the cohort replacement effect contains the effects of cohort experiences and aging. Unless one has a strong basis for assuming one or more of these processes to be producing no effect, it is not possible to achieve a clear resolution of the nature of the other effects.

Let us assume, for example, that the effects of aging on party choice or strength of party loyalty are minimal and that the intracohort effect reflects period influences in the direction of favoring Republicans, especially since the early 1970s through the 1990s. And if aging effects are minimal, the cohort replacement effects would be due to cohort differences rather than the age composition of the cohort categories. The implications of this are that there is no cohort replacement effect on party choice, but there is a cohort replacement effect on party attachment, as Abramson (1983) argues, in that more recently born cohorts are tied less strongly to party affiliations. If we *do not* assume that the intracohort component is all or nearly all due to period factors but that aging is the predominant force, this would mean, contrary to what Glenn (1974) suggests, that aging contributes to conservative party choices. More importantly, this line of interpretation would suggest, since aging should show a negative effect in the cohort replacement component, that the cohort effects for party choice are understated by the cohort replacement component, in that this effect is concealing a negative effect of age composition that is part of the cohort replacement effect. This would mean there is a positive (conservative) cohort effect (i.e., more recent cohorts are more conservative), which is canceling out the negative aging effect. In the case of party attachment, again, by setting aging effects to zero, the period factors would have to drive the intracohort effect in the direction of greater attachment and the cohort replacement component would be a pure cohort effect, in which the more recent cohorts are the more conservative. On the other hand, with period factors set to zero, the presence of an intracohort effect suggests that as people age they grow more attached to the political system, which is consistent with the Campbell and Converse argument (see Converse, 1976).

Which of these two types of interpretations is the most plausible? There is no need for the structure of interpretation to be the same for both the direction of party choice and the degree of party attachment. But we are still left with the following questions:

1. Are the intracohort effects on party choice due to period, or aging, or both? Do people become more conservative with age, or is there a period-type movement of the population in a conservative direction?

2. Are the intracohort effects on strength of party attachment due to the tendency of people to become more attached to the political system with age, or do they reflect the trend toward greater attachment on the part of the entire population to the major political parties?

3. Is the absence of a cohort replacement component of social change for party choice due to the true absence of cohort differences in experience, or is a significant role of cohort differences (with earlier cohorts being more liberal and more recent ones being more conservative) being masked by the operation of a true negative age effect on the cohort replacement component?

4. Is the strong negative cohort replacement effect on party attachment due to a true cohort effect in which the earlier cohorts are most strongly attached and the more recent ones much less so, or is this effect due to aging, that is, an aging effect that promotes greater party loyalty?

The Stability of Political Identities Over the Life Span

As already indicated, the above type of analysis leaves open the question of whether aging processes contribute to political orientations. Despite the past efforts to interpret such patterns, these questions cannot be answered using repeated cross-sectional survey data alone, unless there is a theoretical basis for ruling out either cohort, period, or aging factors. It is important to recall from the above discussion that the interpretation of these effects in terms of cohort replacement and intracohort period effects requires that one essentially rule out the effects of aging on mean levels of the measures. I am not reluctant on the whole to make this assumption, given what seems to be the general scholarly thinking on this topic; however, we must recognize that this is an assumption, and if it is wrong our conclusions are likely to be wrong. Thus, I now turn to an examination of life span stability of three of the above variables, the party choice and attachment measures. Gauging the stability of these variables would inform the extent of change that is linked to age over the life span and would contribute to the overall picture of political development in adulthood.

Molar Stability Estimates

The considerations just discussed lead us back to one of the central questions raised at the outset, specifically, how stable are individuals over their lives? If we can successfully address this question, then we can more productively address the question of the potential for changes due to aging. To confront this issue, I recently engaged in an exploration of varieties of stability in individual differences in psychological characteristics, including personality, intelligence, identities, self-image, and social attitudes (Alwin, 1994a). This research was aimed at integrating psychological and sociological conceptions of human life span development. As noted above, numerous past efforts have attempted to do this, and although that work is certainly impressive in its scope and aims, it has seldom incorporated a commitment to empirically verifying existing hypotheses regarding elements of human constancy and change. This ongoing program of research takes the investigation of human constancy and change as theoretically and empirically problematic, focusing on a wide range of human dispositions.

With this purpose in mind, I presented a theoretical rationale for studying levels of stability over sequential periods of the life span, and I developed an approach to gauging patterns of stability over time. The approach taken to estimating rates of change/stability solves several problems that have plagued past researches on the study of life span trajectories of human stability and change. First, the research uses an approach that directly addresses the unconfounding of measurement errors and true change in longitudinal studies of the same individuals (Block, 1977). Second, the approach is used to assess differences in stability between occasions of measurement, where the reinterview period varies from study to study. The models used to articulate this framework are particularly useful in conjunction with a synthetic-cohort approach, as molar stability estimates can be generated across several cohorts, varying in age. Third, not only does this approach allow a method by which we can compare estimates of stability and change across cohorts differing in age but it also makes it possible to compare molar stability estimates across concepts, or content domains of personality, as well as across studies using remeasurement designs. By thus standardizing rates of change in various human characteristics, one is eventually in a position to be able to develop inferences about the trajectories of constancy and change in specifiable characteristics over the entire life span.

The theoretical framework for this research focuses explicitly on the introduction of the concept of *molar stability,* the persistence of behavior or behavioral orientations as expressed in age-homogenous rates of change over specified periods of time. This concept was introduced as a means of organizing empirical information on human constancy and change and to provide a basis of comparing raw stability estimates across studies having different remeasurement intervals and across different concepts (Alwin, 1994a). Molar stability is defined as $\beta^{j/k}$ where β is the cohort-specific or age-homogenous stability observed empirically, k is the number of years over which raw stability is assessed, and j is the number of years selected to express molar stability. In my research to date, for example, I have chosen j to equal 8 but this is governed in part by the nature of the remeasurement interval and the amount of expected change (see Alwin, 1994a). The goal is to obtain raw stability estimates and convert them into the standardized units of molar stability.

In this research, stability is estimated as the extent of overtime correlation among single variables within groups that are relatively homogenous with respect to age. This type of stability is sometimes referred to as *differential stability* (see Alwin, 1994a; Asendorpf, 1992; Caspi & Bem, 1990; Costa & McCrae, 1980). However, it is a mistake to estimate stability of individual differences over time using simple observed correlations between time points. This is the case because over time correlations confound true change/stability with measurement imprecision (Heise, 1969). Due to the confounding involved, it becomes necessary to separate unreliability of measurement from true instability in order to precisely estimate stability.[4] This is particularly important when measurement errors are correlated with age (see Alwin & Krosnick, 1991a, 1991b). In short, any analysis of the stability of individual differences over time must take into account random errors of measurement.

Of the available approaches, the one that has proven the most useful in our research is the calculation of raw stability estimates from simple, single-variable simplex models (see Alwin, 1988). Such models are characterized by a series of measures (a minimum of three) of the same variable separated in time. The models posit a Markovian (lag-1) restriction to account for change and stability in the underlying latent or "true" variable, which is a highly robust assumption in most change processes. This type of model has been useful in analyzing individual development or change while simultaneously taking random errors of measurement into account. These models are the basic building blocks of a research program aimed at comparing aspects of personality in their trajectories of stability at various stages or points in the life span.

The interest in the present context is in estimates of trajectories of life span stability in the development of political identities in adulthood (see Alwin & Krosnick, 1991a; Alwin et al., 1991). In Table 7.3 are depicted levels of *molar stability,* based on 3-wave panel data for gauging stability and estimated for synthetic cohort data from national samples in National Election Study panels of 1956-1958-1960 and 1972-1974-1976 (see Alwin et al., 1991). The variables of interest are drawn from the measure of party choice given above, including (a) the 3-point party choice variable, (b) the 3-level measure of intensity, and (c) the combined 7-point scale measuring identification with political parties (7 = strong Republican, 6 = moderate Republican, 5 = independent, leaning Republican, 4 = independent, 3 = independent, leaning Democrat, 2 = moderate Democrat, 1 = strong Democrat).

The estimates from the two studies are arrayed according to *life cycle stage.* The similarity of these two sets of results for the 1950s and 1970s panels is remarkable. With one exception (discussed below), these results show that, with respect to political party identification, individuals are relatively unstable when they are young adults but attain increasing levels of stability with age, reaching a very high level of stability by midlife (beginning around age 35), maintaining that level of stability throughout most of their lives, but declining somewhat in old age. This pattern is evident for both the 3-category party choice (Republican/independent/Democrat) variable and the overall combined 7-point measure of party identification. Indeed, these results are hardly distinguishable, suggesting that the main component of the latter results is driven by the basic 3-category party choice measure.

When considered by itself, the intensity component reveals markedly less stability, although it behaves in roughly the same fashion, that is, low levels of stability in young adulthood, with increases to an apex during midlife, and then a decline in old age. As with the directional component, the highest levels of stability are reached roughly by age 35 and maintain themselves through age 60; although as noted, the intensity component is much less stable overall. What is of most interest about the difference between the two components, in light of the foregoing discussion, is that the directional component behaves much more like a trait, whereas the intensity component appears more state-like, to use Nessleroade's (1988) terminology.

Above I noted an exception to this pattern—it is the group that was aged 26-33 in 1972 (see Alwin et al., 1991). This exception represents a unique cohort effect on party loyalties and their stability. This set of cohorts was

Table 7.3. Molar Stability Estimates for Political Party Identification in the National Election Study Panels, 1956-58-60 and 1972-74-76.

| | | | | | Standardized Estimates | | | | | |
| | | | | | Party Choice | | Intensity | | Party Ident. | |
Cohort Category	Age in 1956	N	Age in 1972	N	56-60	72-76	56-60	72-76	56-60	72-76
1947-54			18-25	(191)	—	.430	—	.356	—	.441
1939-46			26-33	(219)	—	.982	—	.706	—	1.000
1931-38	18-25	(83)	34-41	(181)	.442	.922	.370	.511	.534	.953
1923-30	26-33	(212)	42-49	(191)	.623	.817	.476	.646	.637	.927
1915-22	34-41	(227)	50-57	(158)	.920	1.000	.661	.872	.996	.998
1907-14	42-49	(174)	58-65	(132)	.976	.869	.656	.808	1.000	.910
1899-06	50-57	(125)	66-83	(151)	.819	.736	.746	.444	.893	.755
1891-98	58-65	(94)			.766	—	.366	—	.933	—
1873-90	66-83	(92)			.721	—	.410	—	.832	—
Total		(1045)		(1237)	.824	.872	.579	.581	.869	.893

born in the years between 1939 and 1946 and its members were 16-23 years old in the early 1960s. Coming of age in the decade of the 1960s, this cohort experienced its "impressionable years" during one of the most turbulent periods in recent American political history. It seems likely, then, that this cohort may have entered the 1970s with highly crystallized partisan identities, generating highly stable identities somewhat prematurely over the early life course. Unlike their 1950s counterparts—those 26-33 in the mid-1950s— who grew to political maturity in the politically stable and economically prosperous years following World War II, the "pre-Baby Boom" cohorts entered midlife with their political minds made up. The group that grew to political maturity during the 1950s, as indicated in Table 7.3, reveals a gradual increase in the stability of party identification, compared to their juniors; and they are not as highly persistent as the group going before— those 34-41 in the 1950s study. By contrast, those 26-33 in the 1970s study were vastly more stable than their junior counterparts and had reached a level of stability similar to the 34-41 year olds in both studies, again suggesting a premature, historically unique crystallization of identities.

Despite this important and interesting exception, the results shown in Table 7.3 lead to the conclusion that there are relatively durable life cycle factors involved in the development of party loyalties. This pattern of life span trajectories of stability follows a model that suggests that identities are quite malleable in young adulthood, during which time historical factors potentially contribute to cohort experiences, but thereafter identities tend to stabilize to a high degree (see Alwin, 1994a). This interpretation, while acknowledging the possibility of unique cohort departures from the main lines of aging/stability shown here, suggests that the results have considerable generality. However, it would be a mistake to generalize too far beyond the historical context and it would be an even greater mistake to generalize to other domains. I already indicated that the findings for the intensity component of political identification may be a weaker reflection of this pattern, in keeping with the "trait vs. state" interpretation of the difference between direction and intensity. In this sense, intensity may behave much more like measures of attitudes, which generally do not show such high levels of molar stability (see Alwin, 1994a; Alwin & Krosnick, 1991b).

⬡ CONCLUSIONS

Focusing on the relationship between aging and political conservatism, this paper has addressed the broader issues of the linkage between aging and social change. Many interpretations of social change make assumptions about the nature of human stability, particularly those positing processes of cohort replacement. I argued that such interpretations make assumptions, not only about differences in cohort experiences but also about the relative tendency for such differences to remain intact over time via mechanisms of human stability. Similarly, theories that suggest social change occurs via intracohort change, regardless of cohort replacement effects, also make assumptions about the capacity for individuals to change. Thus, my paper has focused on how the study of stability in human lives can help us understand the linkage between social and individual change.

By relying in part on the distinction between the concepts of "trait" versus "state," it is possible to draw some conclusions about the linkage between patterns of stability and cohort replacement effects. The concept of trait is used to represent those stable components of behavioral predispositions, which drive subsequent social change and, conversely, the concept of state is used to represent transitory components of behavior, which are linked to social experiences (including the effects of social change and aging) producing individual-level change. The elaboration of this distinction is viewed as an essential ingredient in the development of a theory that will explain variation in the linkage between individual and social processes across conceptual domains.

The issue of whether human characteristics become relatively stable early in adulthood is, of course, germane to ways in which cohort replacement effects can occur. The presence of high levels of individual stabilities early in adulthood make it possible to interpret cohort replacement effects as cohort effects, rather than life cycle or aging effects. The stability estimates provided above suggest that there is a range of possible patterns of stability over the life span but that throughout midlife there is considerable stability in political orientations. Levels of stability for the directional component of party identification, for example, are decidedly stronger and more "trait-like" than those associated with the intensity component. At the same time, these results may support aging interpretations of the movement toward greater strength in the intracohort component of change.

These results suggest that by considering estimates of stability from panel data, along with the distinction between "traits" and "states," it is possible to give some greater insight into the typical patterns that emerge from the analysis of repeated cross-sectional data. Further research is needed to explore the sources of these patterns of molar stability. Obviously, what we have described in the above do not reflect simply the stability of individuals. In effect what is being assessed is the relative stability of individuals within particular environments, such that estimated stability coefficients summarize the stability of *both* persons and their environments. And although there has been some attention to the issue of the relative role of psychological traits, there has been much less attention to questions of the stability of the elements of environments that persons inhabit. We can distinguish between two complementary sources of stability and change of individuals over time, noting that factors leading to stability may reside both in the person and in the environment. Individuals may differ in their *susceptibility* to change, that is, something inherently different among individuals in their predispositions to stability. Age, for example, is often thought to be a factor that conditions the nature of the individual's flexibility or ability to change. Or, individuals may differ in the *opportunities for change* presented by the social environment, and these may vary over the life course as well as over historical time. We may, thus, contrast explanations of human stability and change that rely on *personological* factors that might implicate differential tendencies of individuals to resist or incorporate change with those *sociological* explanations that target differences in environmentally based experiences in accounting for change and stability.

◎ NOTES

1. The latter are usually called "period" effects. I prefer to use the term "time," or "occasion of measurement" in this context, reserving the term "period" for a broader expanse of survey occasions.

2. This type of "boundaryless" definition of the concept may prove to be more all-encompassing than what may be justified on the basis of cross-disciplinary agreement on what is referred to by the term *personality*. However, lacking a better designation for the conceptual domain of focus, for present purposes I simply equate the term *personality* with individual differences in predispositions to behave in various ways, regardless of their origins, be they biological, social, or some combination of both. Indeed, part of the overall goal of a focus on human stability is to allocate various human characteristics to various realms, as designated by their degree of stability (see Alwin, 1994a).

3. Social change was measured as the difference in the mean scores for the first two surveys of the period compared to the two most recent surveys. For the intracohort and cohort replacement components, I measure statistical significance in terms of the Type I error rate associated with the coefficients b_1 and b_2 in the equation referred to above.

4. There is some recognition in the psychological literature of the need to deal with measurement errors (see Block, 1977, 1981; Epstein, 1980; Rushton, Brainerd, & Pressley, 1983). Although the solutions proposed move in the right direction, they do not accomplish the separation of errors or measurement from true change that I advocate here.

CHAPTER EIGHT

Establishing a Reference Frame
Against Which to Chart
Age-Related Changes

JOHN R. NESSELROADE
DAVID L. FEATHERMAN

◇ OVERVIEW

The representation and assessment of changes in behavioral attributes are among the most challenging tasks faced by students of adult development and aging. Two classes of concepts that we believe warrant some additional evaluative scrutiny in this context are *stability* and *intraindividual variability*. We will examine selected aspects of these two classes of concepts in relation to the matter of representing and measuring change, emphasizing an adult development and aging perspective. But the matters to be raised are germane to other contexts, too. We will recognize explicitly some of the generality before concluding. Because we have a point to make, our treatment of the two classes of concepts admittedly will be somewhat uneven.

   Various scholars have rendered critical evaluations of the pedigree of traditional concepts of stability (e.g., Gergen, 1977; Holling, 1973; Nowak, Vallacher, & Lewenstein, 1994). Despite the sobering points made in such assessments, however, stability concepts retain a privileged seat at the social and behavioral science table. By contrast, some interesting and we believe vitally important intraindividual variability concepts have been forced off to the corner farthest from the principal activities; the corner littered with "noise," error variance, and other embarrassments to a generally equilibrium-oriented household. Our intention is to examine the concepts of stability and intraindividual variability for the purpose of bringing their respective statuses a little more in line with what we perceive to be their potential for furthering developmental research.

In brief, the objective of this chapter is twofold. First, we want to explore, in selective fashion, aspects of stability and intraindividual variability in relation to developmental research, broadly defined. In particular, we will focus on the relative roles and implications of these concepts in the measurement and structuring of changes. As noted earlier, we will feature a life span developmental perspective. Second, we want to draw some implications from current empirical research findings and methodological considerations regarding intraindividual variability concepts for the next round of assaults on the secrets of development and change that nature seems to guard so jealously. We will question the role that stability has played while further promoting what we see to be the expanding role of intraindividual variability in the study of behavior and its development.

⊠ STABILITY AND INTRAINDIVIDUAL VARIABILITY

We will begin with brief definitions of the principal relevant concepts and an identification of their selected aspects to be further considered. We will illustrate many of the abstractions with concrete examples and empirical data drawn from developmental research.

What is Stability?

Just what do we mean by stability? The class of associated concepts has been reviewed and discussed in a number of sources (e.g., Alwin, 1994b; Kagan, 1980; Mortimer, Finch, & Kumka, 1982). Mortimer et al. (1982) summarized extant concepts of stability under four labels; *structural invariance, normative, level,* and *ipsative.*

1. *Structural invariance* refers to consistency in the multivariate patterning of relationships between latent variables and the manifest variables that are used to represent those indicators in empirical research. Invariance of factor loadings (the weights describing the regressions of manifest variables on the latent factors) is the best known and most systematically studied case. Discussions of factor invariance are too numerous and complex to represent here but excellent discussions of the topic are readily available (e.g., Labouvie & Reutsch, 1995; McArdle & Cattell, 1994; Meredith, 1964,

1994). Moreover, the structural modeling literature also contains many informative discussions of the topic.

2. *Normative stability* refers to the extent to which individuals or other entities retain their relative ranks or statuses on attributes of interest across times of measurement.

3. *Level stability* refers essentially to the extent to which scores (either individual or group means) remain invariant across times of measurement.

4. *Ipsative stability* refers to the extent to which the organization of multiple attributes (e.g., relative salience or relative strength of one attribute versus that of others) within the individual remains invariant across times of measurement. Personality research summarized by Block (1971) illustrates well the context for this kind of stability.

Thus, stability is a class of concepts, each member of which has played a significant role in the last several decades of behavioral research and, as pointed out by Gergen (1977), stability has contributed to our understanding of a variety of phenomena. Nevertheless, as traditionally employed even in the context of developmental research, stability emphasizes stasis, equilibrium, constancy, and, in general, the lack of change; at least the lack of differential change.

What is Intraindividual Variability?

The label *intraindividual variability* also encompasses a broad set of concepts, the components of which have been described and systematically researched for nearly three-quarters of a century (Cattell, 1957, 1966; Cattell & Scheier, 1961; Fiske & Rice, 1955; Flugel, 1929; Larsen, 1987, 1992; Nesselroade & Featherman, 1991; Thouless, 1936; Woodrow, 1932). For our purposes here, we will focus explicitly on the following four aspects of intraindividual variability:

1. within-person change that may or may not be reversible and that may or may not be synchronous across individuals (e.g., development, learning, etc.),
2. within-person changes that are more or less reversible and that may or may not be synchronous over individuals (e.g., states, moods, emotions, "transients," "wobble," etc.),
3. patterns of organization of intraindividual variability within the individual. For instance, is the person who is highly variable on one dimension highly variable in others?

4. patterns of intraindividual variation reflecting the profile or organization of an individual's attributes (e.g., Smith puts integrity above all else). Such patterns have been the focus of assessments of ipsative stability as discussed above (see also Block, 1971; Buss, 1979; Emmerich, 1968).

As will be seen subsequently, these four kinds of intraindividual variability are keys to some important potential convergences in the study of personality. It is our view that intraindividual variability, especially the second and third kinds, have been paid too little attention in developmental research (Nesselroade, 1988, 1991; Nesselroade & Featherman, 1991). Subsequently we will identify how this kind of information can be more fully and usefully incorporated into developmental research and theorizing.

⊠ A DEVELOPMENTAL PERSPECTIVE

Stability and intraindividual variability, as empirically derived tendencies within behavior, are inherently developmental constructs (Baltes, 1985; Baltes & Goulet, 1970; Baltes, Reese, & Nesselroade, 1977). That is, both stability and intraindividual variability summarize time- or age-related changes in mind and behavior (Featherman & Petersen, 1986). But more than that, by making explicit one's developmental interpretation of behavioral change within segments of the life course or across the full life span, one potentially alters the relative importance—at least conceptually—of stability versus intraindividual variability.

Developmentalists seek to understand how individuals adapt to but also shape their biocultural environments over the course of life; indeed, the historical dynamics of changes in the life course itself and the evolution of the human genome also are the stuff of developmental study (Featherman & Lerner, 1985). Within such a developmental view, however, we suggest that the conceptual significance of stability versus intraindividual variability becomes highly problematic, and we would go further to suggest that variability becomes far easier to explain, whereas stability becomes more difficult.

For example, Baltes, Lindenberger, and Staudinger (in press), in elaborating a life span perspective, suggested that development entails a sequence of simultaneous gains and losses in capacity and performance. In adapting to both their biological and cultural (environmental) contexts along the life course, persons select goals and means to their achievement that maximize gains over losses, insofar as possible; optimize adaptational outcomes by substituting achievable goals for the unattainable or by changing or modifying situational niches; and, perhaps especially later in life, compensate for loss of capacity or control over outcomes by specialized or selective focusing on one life domain and delimited competencies so as to stem the pace of loss and the range of limitation. Taking such an adaptational, evolutionary, or historical view almost by definition leads one to expect intraindividual variation in behavior and measured latent capacities as the usual background of development. Observed intraindividual variation is not "noise" but rather is the consequence of adaptation to changing, dynamic, biocultural contexts and of attempts, witting or not, to optimize gains over losses.

From the developmental perspective just described, stability, rather than variability, is unusual; at the very least stability becomes conceptually and functionally problematic and must be explained. Perhaps the explanation of stability or invariance (see above for various forms or definitions of invariance) is to be found in the ways by which stability enhances adaptive capacity, especially to the social contexts of adulthood (Featherman, Smith, & Peterson, 1990). For example, Alwin (1994a) studied the persistence and change of attitudes and behaviors of an adolescent college cohort into later life and posited six trajectories that he subsequently observed. His observed levels of stability were not features of attributes per se but rather reflected age-specific patterns in which the middle-adult years showed comparatively more stability but not for all individuals. It is intriguing to speculate that middle-aged adults, at least in American culture, are seen as more "mature" and held in higher esteem to the degree that they project themselves as consistent, stable and thereby, perhaps, more reliable. Although the empirical basis for "midlife crises" remains controversial, the very idea and the pejorative connotation of the label presume the cultural normalcy and functional benefit of stability (but see Sheehy, 1995, for a popularized dissenting view and a commentary on changing cultural valuation of "mature" adult attributes, including constancy of life goals, behavior, and motives).

In summary, as an organizing idea for the study of development, intraindividual variability possesses greater theoretical grounding than stability and should be expected, almost by definition, within the dynamics of adaptation and selective optimization of gains and losses over the course of life. In the following section, we will look in greater detail at some of the ways in which stability and intraindividual concepts have influenced the study of developmental phenomena.

◇ STABILITY AND INTRAINDIVIDUAL VARIABILITY IN DEVELOPMENTAL RESEARCH

What Have Stability Concepts Done for Us?

Central to our thesis is the idea that concepts of stability are closely tied to a static modeling premise that is characterized by lack of change as the norm and, therefore, one from which it follows that change is a departure from the norm. It is clear, however, that stability and change are intimately tied together (Nesselroade & Boker, 1994) in the sense that defining one compels recognition of the other. Certainly, change cannot be evaluated without a stable frame of reference but this is not the same as assuming that the fundamental state of nature is stability with change being a (perhaps) interesting departure from it. Relativity theory did not do away with the need for a reference frame in order to construe changes but rather emphasized that there are alternative reference frames among which to choose—and different reference frames provide different indications of change!

The influence of stability concepts has had both theoretical and methodological impact on the scientific enterprise in general. More to the point, the cluster of concepts to which the term stability refers has literally dominated most areas of social and behavioral science. In reference to stability concepts, Gergen (1977) said that this " overarching analytic template essentially registered stability and eschewed the transitory" (p. 140). From a theoretical perspective the profoundly felt need to conceptualize and demonstrate consistency at some temporal and/or trans-situational level has influenced mightily the shape of research and theorizing about human behavior in the past several decades. For instance, a fierce preoccupation with stability concepts is manifested within the area of adult development and aging research (e.g., Costa & McCrae, 1994). Methodologically, a stability orientation has strongly influenced how measurement is conceptualized, how measuring instruments are developed and evaluated (see e.g., Nunnally, 1967), and how empirical studies are designed and implemented.

There is no doubt that stability concepts have abetted the study of development in valuable ways. Without the concept of *structural invariance*, for example, the quantitative, multivariate study of change with its reliance on repeated measurements, latent variables, and mathematico-statistical modeling would not be the productive activity we know today (Alwin, 1988; Bollen, 1989). In a similar vein, normative stability, especially as incarnated in test-retest correlation coefficients, has helped to stimulate, albeit sometimes in ill-conceived ways, concern for the quality of measurement devices.

Test-retest correlations, however, which are a mainstay both in evaluating the quality of measuring instruments and in conducting substantive research, cannot, in and of themselves, distinguish between the differential changes of individuals and unreliability of the measurement process (Nesselroade, Pruchno, & Jacobs, 1986; Thouless, 1936; Wheaton, Muthén, Alwin, & Summers, 1977).

How Have Stability Concepts Hindered Us?

What are some of the constraints and limitations imposed on our attempts to study developmental and other change phenomena when they occur in a fundamental reference frame of stability? Clearly, the study of change is not precluded as exemplified, for example, in Cattell's (1966) discussion of trait, state, and trait change. However, one is thereby constrained to a limited representation of change. Suppose the course of growth in attribute x is represented as a parabolic function. Other than time itself, the parameters describing the model are fixed rather than time-varying. In more physical terms, change at this level is analogous to velocity (amount of growth per unit of time) rather than being analogous to acceleration (change in amount of growth per unit of time). Time-varying parameters (the antithesis of some aspects of stability), which wreak havoc with traditional modeling approaches, allow one to represent dynamic change patterns (Petersen, 1986, 1990).

Despite efforts to delineate the concept of stability in a more sensitive, productive way (Alwin, 1994a; Mortimer et al., 1982), the concept still tends to be rendered operational by test-retest correlations, reflecting mainly what Mortimer et al. (1982) called normative stability. At best, the naive test-retest approach represents a narrow construction of stability that simply is inadequate as a backdrop for studying dynamics and developmental changes. Moreover, this limiting situation exists at both ends of the stability continuum. High test-retest correlation is "good" when one is focused on interindividual difference dimensions that are putatively stable (traits) whereas low test-retest correlation is "good" when one is measuring episodic or transient dimensions such as emotions (states). But low test-retest values might reflect low reliability of measurement, low stability of the attribute being measured, or both. Stability concepts, especially those rooted in test-retest correlations, have in effect blocked us from the systematic study of intraindividual variability matters that we believe, in the end, will serve the study of development importantly.

Another key feature of the stasis orientation is the reliance on determining a "true score" as the idealized measurement objective. Although the true score can only be known with some error of measurement attached to it (the observed score), the objective of measurement is often perceived to be settling on a single value that characterizes the endowment of a person on a given attribute. Improving one's measures means reducing the amount of "error" associated with these true scores. In theory, true scores can change with time but as the change measurement literature shows, there is much controversy and disagreement about how to represent change within this stability dominated framework or whether it should be done at all (e.g., Cronbach & Furby, 1970).

Acceptance of a stasis orientation, either actively or passively, has greatly limited the enunciation of alternative concepts of stability and change and thereby the representation of complex phenomena. Consider the arguments put forth by Baltes (1985) and by Schulz and Heckhausen (1996) concerning the complexity of the gains and losses pattern of change across the life span. How can one hope to capture this level of complexity with a table of test-retest coefficients? Or, from the standpoint of selection and selection effects (Nesselroade & Jones, 1985), test-retest correlations are based on two occasions of measurement and one interval—the narrowest possible basis from which to estimate stability or assess change.

The essential problem is not with an overt emphasis on stability and equilibrium concepts as much as it is with the more subtle and pervasive command with which stability has held sway over the very concepts, definitions, and basic activities by which we try to represent and understand change. Developmentalists and students of other kinds of change have had to contend with a generic orientation toward stability in both direct and indirect ways. There exists in the literature over a half-century of lively, sometimes rancorous debate concerning the fundamental question of how to represent and evaluate change (Collins & Horn, 1991; Cronbach & Furby, 1970; Harris, 1963; McNemar, 1958; Rogosa, 1988). Some of the more contentious issues can be ascribed to limiting notions about behavioral and social attributes and their measurement that are imposed by a tacit, fundamental acceptance of stability as the primordial condition of the living organism. Of course, there are substantive reasons for the strong emphasis on stability in behavioral research (Nesselroade, 1988; Nesselroade, Featherman, & Tomer, 1997). These include the fact that (a) stability embodies at a very understandable level the scientifically basic idea of invariance, and (b) stability signifies an apparently necessary if not sufficient condition for predictive validity across time and situation. Thus, stability concepts have fundamentally directed and organized behavioral research. Because prediction leads to control and understanding, a central task has been to find those differentiating but stable variables that will enhance prediction.

For us, the central question is: Should stability be an underlying presumption about nature, "departures" from which are the empirical events that need to be explained or should stability be an empirical event that, if found, requires explanation? From a living systems perspective (Ford, 1987), change and intraindividual variability are inherent characteristics of the organism, special cases of which (e.g., zero variability) are various aspects of stability. On the one hand, if stability is an accurate, proper characterization of some attributes of the organism it needs to be acknowledged. On the other hand, however, if stability is a metatheoretical ideal that "drives" the collection, evaluation, and interpretation of empirical information and the development of methodological and analytic tools, and in so doing perpetuates itself, that needs to be recognized and acknowledged also. Such recognition is an important first step toward the consideration and subsequent adoption of other metatheoretical ideals such as inherent change and dynamics that, according to West (1985), are more scientifically advanced than are stability-dominated paradigms.

In summary then, stability has had some positive impacts on the study of development and change but it has also had negative ones. To reiterate our essential argument: stability should be a means to an end, rather than an end in itself. Empirical research that finishes with a few summary stability coefficients implies that stability is an end in itself and stifles further questions regarding the nature of the attributes under consideration. Alwin (1994a), in contrast, focused on stability of various personality attributes but emphasized the information to be drawn from patterns of change and difference in the stabilities of attributes across the life span. Thus, he used stability as a means to an end; as a tool by which additional leverage could be gained on the nature of functioning, development, and other kinds of changes. In a similar vein, asking the developmental question "Are there adaptive advantages to stability and, if so, under what circumstances?" uses the concept of stability as a tool for understanding developmental phenomena rather than as an end in itself.

What Has the Concept of Intraindividual Variability Done for Us?

Earlier, we noted four aspects of intraindividual variability, three of which are particularly germane to our objectives for this chapter. The first directly pertinent aspect had to do with intraindividual changes such as maturation, learning, developmental changes, and so forth. Defining the substance of developmental inquiry in terms of the study of interindividual differences (and similarities) in intraindividual change patterns (Baltes, Reese, & Nesselroade, 1977) critically emphasized both the elemental nature of intraindividual variability (intraindividual change patterns) and the derivative nature of stability concepts (interindividual differences). This idea we likened to the concept of secular change in the economics literature.

The second aspect of intraindividual variability involved often shorter-term, more or less reversible changes such as are involved in states, moods, emotions, and the like. This we likened somewhat to the concept of episodic change in economics. The trait-state distinction, for example, which sprang directly from the study of short-term changes (see e.g., Cattell & Scheier, 1961) has done much to shape measurement and design issues as well as theoretical concerns. For example, the distinction has helped to sharpen the stability versus lability issues underlying this discussion (Nesselroade, Pruchno, & Jacobs, 1986). The trait-state distinction has contributed importantly to the recognition of short-term variability on measurable behavioral and psychological attributes as a set of characteristics that help define both the nature of individuals just as much as do putatively stable traits captured by single scores or measurements (Cattell & Scheier, 1961; Eizenman, Nesselroade, Featherman, & Rowe, 1996; Kim, Nesselroade, & Featherman, 1996; Larsen, 1987, 1992; Mischel, 1991; Nesselroade, 1991; Nesselroade & Featherman, 1991).

There is a strong surge of interest in formulating more "dynamic" representations of interesting behavioral phenomena (Larsen, 1987, 1992; Molenaar, 1985; Thelen & Smith, 1994; Vallacher & Nowak, 1994) that we see as closely linked to the study of short-term, intraindividual variability. Empirical research and modeling efforts in other disciplines make the case as dramatically (and chillingly so!) as does work in human development. In ecology, for example, Holling (1973) argued that

> The present concerns for pollution and endangered species are specific signals that the well-being of the world is not adequately described by concentrating on equilibria and conditions near them. . . . It is at least conceivable that the effective and responsible effort to provide a maximum sustained yield from a fish population or a nonfluctuating supply of water from a watershed (both equilibrium-centered views) might paradoxically increase the chance for extinctions. (p. 2)

But a variety of recent work in behavioral research also illustrates a growing interest in intraindividual variability phenomena that represent the substrate for other behaviors. For example, Hampson (1990) showed that intraindividual variation in the performance of a sample of women on a battery of ability tasks divided into "tests that favored men" and "tests that favored women" reflected intraindividual variation in estrogen levels. The nature of the variation was that higher levels of estrogen correlated with higher performance on tests that favored women (e.g., verbal tasks) and lower levels of estrogen correlated with higher performance on tests that favored men (e.g., spatial relations tasks). May, Hasher, and Stoltzfus (1993) revealed that intraindividual variability in performance associated with time of day can be an important influence on apparent age-related cognitive differences. Butler, Hokanson, and Flynn (1994) demonstrated that lability in self-esteem reports was a more potent predictor of depression proneness than was trait self-esteem. Eizenman et al. (1996) compared intraindividual variability and level in self-reported locus of control scores and found that individual differences in amounts of intraindividual variability greatly enhanced the prediction of mortality 5 years later. Siegler (1993) has pointed to the important role that intraindividual variability plays in cognitive development. Crow (1977) proposed that behavioral variability could be an important unifying behavioral concept because it integrates such a wide array of findings.

Powerful evidence for the predictive value of intraindividual variability has important implications for methodological concerns such as assessment and evaluation as well as for elaboration of our basic understanding of behavior. The empirical evidence that is accruing for the potency and generality of intraindividual variability as fundamental, determining characteristics of the organism can (and should!) tear at the very fabric of our stasis-oriented view of behavior and behavior development. From West's (1985) perspective on the evolution of scientific disciplines, it may be time for such a confrontation if the study of behavior is to advance to the next level. Encouraging applications of dynamical systems modeling to behavioral data suggest that the methodological substrate that will be key to rapid advance is at least partially available already (Thelen & Smith, 1994; Vallacher & Nowak, 1994).

The organization of intraindividual variability has both a temporal and an atemporal aspect to it. As was mentioned earlier, students of personality have focused on patterns of organization of putatively stable traits (ability, temperament, and motivational) within the individual that may or may not change with time (e.g., Block, 1971; Broverman, 1962; Cattell, 1957). From our perspective, a more interesting question is *What is the organization of the rhythms and other intraindividual variability phenomena that characterize the living, behaving organism?* Another example of this more abstract

notion of patterns of organization of intraindividual variability is seen in
work by Mischel (1991; see also Shoda, Mischel, & Wright, 1994) who has
argued that the consistency that personality researchers have been seeking
for so long resides in the nature of intraindividual variability patterns
manifested across situations. For example, aggression may dominate a person's behavior whenever he or she is in situation A but not in situation B.
Thus, Jones is not consistently "aggressive" across all situations as some
versions of "trait" theory would have it but, rather, Jones *varies* consistently;
being aggressive when in situation A but not when in situation B. At one
level, Mischel's (1991) formulation has much in common with Cattell's
(1979) model of modulation that invokes differences in the situation and state
of the organism as modifiers of how an individual's traits are expressed in
his or her actual behavior.

Interest in intraindividual variability has rekindled discussions about
nomothetic versus idiographic aspects of personality research (Lamiell,
1988; Mischel, 1991; Nesselroade & Ford, 1985; Shoda et al., 1994; Zevon
& Tellegen, 1982). The connection is as much structural as conceptual in that
the only way one can generate analyzable multivariate data at the individual
level is by repeatedly measuring, in different temporal and/or spatial contexts. Nevertheless, despite differences in details, one can see a convergence
of ideas concerning the importance of intraindividual variability as a potential locus of consistency in personality. Mischel (1991; see also Shoda et al.,
1994), for example, argued that "Consistent with a cognitive social view of
personality, the locus of expected coherence becomes such intraindividual
stability in patterns of variability, not the cross-situational consistency coefficient" (p. 146).

⊠ SOME CONVERGENCES OF INTRAINDIVIDUAL
VARIABILITY AND STABILITY CONCERNS

There are several aspects of convergence between the intraindividual variability and stability issues we have been discussing. Some of these are
well-recognized in the behavioral and social science literature; others are
not. Certainly, we do not advocate that the concept of stability be done away
with; rather its application needs to be expanded to include phenomena in
addition to scores signifying how much of a given attribute an individual
has. Two examples include the further differentiation of stability coefficients
as exemplified recently by Alwin (1994a) and the application of the concept
of stability to patterns of intraindividual variability. The latter is exemplified

in the work of various researchers working quite independently of each other. We will examine each topic in turn.

Variability in Stability

Earlier, it was noted that stability could be conceptualized as a means to an end, rather than an end in itself. Alwin's (1994a) investigation of stability and variability exemplifies this argument. He treated stability (of a given attribute) as a phenomenon that possibly changed over the individual's life span. Alwin listed six trajectories that might be observed including persistence, lifelong openness, increasing persistence, impressionable years, mid-life stability, and decreasing persistence. Each of these trajectories thus reflects the interplay between intraindividual variability and stability as it is modified by experiences. In other words, level of stability is not a feature of an attribute but a feature of an attribute at a given chronological age of the participants. Alwin's orientation clearly allows for intraindividual variability in the attributes while employing the stability coefficient as a descriptor of some limited features of the intraindividual variability. The model Alwin labels as *Persistence,* for instance, characterizes a trajectory of high test-retest stability between adjacent measurement occasions across the life span. Although such a model seems to be what many personality researchers have in mind when they study traits, two features of *Persistence* need to be recognized. First, it is only one of six different stability trajectories. Second, its demonstration rests on many occasions of measurement, not two or three.

Consistency in Intraindividual Variability

There are several examples of consistency in intraindividual variability that we wish to highlight as examples of convergence between intraindividual variability and stability concerns. One involves the work by Mischel and colleagues (Mischel, 1991; Shoda et al., 1994) mentioned earlier in connection with research on consistency in the patterns of intraindividual variability manifested across situation and time by individuals.

Another example of consistency in intraindividual variability is exemplified by Larsen's (1987; 1992) discussion of "higher order" consistency in which parameters of intraindividual variability dimensions are the "carriers" of individual differences information that can be used for prediction purposes. For example, some individuals might be "high variability" persons and others "low variability" persons. As was indicated earlier, Eizenman et al. (1996) found this to be the case with self-reported locus of control.

Moreover, amount of intraindividual variability tended to be relatively stable across several months and was predictive of mortality 5 years after the measurement of amount of variability was concluded.

The essential point is that (a) repeated measurements show that individuals do vary from occasion to occasion on attributes that are often conceptualized as stable, and (b) aspects of the variability (e.g., magnitude, lability, latency) constitute a class of interindividual differences variables that (c) have been demonstrated to be valid predictors of important outcomes. In the special case of no intraindividual variability, the only meaningful aspect left is the nonvarying value that is the analog of the "true score" of classical test theory. Thus, with living systems, intraindividual variability is a more general target than the long sought after "true score" as the way to characterize the "base" condition of the organism. That said, how interindividual differences in intraindividual variability come about and how they change over time emerge as key questions for developmentalists to ponder.

⊠ CONCLUSION

Concepts of stability and intraindividual variability are critical to the study of behavior and its development. Concepts of stability have tended to dominate the first century or so of scientific research on the pertinent issues. That this would be the case is not a surprise, to the extent that accounts of the nature of progress in science such as West's (1985) are accurate. Concepts of stability, linearity, and additive relations are precursors of concepts of intraindividual variability, nonlinearity, and multiplicative relations.

Before one chooses to let go of a more primitive set of concepts one has to be aware of a desirable, less primitive alternative. Both practice and arguments from a number of quarters are suggesting that behavioral and social scientists are recognizing that the time has come to slip the shackles of the dominant paradigm of the past century or so—stability and equilibrium—in favor of one in which change and variability are regarded as essential characteristics of the living organism. Life involves cycles, oscillations, and fluctuations; all subject to perturbations and disturbances. Even such apparent "stabilities" as standing upright are accomplished by an organism that is constantly making "corrections" that keep it from falling over. That this process is so smooth and continuous as to defy detection is not a tribute to stability but rather a tribute to a mechanism that produces apparent stability upon a substrate of intraindividual variability.

The implications of such an impending shift reach all aspects of the scientific enterprise from the abstract and theoretical to the fundamentals of methodology. From the devising of measurement protocols, the design of data collection schemes, and the analysis of empirical data to the operational definition of key variables and the articulation of theory, a tacit acceptance of intraindividual variability and change exerts a remarkably different influence than does a tacit acceptance of stability. Attempts to capture intraindividual variability and change phenomena by merely extending the old tools and approaches of stability must give way to the development and implementation of new conceptions as has been happening in the physical sciences for some time. For example, deterministic and stochastic nonlinear models in which stability is the construction and intraindividual variability is the substrate (e.g., an attractor) exemplify the kind of shift we believe is already underway in the behavioral and social sciences.

In closing this chapter, we return to the question inherent in its title: What is the appropriate reference frame against which to chart age-related changes? Our conclusion is that they should be charted against a background of intraindividual variability rather than one of putative stability. Descriptively, how does the magnitude and other parameters of intraindividual variability change across the life span? From an explanatory perspective, what are the mechanisms by which intraindividual variability comes about and is modified over the life span? Phrasing developmental questions in these terms gives priority to variation and change. If stability is there, it can still be identified as a special case. The converse is not true. Intraindividual variability is not a special case of stability. An overarching concern with stability should not be allowed to stifle further research on intraindividual variability in behavioral manifestations, the links of which to developmental phenomena are beginning to be glimpsed—and that look exciting and important!

References

Abbott, A. (1992). From causes to events: Notes on narrative positivism. *Sociological Methods and Research, 20,* 428-455.

Abbott, A. (1995). Sequence analysis: New methods for old ideas. *Annual Review of Sociology, 21,* 93-113.

Abbott, A., & Hrycak, A. M. (1990). Measuring resemblance in sequence data. *American Journal of Sociology, 96,* 144-185.

Abrahamse, A., Morrison, P., & Waite, L. J. (1988). *Beyond stereotypes: Who becomes a single teenage mother?* (R-3489-HHS/NICHD). Santa Monica, CA: The RAND Corporation.

Abramson, P. R. (1976). Generational change and the decline of party identification in America, 1952-74. *American Political Science Review, 70,* 469-478.

Abramson, P. R. (1979). Developing party identification: A further examination of life-cycle, generational, and period effects. *American Journal of Political Science, 23,* 78-96.

Abramson, P. R. (1983). *Political attitudes in America.* New York: Freeman.

Agathon (pseudonym; Alfred Tarde & Henri Massis). (1912). *Les jeunes gens d'aujourd'hui.* Paris: Plon Nourrit.

Ageorges, J. (1912). *La marche montante d'une génération (1890-1910).* Paris.

Ainslie, G. (1985). Beyond microeconomics: Conflict among interests in a multiple self as a determinant of value. In J. Elster (Ed.), *The multiple self* (pp. 133-175). Cambridge, UK: Cambridge University Press.

Ainslie, G. (1992). *Picoeconomics: The strategic interaction of successive motivational states within the person.* Cambridge, UK: Cambridge University Press.

Allison, P. D. (1984). *Event history analysis: Regression for longitudinal data.* Beverly Hills, CA: Sage.

Althauser, R. P. (1989). Job histories, career lines and firm internal labor markets: An analysis of job shifts. *Research in Social Stratification and Mobility, 8,* 177-200.

Althauser, R. P., & van Veen, K. (1994). *An algorithm for identifying career lines from job history data.* Manuscript submitted for publication.

Alwin, D. F. (1988). Structural equation models in research on human development and aging. In K. W. Schaie, R. T. Campbell, W. Meredith, & S. C. Rawlings (Eds.), *Methodological issues in aging research* (pp. 71-170). New York: Springer.

Alwin, D. F. (1994a). Aging, personality and social change: The stability of individual differences over the adult life-span. In D.L. Featherman, R.M. Lerner, & M. Perlmutter (Eds.), *Life-span development and behavior* (Vol. 12, pp. 136-185). Hillsdale, NJ: Lawrence Erlbaum.

Alwin, D. F. (1994b). Quantitative methods in social psychology. In K. Cook, G. Fine, & J. House (Eds.), *Sociological perspectives in social psychology* (pp. 650-680). Boston: Allyn & Bacon.

Alwin, D. F. (1995). Taking time seriously: Studying social change, social structure and human lives. In P. Moen, G. H. Elder, Jr., & K. Lüscher (Eds.), *Examining lives in context: Perspectives on the ecology of human development* (pp. 211-262). Washington, D.C.: American Psychological Association.

Alwin, D. F. (1996). Parental socialization in historical perspective. In C. D. Ryff & M. M. Seltzer (Ed.), The parental experience in midlife (pp. 105-167). Chicago: University of Chicago Press.

Alwin, D. F., Cohen, R. L., & Newcomb, T. M. (1991). *Political attitudes over the life-span: The Bennington women after fifty years.* Madison: University of Wisconsin Press.

Alwin, D. F., & Krosnick, J. A. (1991a). Aging, cohorts and the stability of socio-political orientations over the life-span. *American Journal of Sociology, 97,* 169-195.

Alwin, D. F., & Krosnick, J. A. (1991b). The reliability of survey attitude measurement: The influence of question and respondent attributes. *Sociological Methods and Research, 20,* 139-181.

Alwin, D. F., Scott, J., & Braun, M. (1996, August). *Sex-role attitude change in the United States: National trends and cross-national comparisons.* Paper presented at the biennial meetings of the Research Committee on Social Stratification (RC28) of the International Sociological Association. Ann Arbor, MI.

Aminzade, R. (1992). Historical sociology and time. *Sociological Methods and Research, 21,* 456-480.

Anderson, J. E. (1957). Dynamics of development: System in process. In D. B. Harris (Ed.), *The concept of development* (pp. 25-46). Minneapolis: University of Minnesota Press.

Arrow, K. J. (1973). The theory of discrimination. In O. Ashenfelter & A. Rees (Eds.), *Discrimination in labor markets* (pp. 3-33). Princeton: Princeton University Press.

Asendorpf, J. B. (1992). Continuity and stability of personality traits and personality patterns. In J. B. Asendorpf & J. Valsiner (Eds.), *Stability and change in development* (pp. 116-154). Newbury Park, CA: Sage.

Augustine. (1991). *On Genesis against the Manichees.* In R. J. Teske (Trans.), *Saint Augustine on Genesis* (pp. 45-141). Washington, DC: Catholic University of America Press. (Original work published in 388)

Avioli, P. S., & Kaplan, K. (1992). A panel study of married women's work patterns. *Sex Roles, 26,* 227-243.

Bainville, J. (1918). *Histoire de trois générations.* Paris: A. Fayard.

Baldwin, H. (1960, June 5). Turkey's new soldiers. *New York Times.*

Baltes, P. B. (1987). Theoretical propositions of life-span developmental psychology: On the dynamics between growth and decline. *Developmental Psychology, 23,* 611-626.

Baltes, P. B., & Goulet, L. R. (1970). Status and issues of a life-span developmental psychology. In L. R. Goulet & P. B. Baltes (Eds.), *Life-span developmental psychology: Research and theory* (pp. 3-21). San Diego: Academic Press.

Baltes, P. B., Lindenberger, U., & Staudinger, U. M. (in press). Life-span theory in developmental psychology. In W. Damon (Series Ed.) & R. M. Lerner (Vol. Ed.), *Theoretical models of human development: Vol. 1. Handbook of child psychology* (5th ed.). New York: John Wiley.

Baltes, P. B., Reese, H. W., & Nesselroade, J. R. (1977). *Life-span developmental psychology: Introduction to research methods.* Pacific Groves, CA: Brooks/Cole.

Bannerji, H. (1995). *Thinking through.* Toronto: Women's Press.

Baudrillard, J. (1993). *Symbolic exchange and death.* (I. H. Grant, Trans.). London: Sage Ltd. (Original work published 1976)

Bauer, R. A., Inkeles, A., & Kluckhohn, C. (1960). *How the Soviet system works.* New York: Vintage.

Becker, H. S. (1960). Notes on the concept of commitment. *American Journal of Sociology, 66,* 322-340.

Berger, B. M. (1960). How long is a generation? *British Journal of Sociology, 11,* 557-568.

Berger, P. L., & Luckmann, T. (1971). *The social construction of reality.* New York: Penguin Books.

Bernoulli, D. (1954). Exposition of a new theory on the measurement of risk. *Econometrica, 22,* 23-26. (Original work published 1738)

Birren, J. E. (1959). Principles of research on aging. In J. E. Birren (Ed.), *Handbook of aging and the individual* (pp. 3-42). Chicago: University of Chicago Press.

Blalock, H. M. (1984). Contextual effects models: Theoretical and methodological issues. *Annual Review of Sociology, 10,* 353-372.

Block, J. (1971). *Lives through time.* Berkeley, CA: Bancroft.

Block, J. (1977). Advancing the science of personality: Paradigmatic shift or improving the quality of research. In D. Magnusson & N. S. Endler (Eds.), *Psychology at the crossroads: Current issues in interactional psychology* (pp. 37-63). Hillsdale, NJ: Lawrence Erlbaum.

Block, J. (1981). Some enduring and consequential structures of personality. In A. I. Rabin, J. Aronoff, A. M. Barclay, & R. A. Zucker (Eds.), *Further explorations in personality* (pp. 27-43). New York: John Wiley.

Blumer, H. (1939). *Critiques of research in the social sciences I: An appraisal of Thomas and Znaniecki's "The Polish peasant in Europe and America."* (Bulletin 44). New York: Social Science Research Council.

Boas, F. (1911). *Changes in bodily form of descendants of immigrants.* Washington: Government Printing Office.

Bogue, D. J. (1961). Techniques and hypotheses for the study of differential migration: Some notes from an experiment with U.S. data. *International Population Conference, Vol. I,* 405-412.

Böhm-Bawerk, E. (1970). *Capital and interest.* South Holland, IL: Libertarian Press. (Original work published 1889)

Boll, F. (1913). *Die Lebensalter. Ein Beitrag zur antiken Ethnologie und zur Geschichte der Zahlen.* Leipzig: B. G. Teubner.

Bollen, K. A. (1989). *Structural equations with latent variables.* New York: John Wiley.

Boyd, L. H., & Iversen, G. R. (1979). *Contextual analysis: Concepts and statistical techniques.* Belmont, CA: Wadsworth.

Bracker, M. (1954, May 23). There's no class like the class of '29. *New York Times Magazine,* p. 14 et seq.

Brickman, P., & Campbell, D. T. (1971). Hedonic relativism and planning the good society. In M. H. Appley (Ed.), *Adaptation-level theory* (pp. 287-302). New York: Academic Press.

Brim, O. G., Jr. (1964, March). Socialization through the life cycle. *Social Science Research Council Items, 18.*

Brim, O. G., Jr., & Kagan, J. (1980). *Constancy and change in human development.* Cambridge, MA: Harvard University Press

Brinckmann, A. E. (1925). *Spätwerke grosser Meister.* Frankfurt.

Brittain, V. (1949). *Born 1925.* New York: Macmillan.

Broverman, D. M. (1962). Normative and ipsative measurement in psychology. *Psychological Review, 69,* 295-305.

Brown, P. (1985). *The transfer of care: Psychiatric deinstitutionalization and its aftermath.* New York: Routledge.

Bryk, A. S., & Raudenbush, S. W. (1992). *Hierarchical linear models: Applications and data analysis methods.* Newbury Park, CA: Sage.

Bumpass, L. L., Rindfuss, R. R., & Janosik, R. B. (1978). Age and marital status and first birth and the pace of subsequent fertility. *Demography, 15*(1), 75-86.

Burchfield, J. D. (1975). *Lord Kelvin and the age of the Earth.* New York: Science History Publications.

Burt, R. S. (1991). Measuring age as a structural concept. *Social Networks, 13,* 1-34.

Buss, A. R. (1979). Toward a unified framework for psychometric concepts in the multivariate developmental situation: Intraindividual change and inter-and intraindividual differences. In J. R. Nesselroade & P. B. Baltes (Eds.), *Longitudinal research in the study of behavior and development* (pp. 41-59). San Diego: Academic Press.

Butler, A. C., Hokanson, J. E., & Flynn, H. A. (1994). A comparison of self-esteem lability and low trait self-esteem as vulnerability factors for depression. *Journal of Personality and Social Psychology, 66,* 166-177.

Cain, L. D., Jr. (1964). Life course and social structure. In R. E. L. Faris (Ed.), *Handbook of modern sociology* (pp. 272-309). Chicago: Rand McNally.

Campbell, A., Converse, P. E., Miller, W. E., & Stokes, D. E. (1960). *The American voter.* New York: John Wiley.

Campbell, R.T., & O'Rand, A. M. (1988). Settings and sequences: The heuristics of aging research. In J. E. Birren & V. L. Bengston (Eds.), *Emergent theories of aging* (pp. 58-79). New York: Springer.

Caspi, A., & Bem, D. J. (1990). Personality continuity and change across the life course. In L. Pervin (Ed.), *Handbook of personality theory and research* (pp. 549-575). New York: Guilford.

Cattell, R. B. (1957). *Personality and motivation structure and measurement.* New York: World Book.

Cattell, R. B. (1966). Patterns of change: Measurement in relation to state-dimension, trait change, lability, and process concepts. In R. B. Cattell (Ed.), *Handbook of multivariate experimental psychology* (pp. 355-402). Chicago: Rand McNally.

Cattell, R. B. (1979). *Personality and learning theory: Vol. 1. The structure of personality in its environment.* New York: Springer.

Cattell, R. B., & Scheier, I. H. (1961). *The meaning and measurement of neuroticism and anxiety.* New York: Ronald Press.

Center for Political Studies. (1990). *Continuity guide to the American National Election Studies 1952-1988.* Ann Arbor: University of Michigan, Center for Political Studies, Institute for Social Research.

Center for Political Studies. (n.d). *National election studies: 1952-1988 Cumulative Data File, Codebook.* Ann Arbor: University of Michigan, Center for Political Studies, Institute for Social Research.

Changeux, J. P. (1985). *Neuronal man.* (L. Garey, Trans.). New York: Pantheon. (Original work published 1983)

Child, I. L. (1954). Socialization. In G. Lindzey (Ed.), *Handbook of social psychology* (Vol II, pp. 655-692). Cambridge, MA: Addison-Wesley.

Clark, F. L. G., & Dunne, A. (1955). *Ageing in industry.* London: Nuffield Foundation.

Clausen, J., & Yarrow, M. (1955). Pathways to the mental hospital. *Journal of Social Issues, 11,* 25-32.

Clipp, E. C., Pavalko, E. K., & Elder, G. H., Jr. (1992). Trajectories of health: In concept and empirical pattern. *Behavior, Health and Aging, 2,* 159-179.

Collins, L. M., & Horn, J. L. (Eds.). (1991). *Best methods for the analysis of change: Recent advances, unanswered questions, future directions.* Washington, DC: American Psychological Association.

Converse, P. E. (1969). Of time and partisan stability. *Comparative Political Studies, 2,* 139-171.

Converse, P. E. (1976). *The dynamics of party support: Cohort analyzing party identification.* Beverly Hills, CA: Sage.

Converse, P. E. (1979). Rejoinder to Abramson. *American Journal of Political Science, 23,* 97-100.

Corsaro, W. A., & Heise, D. R. (1990). Event structures from ethnographic data. In C. Clogg (Ed.), *Sociological methodology* (pp. 1-57). Oxford, UK: Basil Blackwell.

Costa, P. T., Jr., & McCrae, R. R. (1980). Still stable after all these years: Personality as a key to some issues in adulthood and old age. In P. B. Baltes & O. G. Brim, Jr. (Eds.), *Life-span development and behavior* (Vol. 3, pp. 65-102). San Diego: Academic Press.

Costa, P. T., Jr., & McCrae, R. R. (1994). Set like plaster? Evidence for the stability of adult personality. In T. Heatherton & J. Weinberger (Eds.), *Can personality change?* (pp. 21-40). Washington, DC: American Psychological Association.

Cournot, A. A. (1872). *Considérations sur la marche des idées,* 2 vols. Paris: Hachette.

Crittenden, J. (1962). Aging and party affiliation. *Public Opinion Quarterly, 26,* 648-657.

Cronbach, L. J., & Furby, L. (1970). How should we measure change—Or should we? *Psychological Bulletin, 74,* 68-80.

Crow, L. T. (1977). Is variability a unifying behavioral concept? *The Psychological Record, 27,* 783-790.

Curtius, E. R. (1920). *Die literarischen Wegbereiter des neuen Frankreichs.* Potsdam: G. Kiepenheuer.

Dannefer, D. (1984). Adult development and social theory: A paradigmatic reappraisal. *American Sociological Review, 49,* 100-116.

Dannefer, D. (1988). What's in a name? An account of the neglect of variability in the study of aging. In J. E. Birren & V. L. Bengston (Eds.), *Emergent theories of aging* (pp. 356-384). New York: Springer.

Davis, J. A. (1980). Conservative weather in a liberalizing climate: Change in selected NORC General Social Survey items, 1972-78. *Social Forces, 58,* 1129-1156.

Davis, J. A. (1991). *Changeable weather in a cooling climate atop a liberal plateau: Conversion and replacement in 42 GSS items, 1972-1989.* (Social Change Rep. No. 33). Chicago, IL: National Opinion Research Center.

Davis, J. A., & Smith, T. W. (1994). *General Social Surveys, 1972-1994: Cumulative Codebook.* Chicago, IL: National Opinion Research Center.

Davis, K. (1940). The sociology of parent-youth conflict. *American Sociological Review, 5,* 523-535.

Davis, K., & Moore, W. E. (1945). Some principles of stratification. *American Sociological Review, 10,* 242-247.

Delbrück, M. (1949). A physicist looks at biology. *Transactions of the Connecticut Academy of Arts and Sciences, 38,* 173-190.

Dempsey, D. (1963). First novelists, last words. *Saturday Review, 66,* p. 34.

Dempster, A. P., Rubin, D. B., & Tsutakawa, R. K. (1981). Estimation in covariance components models. *Journal of the American Statistical Association, 76,* 341-353.

DeSisto, M. J., Harding, C. M., & Brooks, G. W. (1995). The Maine and Vermont three decade studies of mental illness, II: Longitudinal course outcomes. *British Journal of Psychiatry, 167*(3), 331-338.

Dilthey, W. (1875). *Über das Studium der Geschichte der Wissenschaften vom Menschen, der Gesellschaft und dem Staat. Abgeordneter Gesammelte Schriften* (Vol. 5, pp. 36-41).

Dilthey, W. (1922) *Leben Schleiermachers,* 2nd edition (vol. 1). Leipzig: Teubner.

Dilthey, W. (1958). *Der Aufbau der geschichtlichen Welt in den Geisteswissenschaften* (2nd. Ed.). B. Groethuysen (Ed.). Stuttgart: B. G. Teubner. (Original work published 1927)

Dilthey, W. (1989). *Introduction to the human sciences.* R. A. Makkreel & F. Rodi (Eds.), (M. Neville, J. Barnouw, F. Schreiner, & R. A. Makkreel, Trans.) Princeton: Princeton University Press. (Original work published 1883)

DiPrete, T. A., & Forristal, J. D. (1994). Multilevel models: Methods and substance. *Annual Review of Sociology, 20,* 331-357.

DiPrete, T. A., & Grusky, D. B. (1990a). Structure and trend in the process of stratification for American men and women. *American Journal of Sociology, 96,* 107-143.

DiPrete, T. A., & Grusky, D. B. (1990b). The multilevel analysis of trends with repeated cross-sectional data. In C. C. Clogg (Ed.), *Sociological methodology* (Vol. 20, pp. 337-368). Oxford: Basil Blackwell.

Dollard, J. (1935). *Criteria for the life history.* New Haven, CT: Yale University Press.

Dowd, J. J. (1987). The reification of age: Age stratification theory and the passing of the autonomous subject. *Journal of Aging Studies, 1*(4), 317-335.

Driberg, J. H. (1958). Age grades. In *Encyclopaedia britannica* (Vol. 1, pp. 344-345). Chicago: Encyclopedia Britannica.

Dromel, J. (1862). *La loi des révolutions, les générations, les nationalités, les dynasties, les réligions.* Paris: Didier.

Duncan, G. J., Coe, R., Corcoran, M., Hill, M., & Morgan, J. (1984). *Years of poverty, years of plenty.* Ann Arbor, MI: Institute for Social Research.

Duncan, G. J., & Kalton, G. (1987). Issues of design and analysis of surveys across time. *International Statistical Review, 55,* 97-117.

Durand, J. D. (1948). *The labor force in the United States, 1890-1960.* New York: Social Science Research Council.

Durkheim, E. (1984). *The division of labor in society* (2nd ed.). (W. D. Halls, Trans.). New York: Free Press. (Original work published 1902)

Easterlin, R. A. (1961). The American baby boom in historical perspective. *American Economic Review, 51,* 869-911.

Easterlin, R. A. (1980). *Birth and fortune.* New York: Basic Books.

Edelman, G. (1987). *Neural Darwinism.* New York: Basic Books.

Eisenstadt, S. N. (1956). *From generation to generation.* New York: Free Press.

Eisenstadt, S. N. (1963). Archetypal patterns of youth. In E.H. Erikson (Ed.), *Youth: Change and challenge* (pp. 24-42). New York: Basic Books.

Eizenman, D. R., Nesselroade, J. R., Featherman, D. L., & Rowe, J. W. (1996). *Intra-individual variability in perceived control: The MacArthur successful aging studies.* Unpublished manuscript, University of Virginia, Charlottesville.

Ekman, G., & Lundberg, U. (1971). Emotional reaction to past and future events as a function of temporal distance. *Acta Psychologica, 35,* 430-441.

Elder, G. H., Jr. (1974). *Children of the great depression.* Chicago: University of Chicago Press.

Elder, G. H., Jr. (1985). Perspectives on the life course. In G. H. Elder, Jr. (Ed.), *Life course dynamics* (pp. 23-49). Ithaca, NY: Cornell University Press.

Elder, G. H., Jr. (1992). Essay on the life course. In E. Borgatta & M. Borgatta (Eds.), *The encyclopedia of sociology* (pp. 1126-1130). New York: Macmillian.

Elder, G. H., Jr. (1995). The life course paradigm: Social change and individual development. In P. Moen, G. H. Elder, & K. Löscher (Eds.), *Examining lives in context: Perspectives on the ecology of human devleopment* (pp. 452-475). Washington, DC: American Psychological Association.

Elder, G. H., Jr., & Hareven, T. K. (1993). Rising above life's disadvantages: From the great depression to war. In G. H. Elder, Jr., J. Modell, & R. D. Parke (Eds.), *Children in time and place* (pp. 47-72). Cambridge, UK: Cambridge University Press.

Elder, G. H., Jr., & O'Rand, A. M. (1995). Adult lives in a changing society. In K. Cook, G. Fine, & J.S. House (Eds.), *Sociological perspectives on social psychology* (pp. 452-475). Needham Heights, MA: Allyn and Bacon.

Elder, G. H., Jr., & Pavalko, E. K. (1993). Work careers in men's later years: Transitions, trajectories, and historical change. *Journal of Gerontology: Social Sciences, 48,* S180-S191.

Elder, G. H., Jr., Pavalko, E. K., & Clipp, E. C. (1993). *Working with archival data.* Newbury Park, CA: Sage.

Elkin, F., & Westley, W. A. (1955). The myth of adolescent culture. *American Sociological Review, 20,* 687-684.

Elster, J., & Loewenstein, G. (1992). Utility from memory and anticipation. In G. Lowenstein & J. Elster (Eds.), *Choice over time* (pp. 213-234). New York: Russell Sage.

Emmerich, W. (1968). Personality development and concepts of structure. *Child Development, 39,* 671-690.

Epstein, S. (1980). The stability of behavior: II. Implications for psychological research. *American Psychologist, 35,* 790-806.

Erikson, E. H. (1950). *Childhood and society.* New York: Norton.

Erikson, E. H. (1963). Youth: Fidelity and diversity. In E.H. Erikson (Ed.), *Youth: Change and challenge* (pp. 1-23). New York: Basic Books.

Evan, W. M. (1959). Cohort analysis of survey data: A procedure for studying long-term opinion change. *Public Opinion Quarterly, 23,* 63-72.

Featherman, D. L. (1986). Biography, society, and history. In A. B. Sørensen, F. E. Weinert, & L. R. Sherrod (Eds.), *Human development and the life course* (pp. 99-149). Hillsdale, NJ: Lawrence Erlbaum.

Featherman, D. L., & Lerner, R. M. (1985). Ontogenesis and sociogenesis: Problematics for theory and research about development and socialization across the lifespan. *American Sociological Review, 50,* 659-676.

Featherman, D. L., & Petersen, T. (1986). Markers of aging: Modeling the clocks that time us. *Research on Aging, 8,* 339-365.

Featherman, D. L., Smith, J., & Peterson, J. G. (1990). Successful aging in a post-retired society. In P. B. Baltes & M. M. Baltes (Eds.), *Successful aging: Perspectives from the behavioral sciences* (pp. 50-93). Cambridge, UK: Cambridge University Press.

Felix, L. (1961). *The modern aspect of mathematics.* New York: Science Editions.

Ferrari, G. (1874). *Teoria dei periodi politici.* Milan: Hoepli.

Fienberg, S. E., & Mason, W. M. (1985). Specification and implementation of age, period and cohort models. In W. M. Mason & S. E. Fienberg (Eds.), *Cohort analysis in social research* (pp. 45-88). New York: Springer.

Firebaugh, G. (1978). A rule for inferring individual-level relationships from aggregate data. *American Sociological Review, 43,* 557-572.

Firebaugh, G. (1989). Methods for estimating cohort replacement effects. In C. C. Clogg (Ed.), *Sociological methodology 1989* (pp. 243-262). Oxford: Basil Blackwell.

Firebaugh, G. (1992). Where does social change come from? Estimating the relative contributions of individual change and population turnover. *Population Research and Policy Review, 11,* 1-20.

Firebaugh, G. (1997). *Analyzing repeated surveys.* Thousand Oaks, CA: Sage.

Firebaugh, G., & Chen, K. (1995). Vote turnout of Nineteenth Amendment women: The enduring effect of disenfranchisement. *American Journal of Sociology, 100,* 972-996.

Firebaugh, G., & Davis, K. E. (1988). Trends in anti-Black prejudice, 1972-1984: Region and cohort effects. *American Journal of Sociology, 94,* 251-272.

Fiske, D. W., & Rice, L. (1955). Intra-individual response variability. *Psychological Bulletin, 52,* 217-250.

Flugel, J. C. (1929). Practice, fatigue, and oscillation. [Monograph] *British Journal of Psychology*(Supplement 4, Whole No. 13).

Foote, N. N. (1958). Anachronism and synchronism in sociology. *Sociometry, 21,* 17-29.

Ford, D. H. (1987). *Humans as self-constructing living systems: A developmental perspective on behavior and personality.* Hillsdale, NJ: Lawrence Erlbaum.

Fortes, M. (1984). Age, generation, and social structure. In D. I. Kertzer & J. Keith (Eds.), *Age and anthropological theory* (pp. 99-122). Ithaca, NY: Cornell University Press.

Freedman, D., Thornton, A., Camburn, D., Alwin, D., & Young-DeMarco, L. (1988). The life history calendar: A technique for collecting retrospective data. *Sociological Methodology, 18,* 3-68.

George, L. K. (1993). Sociological perspectives on life transitions. *Annual Review of Sociology, 19,* 353-373.

Georgescu-Roegon, N. (1971). *The entropy law and the economic process.* Cambridge, MA: Harvard University Press.

Gergen, K. E. (1977). Stability, change, and chance in human development. In N. Datan & H. W. Reese (Eds.), *Life-span developmental psychology: Dialectical perspectives on experimental research* (pp. 135-158). San Diego: Academic Press.

Gergen, K. J. (1980). The emerging crisis in life-span developmental theory. In P. B. Baltes & O. G. Brim, Jr. (Eds.), *Life-span development and behavior* (pp. 32-65). San Diego: Academic Press.

Gerson, K. (1985). *Hard choices: How women decide about work, career, and motherhood.* Berkeley: University of California Press.

Gerth, H. H. (1940). The Nazi party: Its leadership and composition. *American Journal of Sociology, 45,* 530-571.

Giese, F. (1928). Erlebnisform des Alterns. *Deutsche Psychologie, 5*(2).

Glaser, B. G., & Strauss, A. L. (1968). *Time for dying.* Hawthorne, NY: Aldine.

Glaser, E. (1928). *Jahrgang 1902.* Berlin: Gustav Kiepenheuer.

Glendon, M. A. (1989). *The transformation of family law.* Chicago: University of Chicago Press.

Glenn, N. D. (1974). Aging and conservatism. *Annals of the American Academy of Political and Social Science, 33,* 176-186.

Glenn, N. D. (1976). Cohort analysts' futile quest: Statistical attempts to separate age, period, and cohort effects. *American Sociological Review, 41,* 900-904.

Glenn, N. D. (1977). *Cohort analysis.* Beverly Hills, CA: Sage.

Glenn, N. D. (1980). Values, attitudes and beliefs. In O. G. Brim, Jr. & J. Kagan (Eds.), *Constancy and change in human development* (pp. 596-640). Cambridge, MA: Harvard University Press.

Glenn, N. D., & Grimes, M. (1968). Aging, voting, and political interest. *American Sociological Review, 33,* 563-575.

Glenn, N. D., & Hefner, T. (1972). Further evidence on aging and party identification. *Public Opinion Quarterly, 36,* 31-47.

Goffman, E. (1959). *The presentation of self in everyday life.* Garden City, NY: Doubleday.

Goffman, E. (1961). *Asylums.* Hawthorne, NY: Aldine.

Goffman, E. (1974). *Frame analysis.* Cambridge, MA: Harvard University Press.

Goldfarb, N. (1960). *An introduction to longitudinal statistical analysis.* New York: Free Press.

Goldstein, H. I. (1987). *Multilevel models in educational and social research.* Oxford, UK: Oxford University Press.

Goode, W. J. (1962). *World revolution and family patterns.* New York: Free Press.

Graybill, F. A., & Iyer, H. K. (1994). *Regression analysis: Concepts and applications.* Belmont, CA: Duxbury Press.

Griffin, L. J. (1993). Narrative, event structure analysis, and causal interpretation in historical sociology. *American Journal of Sociology, 98,* 1094-1133.

214 ☒ STUDYING AGING AND SOCIAL CHANGE

Grimm, J. (1879). *Über das Alter, Kleinere Schriften,* 2nd edition (vol. 1, pp. 189-211). Berlin: F. Dümmlers.

Gronfein, W. (1985). Incentive and intention in mental health policy: A comparison of the medicaid and community mental health center programs. *Journal of Health and Social Behavior, 26,* 192-206.

Gusfield, J. R. (1957). The problem of generations in an organizational structure. *Social Forces, 35,* 323-330.

Haber, S. (1991). *The quest for authority and honor in the American professions, 1750-1900.* Chicago: University of Chicago Press.

Hagen, E. E. (1962). *On the theory of social change.* Belmont, CA: Dorsey.

Hagestad, G. O. (1990). Social perspectives on the life course. In R. H. Binstock & L. K. George (Eds.), *Handbook of aging and the social sciences* (pp. 151-168). San Diego: Academic Press.

Halbwachs, M. (1992). The social frameworks of memory. (In idem) In L. A. Coser (Ed. and Trans.), *On Collective Memory* (pp. 55-189). Chicago: University of Chicago Press. (Original work published 1925)

Hampson, E. (1990). Variations in sex-related cognitive abilities across the menstrual cycle. *Brain and Cognition, 14,* 26-43.

Harding, C. M. (1988). Course types in schizophrenia: An analysis of European and American studies. *Schizophrenia Bulletin, 14*(4), 633-643.

Harding, C. M., McCormick, R. V., Strauss, J. S., Ashikaga, T., & Brooks, G. W. (1989). Computerized life chart methods to map domains of function and illustrate patterns of interaction in the long-term course trajectories of patients who once met the criteria for DSM-III schizophrenia. *British Journal of Psychiatry, 155*(5), 100-106.

Hardy, M. A., Hazelrigg, L., & Quadagno, J. (1996). *Ending a career in the auto industry.* New York: Plenum.

Harris, C. W. (Ed.) (1963). *Problems in measuring change.* Madison: University of Wisconsin Press.

Hawley, A. H. (1950). *Human ecology.* New York: Ronald.

Hazelrigg, L. (1991). The problem of micro-macro linkage: Rethinking questions of the individual, social structure and autonomy of action. *Current Perspectives in Social Theory, 11,* 229-254.

Hazelrigg, L. (1995). *Cultures of nature: An essay on the production of nature.* Gainesville: University Press of Florida.

Heberle, R. (1951). *Social movements.* Norwalk, CT: Appleton-Century-Crofts.

Hecht, L. (1996). *Managing multiple roles: The organization of home and work role-activities and psychological well-being.* Unpublished doctoral disseration, Indiana University, Bloomington.

Heckman, J., & Robb, R. (1985). Using longitudinal data to estimate age, period, and cohort effects in earnings equations. In W. Mason & S. E. Fienberg (Eds.), *Cohort analysis in social research* (pp. 137-150). New York: Springer.

Heidegger, J. (1927). Sein und Zeit. *Jahrbuch für Philosophie und phänomenologische Forschung, 8,* 384-385.

Heise, D. R. (1969). Separating reliability and stability in test-retest correlation. *American Sociological Review, 34,* 93-191.

Heise, D. R. (1991). Event structure analysis. In N. Fieldling & R. Lee (Eds.), *Using computers in qualitative research* (pp. 136-163). Newbury Park, CA: Sage.

Herberg, W. (1960). *Protestant, Catholic, Jew* (Rev. ed.). Garden City, NY: Doubleday.

Herbst, F. (1823). *Ideale und Irrtümer des akademischen Lebens in unserer Zeit.* Stuttgart.

Hill, R., Stycos, J. M., & Back, K. W. (1959). *The family and population control.* Chapel Hill: University of North Carolina Press.

Hinshaw, R. P. (1944). *The relationship of information and opinion to age.* Unpublished doctoral dissertation, Princeton University, Princeton, New Jersey.

Hogan, D. P. (1981). *Transitions and social change: The early lives of American men.* San Diego: Academic.

Hogan, D. P., & Astone, N. M. (1986). The transition to adulthood. *Annual Review of Sociology, 12,* 109-130.

Hollien, H. (1987). "Old voices": What do we really know about them? *Journal of Voice, 1,* 2-17.

Holling, C. S. (1973). Resilience and stability of ecological systems. *Annual Review of Ecology and Systematics, 4,* 1-23.

Honigsheim, P. (1924). Die Pubertät. *Kölner Vierteljahreshefte für Soziologie, 3*(4).

Hout, M., Brooks, C., & Manza, J. (1995). The democratic class struggle in the United States, 1948-1992. *American Sociological Review, 60,* 805-828.

Hox, J. J., Kreft, I. G. G., & Hermkens, P, L. (1991). The analysis of factorial surveys. *Sociological Methods and Research, 19,* 493-510.

Hughes, R. (1963). *The fox in the attic.* New York: Signet.

Hume, D. (1985). *Essays moral, political and literary* (E. F. Miller, Ed.). Indianapolis: Liberty Classics. (Original work published 1777)

Hyman, H. H. (1959). *Political socialization.* New York: Free Press.

Hyman, H. H., & Sheatsley, P. B. (1964). Attitudes toward desegregation. *Scientific American, 211,* 16-23.

Inglehart, R. (1991). *Culture shift in advanced industrial society.* Princeton, NJ: Princeton University Press.

Isidore of Seville. (c.600) 1911. *Etymologiae.* 2 vols. (W. M. Lindsay, Ed.). Oxford: Clarendon.

Jackson, P. B. (1993). *The context of transition events across the life course: The effects of prior event sequencing on adult mental health.* Unpublished doctoral dissertation, Indiana University, Bloomington.

Jaffe, A. J., & Carleton, R. O. (1954). *Occupational mobility in the United States 1930-1960.* New York: Columbia University Press.

James, W. (1950). *The principles of psychology.* New York: Dover. (Original work published 1890)

Joël, K. (1925). Der sekuläre Rhythmus der Geschichte. *Jahrbuch für Soziologie, 1.*

Johnson, P. (1963, May 9). The new men of the Soviet sixties. *Reporter, 28,* 16-21.

Kagan, J. (1980). Perspectives on continuity. In O. G. Brim, Jr., & J. Kagan (Eds.), *Constancy and change in human development* (pp. 26-74). Cambridge, MA: Harvard University Press.

Kahn, J. R., & Mason, W. M. (1987). Political alienation, cohort size, and the Easterlin hypothesis. *American Sociological Review, 52,* 155-169.

Kant, I. (1952). *Critique of pure reason* (2nd ed.). (J. M. D. Meiklejohn, Trans.) Chicago: Great Books. (Original work published 1787)

Kertzer, D. L. (1983). Generation as a sociological problem. *Annual Review of Sociology, 9,* 125-149.

Kessen, W. (1960). Research design in the study of developmental problems. In P.H. Mussen (Ed.), *Handbook of research methods in child development* (pp. 36-70). New York: John Wiley.

Kim, J. E., Nesselroade, J. R., & Featherman, D. L. (1996). The state component in self-reported world views and religious beliefs of older adults: The MacArthur successful aging studies. *Psychology and Aging, 11,* 396-407.

Kish, L. (1983). Data collection for details over space and time. In T. Wright (Ed.), *Statistical methods and the improvement of data quality* (pp. 73-84). San Diego: Academic Press.

Kohli, M. (1986). The world we forgot: A historical view of the life course. In V. W. Marshall (Ed.), *Later life: The social psychology of aging* (pp. 271-303). Beverly Hills. CA: Sage.

Korschelt, E. (1924). *Lebensdauer, Altern und Tod.* 3rd edition. Jena: G. Fischer.

Kreft, I. G. G., de Leeuw, J., & Kim, K. S. (1990). Comparing four different statistical packages for hierarchical linear regression: GENMOD, HLM, ML2, and VARCL (CSE Tech. Rep. No. 311). Los Angeles, CA: Center for Research Evaluation.

Kummer, F. (1900). *Deutsche Literaturgeschichte des 19. Jahrhunderis, Dargestellt nach Generationen.* Dresden: Reissner.

Labouvie, E. W., & Ruetsch, C. (1995). Testing for equivalence of measurement scales: Simple structure and metric invariance reconsidered. *Multivariate Behavioral Research, 30,* 63-76.

Laird, N. M., & Ware, H. (1982). Random-effects models for longitudinal data. *Biometrics, 38,* 963-974.

Lamiell, J. T. (1988). *Once more into the breach: Why individual differences in research cannot advance personality theory.* Paper presented at the meeting of the American Psychological Association, Atlanta, GA.

Landsberger, F. (1927). Das Generationsproblem in der Kunstgeschichte. *Kritische Berichte,* 1927/2.

Larsen, R. J. (1987). The stability of mood variability: A spectral analytic approach to daily mood assessments. *Journal of Personality and Social Psychology, 52,* 1195-1204.

Larsen, R. J. (1992). A process approach to personality psychology: Utilizing time as a facet of data. In D. Buss & N. Cantor (Eds.), *Personality psychology: Recent trends and emerging issues* (pp. 177-193). New York/Berlin: Springer-Verlag.

Lee, R. D. (1994). The formal demography of population aging. In L. G. Martin & S. H. Preston (Eds.), *Demography of aging* (pp. 8-49). Washington, DC: National Academy Press.

Lesthaeghe, R., & Surkyn, J. (1988). Cultural dynamics and economic theories of fertility change. *Population and Development Review, 11,* 1-45.

Levy, M. J., Jr. (1949). *The family revolution in modern China.* Cambridge, MA: Harvard University Press.

Levy, M. J., Jr. (1952). *The structure of society.* Princeton, NJ: Princeton University Press.

Lewin, K. (1939). Field theory and experiment in social psychology: Concepts and methods. *American Journal of Sociology, 44,* 868-896.

Lipset, S. M., Lazarsfeld, P. G., Barton, A. H., & Linz, J. (1954). The psychology of voting: An analysis of political behavior. In G. Lindzey (Ed.), *Handbook of social psychology* (pp. 112-175). Reading, MA: Addison-Wesley.

Loewenstein, G. (1992). The fall and rise of psychological explanations in the economics of intertemporal choice. In G. Loewenstein & J. Elster (Eds.), *Choice over time* (pp. 3-34). New York: Russell Sage.

Loewenstein, G., & Prelec, D. (1992). Anomalies in intertemporal choice. In G. Loewenstein & J. Elster (Eds.), *Choice over time* (pp. 119-145). New York: Russell Sage.

Lorenz, O. (1886 & 1891). *Die Geschichteswissenschaft in Hauptrichtungen und Aufgaben kritisch erörtert,* 2 vols. Berlin: W. Hertz.

MacIver, R. M. (1963). *The challenge of the passing years.* New York: Pocket Books.

Maine, H. S. (1963). *Ancient law.* Boston: Beacon. (Original work published 1861)

Mannheim, K. (1952a). On the nature of economic ambition and its significance for the social education of man. In P. Kecskemeti (Ed.), *Essays in the sociology of knowledge* (pp. 230-275). Boston: Routledge & Kegan Paul. (Original work published 1930)

Mannheim, K. (1952b). The problem of generations. In P. Kecskemeti (Ed.), *Essays in the sociology of knowledge* (pp. 276-322) . Boston: Routledge & Kegan Paul. (Original work published 1927).

Mannoni, D. O. (1956). *Prospero and Caliban.* New York: Methuen.

Manski, C. F. (1993). Identification problems in the social sciences. *Sociological Methodology, 23,* 1 56.

Marshall, A. (1961). *Principles of economics* (9th ed.). New York: Macmillan. (Original work published 1890)

Marshall, V. W. (1996). The state of theory in aging and the social sciences. In R. H. Binstock & L. K. George (Eds.), *Handbook of aging and the social sciences* (4th ed.) (pp. 12-30). San Diego: Academic Press.

Martel, L., & Biller, H. (1987). *Stature and stigma.* Lexington, MA: D. C. Heath.

Martineau, H. (n.d.). *The positive philosophy of Auguste Comte,* Vol. II. London: Trubner.

Marx, K. (1973). *Grundrisse: Foundations of the critique of political economy* (M. Nicolaus, Trans.). New York: Vintage.

Marx, K. (1976). Theses on Feuerbach. In *Collected works* (Vol. 5, pp. 3-5). New York: International Universities Press.

Mason, K. O. (1991). Multilevel analysis in the study of social institutions and demographic change. In J. Huber (Ed.), *Macro-micro linkages in sociology* (pp. 223-230). Newbury Park, CA: Sage.

Mason, K. O., & Lu, Y. H. (1988). Attitudes toward women's familial roles: Changes in the United States, 1977-1985. *Gender and Society, 2,* 39-57.

Mason, K. O., Mason, W. M., Winsborough, H. H., & Poole, W. K. (1973). Some methodological issues in cohort analysis of archival data. *American Sociological Review, 38,* 242-258.

Mason, W. M., & Fienberg, S. E. (Eds.). (1985). *Cohort analysis in social research: Beyond the identification problem.* New York/Berlin: Springer-Verlag.

Mason, W. M., Wong, G. M., & Entwisle, B. (1983). Contextual analysis through the multilevel linear model. In S. Leinhardt (Ed.), *Sociological Methodology* (pp. 72-103). San Francisco: Jossey-Bass.

Matza, D. (1964). Position and behavior patterns of youth. In R. E. L. Faris (Ed.), *Handbook of modern sociology* (pp. 191-216). Chicago: Rand McNally.

May, C. P., Hasher, L., & Stoltzfus, E. R. (1993). Optimal time of day and the magnitude of age differences in memory. *Psychological Science, 4,* 326-330.

Mayer, K. U., & Tuma, N. B. (1990). *Event history analysis in life course research.* Madison: University of Wisconsin Press.

Mayr, E. (1976). *Evolution and the diversity of life.* Cambridge: Harvard University Press.

McArdle, J. J., & Cattell, R. B. (1994). Structural equation models of factorial invariance in parallel proportional profiles and oblique cofactor problems. *Multivariate Behavioral Research, 29,* 63-113.

McDonald, R. P. (1994). The bilevel reticular action model for path analysis with latent variables. *Sociological Methods and Research, 22(3),* 399-413.

McGuire, W. J. (1989). The structure of individual attitudes and attitude systems. In A. R. Pratkanis, S. J. Breckler, & A. G. Greenwald (Eds.), *Attitude structure and function* (pp. 37-69). Hillsdale, NJ: Lawrence Erlbaum.

McNemar, Q. (1958). On growth measurement. *Educational and Psychological Measurement, 18,* 47-55.

McTaggart, J. E. (1908). The unreality of time. *Mind, 18,* 457-474.

Mead, G. H. (1913). The social self. *Journal of Philosophy, 10,* 374-380.

Mead, G. H. (1938). *The philosophy of the act.* (C. Morris, Ed.) Chicago: University of Chicago Press.

Mead, M. (1953). *Cultural patterns and technical change.* Paris: UNESCO.

Mechanic, D. (1989). *Mental health and social policy* (3rd ed.). Englewood Cliffs, NJ: Prentice Hall.

Mentré, F. (1920). *Les générations sociales.* Paris: Editions Bossard.

Meredith, W. (1964). Notes on factorial invariance. *Psychometrika, 29,* 177-185.

Meredith, W. (1994). Measurement invariance, factor analysis and factorial invariance. *Psychometrika, 58,* 525-543.

Meyer, J. W. (1986). The self and the life course: Institutionalization and its effects. In A. B. Sørensen, F. E. Weinert, & L. R. Sherrod (Eds.), *Human development and the life course: Multidisciplinary perspectives* (pp. 199-216). Hillsdale, NJ: Lawrence Erlbaum.

Meyer, J. W. (1988). Levels of analysis: The life course as a cultural construction. In M. W. Riley (Ed.), *Social structures and human lives: Vol. 1. Social change and the life course* (pp. 49-62). Newbury Park, CA: Sage.

Mills, C. W. (1959). *The sociological imagination.* New York: Oxford University Press.

Mischel, W. (1991). *Finding personality coherence in the pattern of variability.* Paper presented at the meeting of the Eastern Psychological Association, New York, NY.

Mischel, W., Shoda, Y., & Peake, P. K. (1988). The nature of adolescent competencies predicted by preschool delay of gratification. *Journal of Personality and Social Psychology, 54,* 687-696.

Modell, J. (1989). *Into one's own: From youth to adulthood in the United States, 1920-1925.* Berkeley: University of California Press.

Modell, J., Furstenburg, F., Jr., & Hershberg, T. (1976). Social change and transitions to adulthood in historical perspective. *Journal of Family History, 1,* 7-31.

Moen, P. (1985). Continuities and discontinuities in women's labor force activity. In G. H. Elder, Jr. (Ed.), *Life course dynamics* (pp. 113-155). Ithaca, NY: Cornell University Press.

Moen, P., Demptser-McClain, D., & Williams, R. M., Jr., (1992). Successful aging: A life course perspective on women's multiple roles and health. *American Journal of Sociology, 97,* 1612-1638.

Molenaar, P. C. M. (1985). A dynamic factor model for the analysis of multivariate time series. *Psychometrika, 50,* 181-202.

Moore, W. E. (1946). *Industrial relations and the social order.* New York: Macmillan.

Mortimer, J. T., Finch, M. D., & Kumka, D. (1982). Persistence and change in development: The multidimensional self-concept. In P. B. Baltes & O. G. Brim, Jr. (Eds.), *Life-span development and behavior* (Vol. 4, pp. 264-313). San Diego: Academic Press.

Moss, H. A., & Susman, E. J. (1980). Longitudinal study of personality development. In O.G. Brim, Jr. & J. Kagan (Eds.), *Constancy and Change in human development* (pp. 530-595). Cambridge, MA: Harvard University Press.

Musgrove, F. (1977). *Margins of the mind.* New York: Methuen.

Muthén, B. O. (1994). Multilevel covariance structure analysis. *Sociological Methods and Research, 22*(3), 376-398.

National Opinion Research Center. (1994). *General social surveys, 1972-1994: Cumulative codebook.* Chicago: University of Chicago, NORC.

Nesselroade, J. R. (1988). Some implications of the trait-state distinction for the study of development over the life span: The case of personality. In P. B. Baltes, D. L. Featherman, & R. M. Lerner (Eds.), *Life-span development and behavior* (pp. 163-189). Hillsdale, NJ: Lawrence Erlbaum.

Nesselroade, J. R. (1990). Adult personality development: Issues in assessing constancy and change. In A. I. Rabin, R. A. Zucker, R. A. Emmons, & S. Frank (Eds.), *Studying persons and lives* (pp. 41-85). New York: Springer.

Nesselroade, J. R. (1991). The warp and the woof of the developmental fabric. In R. Downs, L. Liben, & D. S. Palermo (Eds.), *Visions of aesthetics, the environment, & development: The legacy of Joachim F. Wohlwill* (pp. 213-240). Hillsdale, NJ: Lawrence Erlbaum.

Nesselroade, J. R., & Boker, S. M. (1994). Assessing constancy and change. In T. Heatherton & J. Weinberger (Eds.), *Can personality change?* (pp. 121-147). Washington, DC: American Psychological Association.

Nesselroade, J. R., & Featherman, D. L. (1991). Intraindividual variability in older adults' depression scores: Some implications for developmental theory and longitudinal re-search. In D. Magnusson, L. Bergman, G. Rudinger, & B. Törestad (Eds.), *Stability and change: Methods and models for data treatment* (pp. 47-66). Cambridge, UK: Cambridge University Press,

Nesselroade, J. R., Featherman, D. L., & Tomer, A. (1997). *Intraindividual variability and change from an individual differences perspective.* Thousand Oaks, CA: Sage.

Nesselroade, J. R., & Ford, D. H. (1985). P-technique comes of age: Multivariate, replicated, single subject designs for research on older adults. *Research on Aging, 7,* 46-80.

Nesselroade, J. R., & Jones, C. J. (1985). Multi-modal selection effects in the study of adult development: A perspective on multivariate, replicated, single-subject, repeated measures. *Experimental Aging Research, 11,* 21-27.

Nesselroade, J. R., Pruchno, R., & Jacobs, A. (1986). Reliability and stability in the measurement of psychological states: An illustration with anxiety measures. *Psychologische Beitraege, 28,* 255-264.

Neugarten, B. L., Moore, J. W., & Lowe, J. C. (1965). Age norms, age constraints and adult socialization. *American Journal of Sociology, 70,* 710-717.

Neumann, S. (1942). *Permanent revolution.* New York: Harper.

Nohl, H. (1914). Das Verhältnis der generationen in der Pädagogik. *Die Tat,* May.

Nowak, A., Vallacher, R. R., & Lewenstein, M. (1994). Toward a dynamical social psychology. In R. R. Vallacher & A. Nowak (Eds.), *Dynamical systems in social psychology* (pp. 279-293). San Diego: Academic Press.

Nunnally, J. C. (1967). *Psychometric theory.* New York: McGraw-Hill.

Oaklander, L. N., & Smith, Q. (Eds.) (1994). *The new theory of time.* New Haven, CT: Yale University Press.

O'Rand, A. M., & Henretta, J. C. (1982). Delayed career entry, industrial pension structure, and retirement in a cohort of unmarried women. *American Sociological Review, 47,* 365-373.

O'Rand, A. M., & Krecker, M. L. (1990). Concepts of the life cycle. *Annual Review of Sociology, 16,* 241-262.

Ortega y Gasset, J. (1928). *Die Aufgabe unserer Zeit.* Zürich: H. Girsberger.

Ortega y Gasset, J. (1933). *The modern theme.* New York: W. W. Norton.

Otto, L. B., Spenner, K. L., & Call, V. R. A. (1980a). *Career line prototypes.* Boys Town, NB: Boys Town Center for the Study of Youth Development.

Otto, L. B., Spenner, K. L., & Call, V. R. A. (1980b). *Career line prototypes II.* Boys Town, NB: Boys Town Center for the Study of Youth Development.

Pampel, F. C., & Peters, H. E. (1995). The Easterlin effect. *Annual Review of Sociology, 21,* 163-194.

Parsons, T. (1951). *The social system.* New York: Free Press.

Parsons, T. (1959). The school class as a social system: Some of its functions in American society. *Harvard Educational Review, 20,* 297-318.

Pavalko, E. K., Elder, G. H., Jr., & Clipp, E. C. (1993). Worklives and longevity: Insights from a life course perspective. *Journal of Health and Social Behavior, 34,* 363-380.

Perruci, R., & Targ, D. B. (1982). *Mental patients and social networks.* Westport, CT: Auburn House.

Pescosolido, B. A. (1991). Illness careers and network ties: A conceptual model of utilization and compliance. In G. Albrecht & J. Levy (Eds.), *Advances in medical sociology* (Vol. 2, pp. 161-184). Greenwich, CT: JAI.

Pescosolido, B. A. (1992). Beyond rational choice: The social dynamics of how people seek help. *American Journal of Sociology, 97*(4), 1096-1138.

Petersen, J. (1925). *Die Wesensbestimmung der deutschen Romantik.* Leipzig: Quelle.

Petersen, J. (1930). *Die Literarischen Generationen.* Berlin: Junker and Dunnhaupt.

Petersen, T. (1986). Fitting parametric survival models with time-dependent covariates. *Journal of the Royal Statistical Society Ser. C., 35,* 281-288.

Petersen, T. (1990). Analyzing event histories. In A. von Eye (Ed.), *Statistical methods in longitudinal research* (Vol. 2) (pp. 69-95). San Diego: Academic Press.

Petersen, T. (1991). The statistical analysis of event histories. *Sociological Methods and Research, 19,* 270-323.

Petersen, T., & Spilerman, S. (1990). Job quits from an internal labor market. In K. U. Mayer & N. B. Tuma (Eds.), *Event history analysis in life course research* (pp. 69-95). Madison: University of Wisconsin Press.

Peyre, H. (1948). *Les générations litteraires.* Paris: Bowin.

Pienta, A. M., Burr, J. A., & Mutchler, J. E. (1994). Women's labor force participation in later life: The effects of early work and family experiences. *Journal of Gerontology: Social Sciences, 49,* S231-S239.

Pinder, W. (1926). *Kunstgeschichte nach Generationen. Zwischen Philosophie und Kunst.* Leipzig: E. Pfeiffer.

Pinder, W. (1926). *Das Problem der Generation in der Kunstgeschichte Europas.* Berlin: Frankfurter Verlags-Anstalt.

Pittam, J. (1994). *Voice in social interaction.* Thousand Oaks, CA: Sage.

Pitts, J. (1960). The family and peer groups. In N.W. Bell & E.F. Vogel (Eds.), *A modern introduction to the family* (pp. 266-286). New York: Free Press.

Platz, H. (1922). *Geistige Kampfe in modernen Frankreich.* Munich: Kösel & Pustet.

Powell, B., & Steelman, L. C. (1990). Beyond sibship size: Sibling density, sex composition, and educational outcomes. *Social Forces, 69*(1), 181-206.

Powell, B., & Steelman, L. C. (1993). The educational benefits of being spaced out: Sibship density and educational progress. *American Sociological Review, 58*(3), 367-381.

Powell, B., & Steelman, L. C. (1995). Feeling the pinch: Child spacing and constraints on parental economic investments in children. *Social Forces, 73*(4), 1465-1486.

Pressey, S. L., & Kuhlen, R. G. (1957). *Psychological development through the life span.* New York: Harper.

Putnam, F. W. (1989). *Diagnosis and treatment of multiple personality disorder.* New York: Guilford.

Quadagno, J. (1989). Generational equity and the politics of the welfare state. *Politics & Society, 17,* 353-376.

Ralea, M. (1962). Le problème des générations et la jeunesse d'aujourd'hui. Rencontres Internationales de Geneve. *La vie et le temps.* Neuchatel: Baconniere, pp. 59-73.

Reiss, A. J., Jr. (1960). Sex offenses: The marginal status of the adolescent. *Law and Contemporary Problems, 25,* 309-333.

Renouard, Y. (1953). La notion de génération en histoire. *Revue Historique, 209,* 1-23.

Rexroat, C. (1992). Changes in employment continuity of succeeding cohorts of young women. *Work and Occupations, 19,* 18-34.

Riesman, D., Denney, R., & Glazer, N. (1950). *The lonely crowd.* New Haven, CT: Yale University Press.

Riley, M. W. (1973). Aging and cohort succession: Interpretations and misinterpretations. *Public Opinion Quarterly, 37,* 35-49.

Riley, M. W. (1987). On the significance of age in sociology. *American Sociological Review, 52,* 1-14.

Riley, M. W., Foner, A., & Waring, J. (1988). Sociology of age. In N. J. Smelser (Ed.), *Handbook of sociology* (pp. 243-290). Newbury Park, CA: Sage.

Riley, M. W., Johnson, M., & Foner, A. (Eds.). (1972). *Aging and society: Vol. 3. A sociology of age stratification.* New York: Russell Sage Foundation.

Rindfuss, R. R., Morgan, S. P., & Swicegood, G. (1988). *First births in America: Changes in the timing of parenthood.* Berkeley: University of California Press.

Rindfuss, R. R., Swicegood, C. G., & Rosenfeld, R. A. (1987). Disorder in the life course: How common and does it matter? *American Sociological Review, 52,* 785-801.

Rintala, M. (1958). The problem of generations in Finnish communism. *American Slavic and East European Review, 17,* 190-202.

Rodgers, W. L. (1990). Interpreting the components of time trends. In C. C. Clogg (Ed.), *Sociological methodology 1990* (pp. 421-438). Oxford, UK: Basil Blackwell.

Rogosa, D. R. (1988). Myths about longitudinal research. In K. W. Schaie, R. T. Campbell, W. Meredith, & S. C. Rawlings (Eds.), *Methodological issues in aging research* (pp. 171-209). New York: Springer.

Rosenbaum, J. (1984). *Career mobility in a corporate hierarchy.* San Diego: Academic Press.

Rosenberg, H. (1959). *The tradition of the new.* New York: Horizon Press.

Ross, M. (1989). Relation of implicit theories to the construction of personal histories. *Psychological Review, 96,* 341-357.

Rostow, W. W. (1960). *The stages of economic growth.* New York: Cambridge University Press.

Rümelin, G. (1875). Über den Begriff und die Dauer einer Generation. *Reden und Aufsätze,* vol. 1. Tübingen: Laupp.

Rushton, J. P., Brainerd, C. J., & Pressley, M. (1983). Behavioral development and construct validity: The principle of aggregation. *Psychological Bulletin, 94,* 18-38.

Ryder, N. B. (1956). La mesure des variations de la fécondité au cours du temps. *Population, 11,* 29-46.

Ryder, N. B. (1965). The cohort as a concept in the study of social change. *American Sociological Review, 30,* 843-861.

Sacks, O. (1985). *The man who mistook his wife for a hat and other clinical tales.* New York: Summit.

Sampson, R. J., & Laub, J. H. (1993). *Crime in the making: Pathways and turning points through life.* Cambridge, MA: Harvard University Press.

Scheff, T. J. (1966). *Being mentally ill: A sociological theory.* Hawthorne, NY: Aldine.

Scherer, W. (1885). *Geschichte der deutschen Literatur,* 3rd edition. Berlin: Weidmann.

Schulz, R., & Heckhausen, J. (1996). A life span model of successful aging. *American Psychologist, 51,* 702-714.

Schuman, H., & Scott, J. (1989). Generations and collective memories. *American Sociological Review, 54,* 359-381.

Schurtz, H. (1902). *Altersklassen und Männerbünde. Eine Darstellung der Grundformen der Gesellschaft.* Berlin: G. Reimer.

Sears, D. O. (1981). Life-stage effects on attitude change, especially among the elderly. In S. B. Kiesler, J. N. Morgan, & V. K. Oppenheimer (Eds.), *Aging and social change* (pp. 183-204). San Diego: Academic Press.

Sears, D. O. (1983). The persistence of early political predispositions: The roles of attitude object and life stage. *Review of Personality and Social Psychology, 4,* 79-116.

Sewell, W. H. (1963). Some recent developments in socialization theory and research. *Annals, 349,* 163-181.

Shakespeare, W. (1598). *As you like it.*

Sheehy, G. (1995). *New passages: Mapping your life across time.* New York: Random House.

Shoda, Y., Mischel, W., & Wright, J. C. (1994). Intraindividual stability in the organization and patterning of behavior: Incorporating psychological situations into idiographic analysis of personality. *Journal of Personality and Social Psychology, 67,* 674-687.

Siegler, R. S. (1993). *Children's thinking: How does change occur?* Paper presented at the meeting of the Society for Research in Child Development, New Orleans, LA.

Simmel, G. (1956). The persistence of social groups. In E. F. Borgatta & H. J. Meyer (Eds.), *Sociological theory* (pp. 334-358). New York: Knopf.

Slemrod, J. (1984). The economic impact of nuclear fear. *Bulletin of the Atomic Scientists, 40,* 42-43.

Slemrod, J. (1986). Saving and the fear of nuclear war. *Journal of Conflict Resolution, 30,* 403-419.

Smith, T. W. (1989). *Liberal and conservative trends in the United States since World War II.* (GSS Social Change Report No. 29). Chicago: National Opinion Research Center.

Sorokin, P. A. (1941). *Social and cultural dynamics.* New York: American Book Company.

Sorokin, P. A. (1947). *Society, culture and personality.* New York: Harper.

Spilerman, S. (1977). Careers, labor market structure and economic achievement. *American Journal of Sociology, 83,* 551-593.

Spranger, E. (1925). *Die Psychologie des Jugendalters.* Leipzig: Quelle & Meyer.

Stark, R., & Roberts, L. (1996). *Contemporary social research methods.* Bellevue, WA: Micro-Case Corp.

Steyer, R., & Schmitt, M. J. (1990). Latent state-trait models in attitude research. *Quality and Quantity, 24,* 427-445.

Strauss, A. L. (1959). *Mirrors and masks.* New York: Free Press.

Strauss, J. S., Hafez, H., Lieberman, P., & Harding, C. M. (1985). The course of psychiatric disorder: III. Longitudinal principals. *American Journal of Psychiatry, 11*(4), 199-204.

Strelau, J. (1987). The concept of temperament in personality research. *European Journal of Personality, 1,* 107-117.

Sullivan, H. S. (1953). *An interpersonal theory of psychiatry.* New York: Norton.

Taeuber, I. B. (1964). China's population: An approach to research. *Social Science Research Council Items, 18,* 13-19.

Talmon-Garber, Y. (1959). Social structure and family size. *Human Relations, 12,* 121-146.

Tannenbaum, A. S. (1961, October). Adaptability of older workers to technological change. *Institute for Social Research Newsletter.*

Teachman, J. D., & Schollaert, P. T. (1989). Gender of children and birth timing. *Demography, 26*(3), 411-423.

Thelen, E., & Smith, L. B. (1994). *A dynamic system approach to the development of cognition and action.* Cambridge: MIT Press.

Thomas, A., & Chess, S. (1977). *Temperament and development.* New York: Bruner-Mazel.

Thomas, W. I., & Znaniecki, F. (1919). *The Polish peasant in Europe and America: Vol. III. Life record of an immigrant.* Boston: Gorham.

Thouless, R. H. (1936). Test unreliability and function fluctuation. *British Journal of Psychology, 26,* 325-343.

Tuma, N. B., & Hannan, M. T. (1984). *Social dynamics: Models and methods.* San Diego: Academic Press.

Tversky, A., & Kahneman, D. (1973). Availability. *Cognitive Psychology, 5,* 207-232.

Ussher, J. (1658). *Annals of the World.* London: Printed by E. Tyler for J. Crook and G. Bedell.

Vallacher, R. R., & Nowak, A. (1994). *Dynamical systems in social psychology.* San Diego: Academic Press.

Valois, G. (1921). *D'un siècle à l'autre. Chronique d'une génération (1885-1920).* Paris: Nouvelle librairie nationale.

van de Stadt, H., Kapteyn, A., & van de Geer, S. (1985). The relativity of utility. *Review of Economics and Statistics, 67,* 179-187.

Van Velsor, E., & O'Rand, A. M. (1984). Family life cycle, work career patterns and women's wages at midlife. *Journal of Marriage and the Family, 46,* 365-373.

Verbrugge, L. M., Reoma, J. M., & Gruber-Baldini, A. L. (1994). Short-term dynamics of disability and well-being. *Journal of Health and Social Behavior, 35,* 97-117.

Volkart, E. H. (1951). *Social behavior and personality.* New York: Social Science Research Council.

von Wiese, L. (1924). *Allgemeine Soziologie als Lehre von den Beziehungsgebilden.* Munich and Leipzig: Duncker & Humblot.

von Wiese, L. (n.d.). Väter und Söhne. *Die Neue Strom, 1*(3).

Wagner, H. R. (1956). A new generation of German labor. *Social Research, 23,* 151-170.

Weber, M. (1946). The social psychology of the world religions. H. H. Gerth & C. Wright Mills (Eds. and Trans.), *From Max Weber* (pp. 267-301). New York: Oxford University Press. (Original work published 1915)

Weber, M. (1946). Science as a vocation. H. H. Gerth & C. Wright Mills (Eds. and Trans.), *From Max Weber* (pp. 129-156). New York: Oxford University Press. (Original work published 1919)

Weber, M. (1968). *Economy and society* (G. Roth & C. Wittich, Eds.; G. Roth et al., Trans.). New York: Bedminster. (Original work published 1922)

Wegner, E. L. (1990). Deinstitutionalization and community-based care for the chronically mentally ill. *Research and Community and Mental Health, 6,* 295-324.

Welford, A. T. (1958). *Ageing and human skill.* New York: Oxford University Press.

Wells, L. E., & Stryker, S. (1988). Stability and change in the self over the life course. In P. B. Baltes, D. L. Featherman, & R. M. Lerner (Eds.), *Life-span development and behavior* (pp. 191-229). Hillsdale, NJ: Lawrence Erlbaum.

West, B. J. (1985). *On the importance of being non-linear.* New York/Berlin: Springer-Verlag.

Wheaton, R. B., Muthén, B., Alwin, D. F., & Summers, G. F. (1977). Assessing reliability and stability in panel models. In R. Heise (Ed.), *Sociological methodology* (pp. 85-136). San Francisco: Jossey-Bass.

White, H. C. (1992a). *Identity and control.* Princeton, NJ: Princeton University Press.

White, H. C. (1992b). Succession and generations: Looking back on chains of opportunity. In H. A. Becker (Ed.), *Dynamics of cohort and generations research* (pp. 31-51). Amsterdam: Thesis Publishers.

Whitehead, A. N. (1978). *Process and reality* (Corrected ed.). (D. R. Griffin & D. W. Sherburne, Eds.). New York: Free Press. (Original work published 1929)

Wilensky, H. L. (1961). Orderly careers and social participation: The impact of work history on social integration in the middle mass. *American Sociological Review, 26,* 521-539.

Wiley, D., & Wiley, J. A. (1970). The estimation of measurement error in panel data. *American Sociological Review, 35,* 112-117.

Willms, J. D., & Raudenbush, S. W. (1989). A longitudinal hierarchical linear model for estimating school effects and their stability. *Journal of Educational Measurement, 26,* 209-232.

Wineberg, H., & McCarthy, J. (1989). Child spacing in the United States: Recent trends and differentials. *Journal of Marriage and the Family, 51,* 213-228.

Winston, G. C. (1982). *The timing of economic activities.* Cambridge, UK: Cambridge University Press.

Woodrow, H. (1932). Quotidian variability. *Psychological Review, 39,* 245-256.

Wrong, D. H. (1961). The oversocialized conception of man. *American Sociological Review, 26,*185-193.

Yamaguchi, K. (1991). *Event history analysis.* Newbury Park, CA: Sage.

Young, M. (1958). *The rise of the meritocracy.* New York: Penguin.

Zeuthen, H. G. (1909). Quelques traits de la propagation de la science de génération en génération. *Rivista di Scienza.*

Zevon, M. A., & Tellegen, A. (1982). The structure of mood change: An idiographic/nomothetic analysis. *Journal of Personality and Social Psychology, 43,* 111-122.

Zihlman, A. (1985). *Australopithecus afarensis:* Two sexes or two species? In P. V. Tobias (Ed.), *Hominid evolution* (pp. 213-220). New York: Alan R. Liss.

Index

About the Authors

Duane F. Alwin is Professor of Sociology and Senior Research Scientist in the Survey Research Center of the Institute for Social Research, University of Michigan. He received a Ph.D. in sociology from the University of Wisconsin in 1972. Over the past decade, his work has focused on human development, the family, socialization, and social change. He is particularly well known for innovative contributions to the study of social change and the role of lifecourse factors in the development of family-related attitudes, beliefs, and values, as well as political attitudes and identities.

David L. Featherman is Director of the Institute for Social Research at the University of Michigan. He is well known for his groundbreaking research in social stratification and for his more recent research on the social patterning of the adult life course and the impact of work and career structure on cognitive and personality systems in later adulthood and old age.

Glenn Firebaugh is Professor of Sociology at Pennsylvania State University and a faculty member of the Institute for Social Research Summer Institute at the University of Michigan. He received his PhD in sociology from Indiana University in Bloomington, Indiana, in 1976. He has recently published papers in *Sociological Methodology, American Journal of Sociology,* and the *American Sociological Review*. He is well known for his methodological work.

Melissa A. Hardy is Director of the Pepper Institute on Aging and Public Policy and Professor of Sociology at Florida State University. Her research focuses on issues of income inequality, retirement, pensions, and social policy. Recent publications include *Ending a Career in the Auto Industry* (with Lawrence Hazelrigg and Jill Quadagno); *Regression with Dummy Variables,* a widely used resource in graduate seminars on quantitative analysis; and articles in *Social Forces,* the *Journal of Gerontology,* and *Research on Aging.*

Dana L. Haynie is a PhD candidate in the Department of Sociology at Pennsylvania State University. Her interests include labor market analyses of gender and race inequality, criminology, and the study of social change.

Lawrence Hazelrigg is Professor of Sociology at Florida State University. He received his PhD in sociology from the University of Texas in 1970. He has published widely in the area of stratification and social theory. The third volume of his three-volume theoretical work, *Social Science and the Challenge of Relativism,* was published in 1995; that project was partially funded by an NIH Career Development Award. In his recent work, he has examined the "micro/macro" issue and its implications for social science research.

Karl Mannheim (1893-1947) began his professional career in his native Hungary, continued in Germany (first at Heidelberg, then at Frankfurt) until 1933 when he moved to the London School of Economics, thence to the University of London. Mannheim's major works include *Ideology and Utopia* (1929), *Man and Society in an Age of Reconstruction* (1940), and essays posthumously collected as *Essays on the Sociology of Knowledge* (1952) and *Essays on the Sociology of Culture* (1956).

John R. Nesselroade is Hugh Scott Hamilton Professor of Psychology at the University of Virginia. He received his PhD in psychology from the University of Illinois at Urbana-Champaign in 1967. Among his primary research interests is developing methodology for structuring and measuring change. He has published extensively in the area of individual development and social change, life span developmental psychology, and is well known for his important contributions to the field of methodology.

Eliza K. Pavalko is Assistant Professor of Sociology at Indiana University in Bloomington, Indiana. She received her PhD from Florida State University in 1987. She has published in the *American Journal of Sociology* and the *Journal of Health and Social Behavior.* She is currently conducting research on the relationship between work and health among older women, a study funded by the National Institute on Aging. With Glen Elder, she coauthored a monograph for Sage's series in *Quantitative Applications in the Social Sciences* on the uses of archival data for studying life histories.

Norman B. Ryder began his professional career as a demographer with the Dominion Bureau of Statistics in his native Canada in 1950. A professor of sociology at the University of Wisconsin when his article on cohorts was published in the American Sociological Review, Ryder has been since 1971 at the Office of Population Research, Princeton University, where he is now Professor Emeritus. Later publications include *The Contraceptive Revolution* (1977). Ryder has been editor of the *American Sociological Review* (1966-69), president of the Population Association of America (1972), and a fellow both of the American Statistical Association and of the American Academy of Arts and Sciences.

Linda Waite is Professor of Sociology at the University of Chicago, where she directs the Center on Aging. She is Past President of the Population Association of America. Her research focuses primarily on the family; she has studied women's employment, marriage, cohabitation, divorce, child care, the transition to adulthood and intergenerational support and exchange.